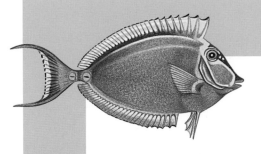

DIVE the WORLD
the most fascinating diving sites

WS
WHITE STAR PUBLISHERS

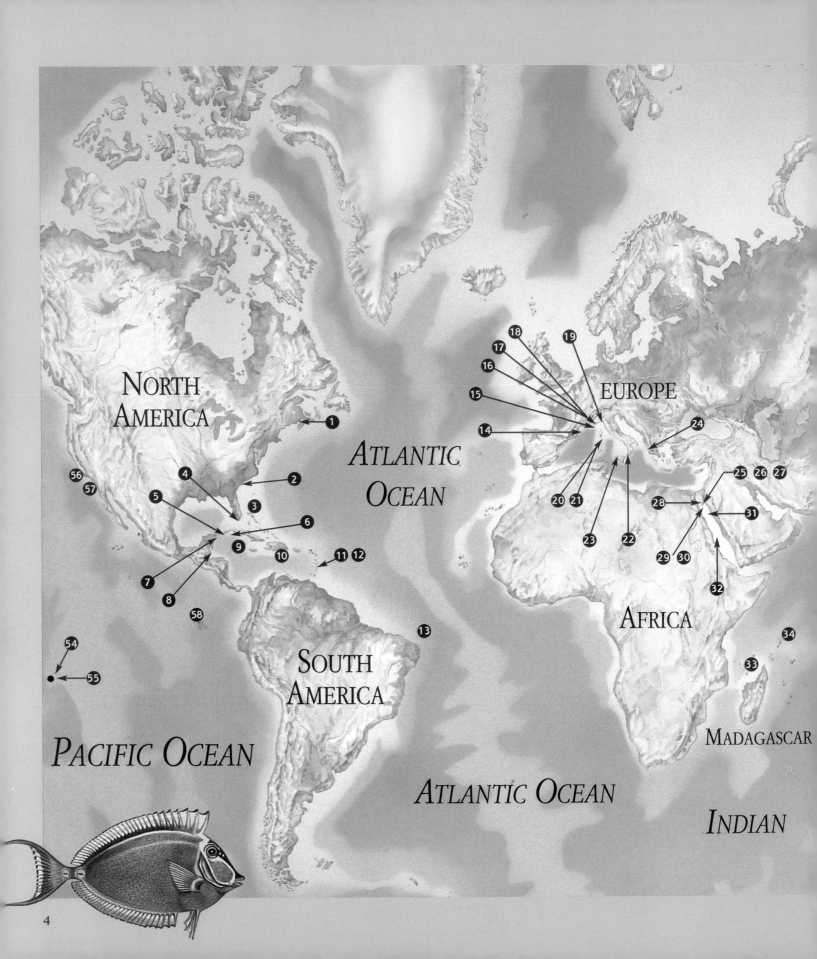

NORTH
AMERICA

ATLANTIC
OCEAN

EUROPE

AFRICA

SOUTH
AMERICA

PACIFIC OCEAN

ATLANTIC OCEAN

MADAGASCAR

INDIAN

4

DIVE the WORLD
the most fascinating diving sites

Edited by Egidio Trainito

TEXT AND PHOTOGRAPHS	GIORGIO MESTURINI	ILLUSTRATORS
KURT AMSLER	VINCENZO PAOLILLO	DOMITILLA MÜLLER
JONATHAN BIRD	ROBERTO RINALDI	AURORA ANTICO
BRANDON COLE	EGIDIO TRAINITO	
ELEONORA DE SABATA	JAMES TRETER	GRAPHIC DESIGN
		CLARA ZANOTTI

List of the sites

1 A tiny wrasse peeks out from its den.
© Claudio Cangini

2–3 Halcyons, madrepore and sponges along the ciliate of the reef. © Roberto Rinaldi.

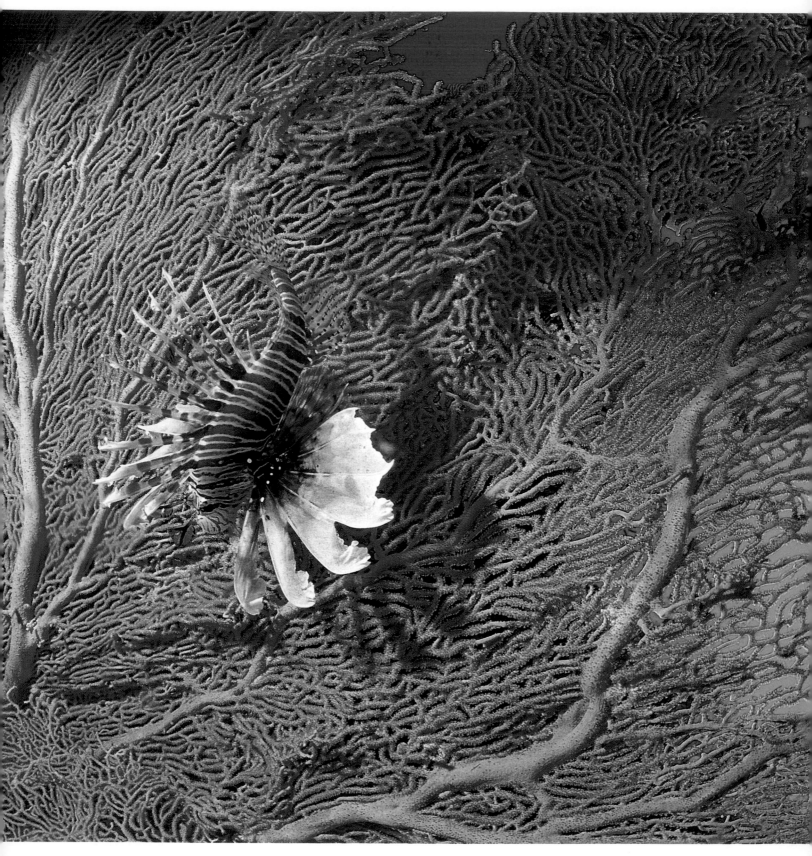

GENERAL INTRODUCTION

BY EGIDIO TRAINITO

Seventy-five percent of the surface of the earth is covered by seas and oceans, but even this enormous liquid expanse represents very little of the entire mass of the planet. Imagine the earth as a tennis ball that you submerge in a bucket of water; the water on the surface of the planet is the equivalent of what remains on the tennis ball after you take it out of the bucket. Yet we know this relatively small quantity of water very little. The aquatic environment has rules and conditions profoundly different from those for which our body has been structured, and even if we have managed to conquer almost every square foot of the land, our exploration below the surface of the seas is very recent, the result of limited and unsystematic research. Then there is the problem of depth: almost anyone can descend to 70 feet (20 meters) below the surface of the sea, and as far as 160 feet (50 meters) in relative tranquility using modern technology, but beyond that depth technical, organizational, economic, and physiological problems are so great as to reduce to insignificance the numbers of people able to do so and the time dedicated to it worldwide.

Despite these limitations in our knowledge of marine environments, millions of ordinary people have begun to visit the seabed in hundreds of tourist resorts and cruise destinations around the world; in some areas and stretches of coast, we know every single cranny down to a depth of 130 feet (40 meters). We recognize a large number of different forms of life, and many creatures have become stars, with divers lining up to observe them. Most of the activity takes place in the warm waters of the planet, where barrier reefs proliferate, but less warm waters such as the Mediterranean are also visited, and even downright cold ones farther north or in the extreme south have their enthusiasts. Every dive has its own attraction, whether you are observing the colors of a barrier reef, swimming through a forest of kelp, moving slowly over a sandy seabed, or visiting the architectural wonders below the surface of the Mediterranean. And there is no more beautiful place

6-7 A lionfish (Pterois volitans) spreads its long fins among the intricate ramifications of a large gorgonian.
Photograph by Roberto Rinaldi.

7 top left The garibaldi (Hypsypops rubicundus), local to the kelp forests in the eastern Pacific.
Photograph by Vincenzo Paolillo.

7 bottom left This close-up gives an unusual sight of a group of pygmy sweepers (Parapriacanthus ransonneti) at Hin Daeng in Thailand.
Photograph by Egidio Trainito.

7 top right Red and yellow gorgonians (Paramuricea clavata) on Mount Scilla contradict the general view that the Mediterranean is a murky, colorless sea.
Photograph by Roberto Rinaldi.

7 bottom right Soft corals, gorgonians, and crinoids frame the body of a sponge; the variety of life forms that contend for living space on the vertical walls of a reef in the Philippines is extraordinary.
Photograph by Vincenzo Paolillo.

8 An enormous barrel sponge (Xestospongia testudinaria) dominates the amphitheater of the reef at Mari Mabuk in Sulawesi. Photograph by Egidio Trainito.

8-9 An angelfish (Pomacanthus sp.) with unusual coloring swims at Careless Reef in the Red Sea. Photograph by Vincenzo Paolillo.

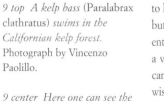

9 top A kelp bass (Paralabrax clathratus) swims in the Californian kelp forest. Photograph by Vincenzo Paolillo.

9 center Here one can see the rich and variegated forms of life in the Caribbean. Photograph by Egidio Trainito.

than where you are, even if each diver has his or her own favorite site.

This last factor has also been a problem in drawing up a guide of the fifty loveliest dives in the world. Choosing from the multicolored kaleidoscope of the depths of the whole planet is not only a difficult task in itself, it is also arbitrary. However, the dives described in this guide are all superlative, and not just for their geographical context; more importantly, they are all within the reach of the normal underwater tourist.

This book can be read on different levels. For experienced divers who have traveled around the world, it can serve as a souvenir album to refresh fading memories and perhaps help put names to underwater plants or creatures. For those considering diving for the first time, it can be used to choose where to go, to kindle particular interests, or just to stimulate daydreams on the sofa at home.

The book is laid out so that you can see at a glance the differences and similarities between places or the organisms that populate them; it also allows you to find out where to see whale sharks, large groupers, a particular small fish, or a special symbiotic relationship. Not only does it bring to life the deeps in individual parts of the globe, but its distribution map of individual species or entire groups covers the seas worldwide, creating a veritable atlas of marine species. Each of you can choose, as you do underwater, the theme you wish to explore—for example, the waters of the Indian or Pacific Oceans, or the enormous variety of groupers inhabiting the deep waters of the world's seas, or perhaps the extraordinary diversity of the small group of fish that nearly everyone calls anemonefish, but which contains thirty different species, sometimes restricted to very narrowly defined areas. The book also allows you to build up an overall picture of the varied world of invertebrates (though without any pretense of going into great detail), demonstrating that the menagerie below the waves is not very difficult to understand, as the

9 bottom Two shy clownfish
hide among the tentacles of
an anemone.
Photograph by
Vincenzo Paolillo.

10-11 A bank of thousands
of barracuda (Sphyraena sp.)
create a circular movement
that seems to ring the sun;
the dynamics of the group are
based on eye contact, with
each individual maintaining
an equal distance from its
neighbors.
Photograph by
Vincenzo Paolillo.

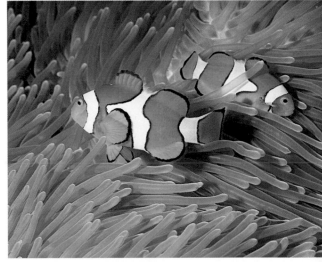

basis of life is the same for all aquatic creatures.

Many of the dives described are contained within protected areas, and often this is the reason for the exceptional beauty of the sites and the richness and peculiarities of their life forms. Here the diver might find organisms that would otherwise be very difficult to approach. Natural interest, aesthetic value, and effective conservation measures are so closely linked as to be almost inseparable, and together they help to distinguish the world's most beautiful underwater sites.

Finally, one can just leaf through this book to make one's personal, virtual journey below the waves, bearing in mind the words of Christopher Columbus: "And the sea will give every man new hopes, just as sleep brings dreams."

ATLANTIC OCEAN AND CARIBBEAN SEA:

INTRODUCTION BY EGIDIO TRAINITO

The Caribbean is located in the middle western area of the Atlantic Ocean. The huge basin covers 1,700 square miles (2,754,000 square kilometers) and is bounded to the north and east by the archipelagos of the Greater and Lesser Antilles, and to the west and south by the coast of central America between Capo Catoche in Yucatán and Punta Peñas in Venezuela. Its waters communicate with the Gulf of Mexico through the Yucatán Channel, and the sea has its deepest point in the Cayman trench at 25,000 feet (7,680 meters) below sea level. The western area of the sea is subject to frequent cyclones and hurricanes. The Caribbean represents little more than 2 percent of the area of the Atlantic and is traversed by the southern equatorial current that flows into the Gulf of Mexico to join the Gulf Current. This current then heads north toward Florida, the Bahamas, and the Turks and Caicos Islands; although outside the Caribbean, these are considered part of it by some scholars and are similar from a biogeographical standpoint.

The islands in the Caribbean are flung across an arc of roughly 1,200 miles (2,000 kilometers). The remaining fragments of an ancient bridge of land that once united North and South America, they mainly consist of limestone, but some are of volcanic origin. The water temperature oscillates between 72°F (22°C) in winter and 84°F (29°C) in summer and encourages the development of broad coral reefs. The largest coral reef in the Caribbean and the second largest in the world, at 175 miles (280 kilometers) in length, is located not around the islands but along the coast of Belize. In this area and elsewhere in the zone, fascinating "blue holes" can be explored: these are formed by submerged caverns whose ceiling has collapsed, opening chasms close to the surface. As you penetrate, you will be amazed by their roundness and by the blue of the water.

The second largest barrier reef is the Andros Reef, named after one of the 3,000 islands and rocks that make up the Bahamas. This coral reef is roughly 140 miles (230 kilometers) long and also offers blue holes, grottoes, and caverns to the diver.

The formations of corals and other organisms in Caribbean barrier reefs differ from those in other oceans in both composition and appearance. Caribbean reefs are fragmented and less ordered, with pinnacles or walls that sometimes plunge straight into the depths, and are often broken into sections, separated by expanses of fine white sand. The main scenic elements are the fans of gorgonians and large stick and barrel sponges with intricate branches colored bright yellow, orange, blue, and violet. Caribbean barrier reefs offer a notable variety of organisms but cannot boast the biodiversity of the Indian or Pacific reefs. A comparison of the number of known species of fish in the more fertile waters of the Caribbean with those in various localities of the Indian and Pacific Oceans makes the difference evident: the Caribbean is home to only 50 percent of the species known in the Red Sea, 33 percent of those in the Great Barrier Reef, and just 20 percent of those in the Philippines. The number is equal to that of the colder waters of the Mediterranean, where there are no barrier reefs.

The Caribbean is far and away the area of the planet most heavily visited by divers, mainly because of its proximity to North America, with its many diving tourists. The most popular sites are in the Florida Keys, in the Bahamas, and in the Cayman Islands, where some localities have transformed themselves into diving resorts—Stingray City, for example, where you swim in a few yards of water over white sand while watching enormous rays, and Crystal River, where you can have close encounters with friendly manatees, or the Bahamas, where you will assuredly meet sharks and dolphins. But there are many destinations, nearly always of excellent diving quality: the Mexican coast of the Yucatán, the marine park at Cozumel, the western parts of Cuba, Isla de la Juventud, Cayo Largo and Los Jardines de la Reina, the islands off the coast of Venezuela, with the national park of Los Roques, and the Dutch Antilles, where Bonaire is considered by the diving press to be the capital of Caribbean macrophotography and Aruba is one of the top four destinations in the world for wrecks.

For diving enthusiasts, the Caribbean is not the only destination in the Atlantic, but there are precious few other coral environments in this ocean. The island of Bermuda can boast the northernmost formations of coral and an extraordinary concentration of wrecks, and there are a few species of coral at Fernando de Noronha on the Brazilian coast and an even smaller number in the shallows of the Cape Verde islands off the coast of western Africa.

Fernando de Noronha

Text and photographs by Jonathan Bird – Illustrations by Aurora Antico

MAINE

◆ *Eastport*

Atlantic Ocean

MAINE—PASSAMAQUODDY BAY
EASTPORT

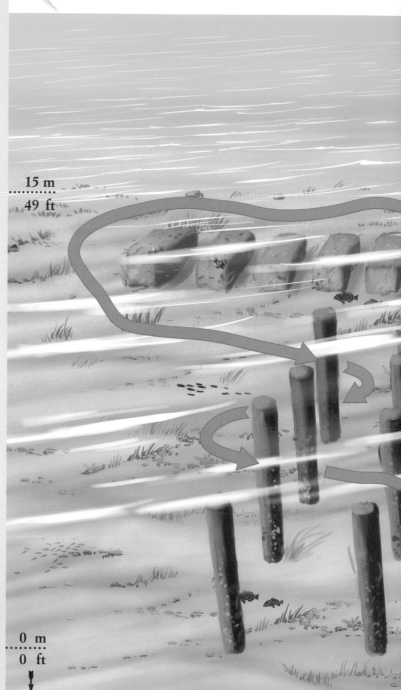

The underwater topography of the rocky New England coast provides an excellent environment for sea life, with countless precipices and ledges that attract fish and invertebrates. The further north we go, the wider the range of flora and fauna, with the biggest variety to be found along the northern coast of Maine, in and around Passamaquoddy Bay. Here the high tides, which can be over 45 feet (13 meters), produce violent currents, in excess of 10 knots (11 mph). Nevertheless, when at slack time, divers can observe a variety and density of plant and animal life that few other sites can match.

Many significant points of interest are accessible from the coast. Moreover, many sites have such steep slopes that it is difficult to anchor boats, so it is simpler to dive directly from the shore.

One of the area's best diving sites is right in the heart of Eastport, where the town's old pier used to be. The granite posts and slabs can still be seen at low tide. The local divers call this point "The Bottle Dump," revealing the site's

14 top High tide in Passmaquoddy Bay, in the Bay of Fundy. Here the tide surges 33 feet (10 meters), for the greatest rise anywhere in the world.

14 bottom The "wolf fish" (Anarhichas lupus) is well-equipped to eat shellfish by crushing their shells, and thrives on crabs, mussels, and other shellfish.

15 m
49 ft

0 m
0 ft

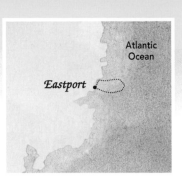

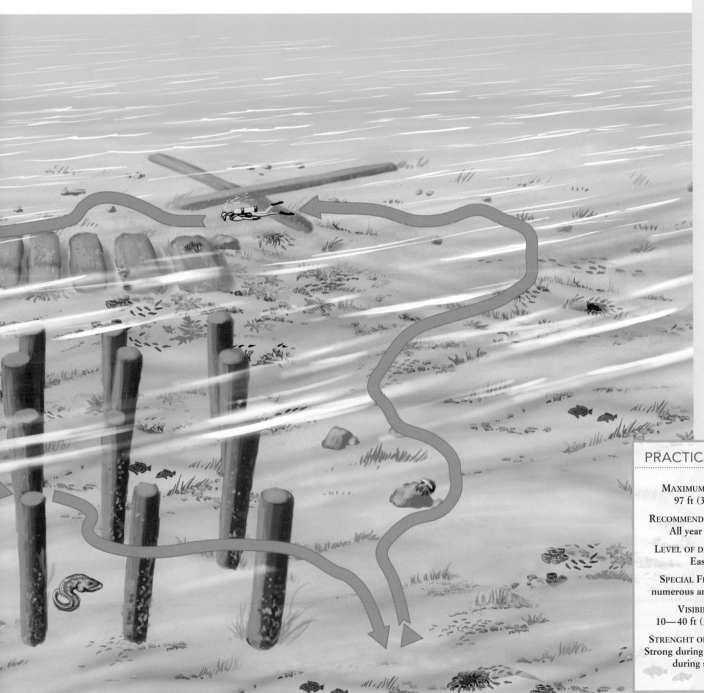

PRACTICAL TIPS

MAXIMUM DEPTH:
97 ft (30 m)

RECOMMENDED PERIOD:
All year round

LEVEL OF DIFFICULTY:
Easy

SPECIAL FEATURES:
numerous artic species

VISIBILITY:
10—40 ft (3—12 m)

STRENGHT OF CURRENT:
Strong during tides, Weak
during slacks

16 top The Tealia crassiformis *thrives in the waters off Seaport, where a hidden underwater garden offers a wealth of artic and acclimatized species.*

16 bottom left Divers frequently encounter clams of the Chlamys islandica, *or* Pecten islandicus, *species in Eastport waters. Here we see some quite active ones.*

16 bottom right The Cancer irroratus *crustacean is widespread in northwestern Atlantic waters, and is found from Labrador to the Carolinas.*

lengthy former use, but this is where we need to be to take photos! I still recall the wonder of the first time I visited here. I actually found an underwater paradise under the derelict pier, which is extremely rare so close to the coast and these depths so far south. A huge assortment of artic invertebrates, soft pink corals and basket stars, nudibranchs, tunicates, and sunflower sea stars (*Pycnopodia helianthoides*), mingle with other species acclimatized outside of their natural habitat, such as the Atlantic wolf fish (*Anarhichas lupus*), the ocean pout (*Macrozoarces americanus)*, and Tealia lofotensis anemones, in every color of the rainbow. The old pier's huge submerged posts have become a refuge for numerous red-gilled nudibranchs (*Coryphella rufibranchialis*), which are rare in more southern areas. Equally widespread are the nudibranchs of the brown or violet *Dendronotus frondosus* species.

The abandoned pier's granite slabs form a wall that reaches down 25 to 50 feet (7 to 15 meters), depending on the tide. From this point onwards the seabed is sandy and scattered with tiny rocks. Here we can enjoy the coin-sized hydroids, the soft corals, Bernard's hermit crabs, cottids, basket stars, and the extraordinary common sun star (*Crossaster papposus*), with its 12 arms and a habit of feeding off other starfish. These beds are also home to the very rare wrinkled sea star *Pteraster militaris*, who "nurses" its young in a special protective "pouch," and is normally found much closer to the Artic Circle. The high tide will increase depths up to 100 feet (30 meters).

Passamaquoddy Bay is sheltered from the ocean, so it is possible to dive all year round and in all weather conditions. The water temperature is milder from June to November, but cool even in summer, so it is advisable to wear a dry suit. The strong ocean currents, in fact, drag deep waters up to the surface. In summer the surface water temperature can rise even to 10°C (50°F) , but just 20 feet (6 meters) down, it will still be 4°C (40°F). Visibility is acceptable, from 10-40 feet (6-12 meters), even when the coast is suffering gales. It is a good idea to check the local tide timetables and dive during slack, when the current is almost non-existent, avoiding risky moments of ebb and flow.

Just a few feet from the diving site, off the old pier, we find Eastport's Motel East, which is a fine, recently built hotel where they even let divers rinse off their equipment. Anyone on a tight budget may prefer the Seaview Campsite or any one of several B&Bs.

17 Eastport's biological diversity is remarkable and quite rare in consideration of its nearness to the coast and the water's depth.

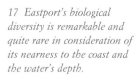

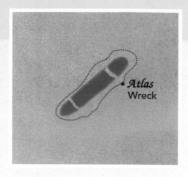

NORTH CAROLINA

Morehead City

Atlas Wreck

Cape Lookout National Seashore

Atlantic Ocean

N

Atlas Wreck

PRACTICAL TIPS

MAXIMUM DEPTH:
25 ft (38 m)

RECOMMENDED PERIOD:
April—October

LEVEL OF DIFFICULTY:
Average/High

SPECIAL FEATURES:
sand tiger sharks
and lionfish

VISIBILITY:
30—60 ft (9—18 m)

STRENGHT OF CURRENT:
Moderate

Text and photographs by Jonathan Bird – Illustrations by Aurora Antico

NORTH CAROLINA
Morehead City
Atlas Wreck
Atlantic Ocean

NORTH CAROLINA—CAPE LOOKOUT
THE *ATLAS* WRECK

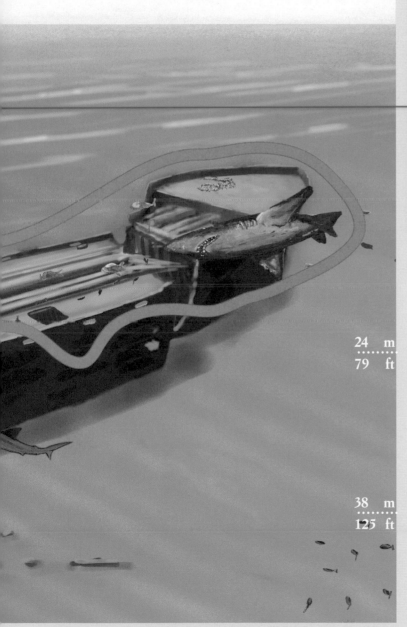

24 m
79 ft

38 m
125 ft

How could I ever forget my first dive in the North Carolina waters? The waters close to the shore were as cloudy as mud but further out they turned a Caribbean blue, as if we had crossed some imaginary line. Flying fish began to shoot past the prow and a small school of dolphins even arrived to keep us company. Of course there are always two sides to every story: off the North Carolina shore the weather conditions are often adverse and diving can be fraught with difficulty. When the day is fine, on the other hand, the waters are amongst the most spectacular diving sites in the world.

The waters off North Carolina are a cemetery of ships that sunk on the dangerous shoals and menacing reefs. Besides which, during World War II, German U-boats sank hundreds of merchant navy ships. As time passed, these wrecks became popular underwater sites thanks to the

19 top The bull shark (Odontaspis taurus) is a habitué of the many wrecks scattered along the coast of North Carolina, which is very dangerous to ships because of its many shoals and reefs.

19 bottom A bull shark searches the remarkably blue clear waters surrounding the wreck of the Atlas.

fact that the wrecks here, unlike those off New Jersey and the state of New York, are in waters warmed by the Gulf current.

In the 1980s several diving expeditions around North Carolina wrecks began noticing the presence of sand tiger sharks *(Odontaspis taurus)* concentrated around the ships. They did show a preference for just some of the vessels, but about 50 to 60 sharks were to be seen grouped together. So some wrecks became popular with shark enthusiasts, thanks to the diver grapevine and magazine articles. Biologists say that sharks concentrate around wrecks because food is plentiful there and also to reproduce. While the females reside near ship hulls, the males stay only for the mating period and then go back to the open sea. Sharks are not aggressive towards divers and tolerate their presence, as long as they are not touched.

Of all the wrecks, the Atlas is considered one of the best sites worldwide for observing sand tiger sharks. It is a 440-feet (135-meters) petrol tanker that was sunk in 1942 by the German submarine U-552, and lies at 125 feet (38 meters) below sea level, off Morehead City. The current around the wreck may be moderate and visibility can vary enormously, depending on weather conditions, but will usually be about 50 feet (15 meters). The bridge is about 80 feet (24 meters) down, so nitrox tanks are a good idea for extending the amount of time spent on the seabed.

The *Atlas* lies on the sand in the sailing position. The holds are open and easy to cross. Often the sand tiger sharks swim inside and play together. Nevertheless, close up this can turn into a dangerous game. I once heard a thud behind me and as I turned around I saw a shark shooting off in the opposite direction. I sup-

20 left, top and center Sand tiger sharks prefer wrecks like that of the Atlas (an oil tanker sunk by a German U-boat in 1942). In particular, females find them excellent places for reproduction.

20 bottom left A surprising encounter with a lionfish (Pterois volitans), *typical of more southern waters.*

20 bottom right When treated
with the required caution, the
bull sharks in wrecks don't
attack divers.

20-21 A great view of a bull
shark, taken from the bridge of the
Atlas, as it swims close to the ill-
fated tanker's anti-aircraft battery.

posed the animal had been frightened and in its
haste to flee had bumped against something.
Then I realized that the thudding was simply
the sudden sweep of its tail to make a quick
move away. Such is the power of the caudal fin
that it makes a dull sound, like the lash of a
whip. It is best to avoid frightening sharks
simply to steer clear of the range of action of
their tails!

A few years back, divers began to sight

examples of lionfish (Pterois volitans) on the
Atlas wreck. They had probably escaped from a
Florida aquarium and now prosper on North
Carolina wrecks, offering a unique chance to
observe tropical fish from the Pacific in this
unexpected habitat.

The best season for visiting North Carolina's wrecks is April to October, when the water
temperature is 20 to 27°C (68 to 80°F). The
water gets warmer as the season progresses.

Atlantic Ocean

FLORIDA · *Little Bahama Bank*

Gulf of Mexico

Caribbean Sea

Text and photographs by Vincenzo Paolillo – Illustrations by Domitilla Müller

BAHAMAS—GRAND BAHAMA
LITTLE BAHAMA BANK

Bahama Bank is an area of about 70,000 square miles (180,000 square kilometers) of sandbanks and fairly shallow coral banks inhabited by subtropical flora and fauna. Nourishment arrives with a warm sea current pushed from the center of the Atlantic by the trade winds.

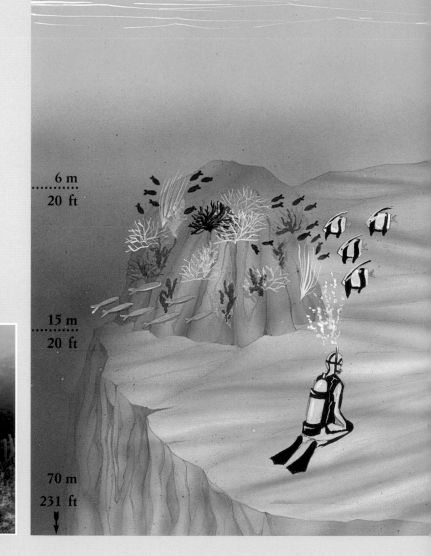

6 m
20 ft

15 m
20 ft

70 m
231 ft

22 top The gray angelfish (Pomacanthus arcuatus) is the perfect symbol of the Caribbean Sea.

22 bottom The light of the flashlight makes it possible to admire the brilliant red color of a sponge growing on the seabed of Mount Olympus.

Little Bahama
Bank

BAHAMAS

Grand Bahama

N

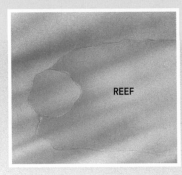

REEF

PRACTICAL TIPS

MAXIMUM DEPTH:
50 ft (15 m)

RECOMMENDED PERIOD:
September — April

LEVEL OF DIFFICULTY:
Easy

SPECIAL FEATURES:
swimming with dolphins

VISIBILITY:
over 99 ft (30 m)

STRENGTH OF CURRENT:
Weak

The environment is typical of the Caribbean. There are no barrier reefs, as there are no coral builders, but instead formations of limestone and lava on which a unique and very strange vegetation lives. The bright colors of the underwater worlds of the Red Sea or equatorial Pacific are nowhere to be seen; here pale, delicate colors predominate in an infinite variety of white, yellow, pink, gray, and green.

Little Bahama Bank is part of the bank that lies along the northern side of Grand Bahama Island, a platform that never exceeds 50 feet (15 meters) in depth. Its sandy bed is strewn with small rocks inhabited by sea fans, sea whips, coral, sponges of all shapes and sizes, stupendous French angelfish (*Pomacanthus paru*), queen angelfish (*Holocanthus ciliaris*), gray angelfish (*Pomacanthus arcuatus*), colorful schools of grunts (*Haemulon flavolin-*

24-25 Schools of grunts (Haemulon sciurus *and* Haemulon flavolineatus) *swim among the structures of a wreck, in the shadow of the sea fans.*

25 top left Meeting rays (this one is Dasyatis americana) *is a common experience on the sand flats of the Bahamas.*

25 center left The French angelfish (Pomacanthus paru)*, two of which are shown in the photo, like the shallowest areas of the reefs where sea fans grow.*

25 top right Mount Olympus is characterized by a host of sea fans, in the midst of which beautiful Caribbean sponges are growing.

25 bottom A redtail parrotfish (Sparisoma chrysopterum) *prepares to pass the night.*

26 center left A school of enormous yellow mullet (Mulloidichthys martinicus) swims in a compact formation, perhaps attempting to escape from the perceived menace of the photographer.

26 bottom left A nurse shark (Ginglymostoma cirratum) finds an ideal habitat on the stretches of sandbanks.

26 right A school of three Atlantic spotted dolphins seems to want to play with a diver. Photograph by Gianfranco D'Amato.

26-27 A reef shark (Carcharhinus perezi), accompanied by remoras, doesn't run from a meeting with the diver. Photograph by Gianfranco D'Amato.

26 top left A large candelabra-shaped sea fan grows exuberantly on the Mount Olympus reef.

eatum, *Haemulon plumieri, Haemulon sciurus,* and so on), snappers (*Lutjanus* sp.), mullet, Nassau groupers (*Epinephelus striatus*), nurse sharks (*Ginglymostoma cirratum*), rays, barracuda, and many more.

There are many lovely sites for dives—for example, Mount Olympus, with its magnificent forest of gorgonians and soft corals where yellow and silver fish play hide-and-seek, and Sugar Wreck, the wreck of a ship that carried a cargo of sugar and is now literally covered with sea fans, some with pink and some with yellow stems, in whose shadows shoals of coral fish conceal themselves; at night enormous leatherback turtles (*Dermochelys coriacea*) and reef sharks patrol the wreck.

What makes this area unique is that hardly any dive can be made without encountering dolphins. The bank is home to large groups of striped dolphins (*Stenella coeruleoalba*) and bottle-nosed dolphins (*Tursiops truncatus*), sometimes ten to twenty together but occasionally also from fifty up to a hundred if you are lucky. All you need do is ride out over the bank, especially in the afternoon, and they will come to meet you. Unusually, the dolphins of the Little Bahama Bank are friendly and confident; the striped dolphins will come right up to divers and spend ten or fifteen minutes playing with them, coming and going, stopping and looking, almost inviting divers to leave the world of the humans and stay with them. This incredible experience alone makes the trip worthwhile, and confirms the intelligence of these wonderful mammals.

KEY LARGO

Key Largo
National Marine
Sanctuary

◆ *Molasses
Reef*

N

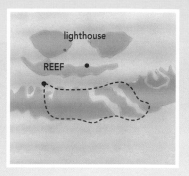

lighthouse

REEF

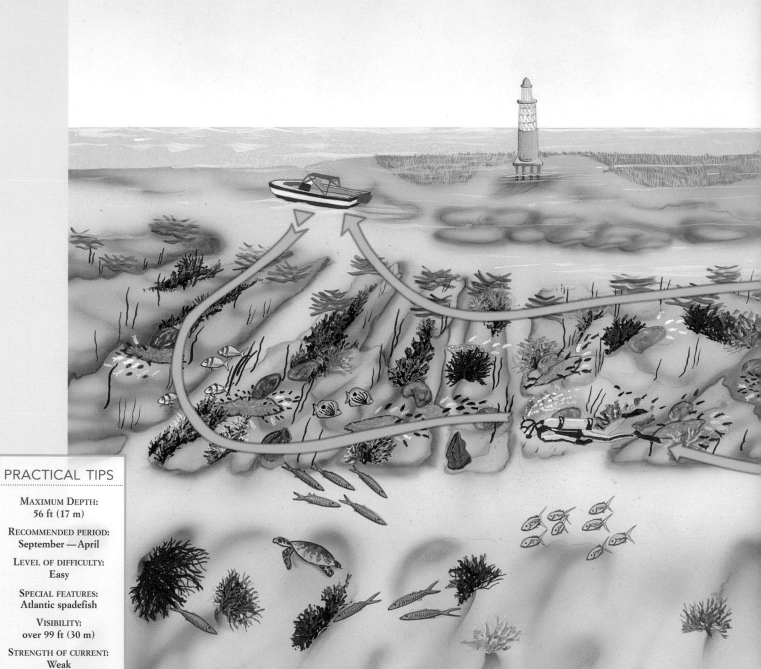

PRACTICAL TIPS

MAXIMUM DEPTH:
56 ft (17 m)

RECOMMENDED PERIOD:
September — April

LEVEL OF DIFFICULTY:
Easy

SPECIAL FEATURES:
Atlantic spadefish

VISIBILITY:
over 99 ft (30 m)

STRENGTH OF CURRENT:
Weak

Text and photographs by Kurt Amsler – Illustrations by Domitilla Müller

FLORIDA KEYS—KEY LARGO
MOLASSES REEF

T he Florida Keys is an archipelago of over 200 islands in the shape of a long arc to the south of mainland Florida, running northeast to southwest for 130 miles (212 kilometers). The subtropical vegetation and the mild climate are the result of the location of the chain of islands along Florida's coral bank, which channels the warm waters of the Gulf Stream.

Of the 200 islands, thirty-four are connected by forty-two bridges to form the famous U.S. Highway 1. The road is lined with mile markers, which are of vital importance for knowing your position in the Keys. Key Largo is located at mile marker 100.

Comparison of the topography of the seabed of the Keys with that of the Bahamas shows that the actual coral banks lie at a great distance from the coast. The coastal zones are formed by man-

29 top A small group of Atlantic spadefish (Chaetodipterus faber) take shelter in a recess; this species is confident in the presence of divers and seems attracted by bubbles.

29 bottom Although great barracuda (Sphyraena barracuda) are not aggressive in clear water, their powerful teeth are always an impressive sight seen close up; the largest barracuda can exceed 7 feet (2 meters) in length.

6 m
20 ft

17 m
56 ft

30 center left The tail, yellow fins, and diagonal stripes on its sides help to identify the French grunt (Haemulon flavolineatum), *the most widespread species in the Caribbean and Florida.*

30 bottom left A trumpetfish (Aulostomus maculatus), *immobile among the gorgonians and corals, monitors the movements of the photographer; this species changes color and posture to best adapt to its environment.*

30 right A group of spiral tube worms (Bispira brunnea) *has grown among the madrepore; this species reproduces asexually by splitting in half, so it is normal to find many of them together.*

30 top left A large coralline concretion rises from the white sand, crowned by sea fans and large sponges of various species.

grove swamps and grasswrack (*Zostera marina*); these shallow but vast areas are very important from an ecological point of view, as they are the breeding ground for many of the inhabitants of the sea. This is where fry spend the first period of their lives.

The midreef is formed by single blocks of coral, often surrounded by grasswrack. Here the seabed is slightly deeper, from 10 to 15 feet (3 to 5 meters). The offshore coral zone is also formed by blocks of coral that grow until they almost reach the surface, and it is from this point that an interesting dive area begins, where the water is especially clear. The seabed slopes gradually toward the deep reef, and the corals form gullies, grottoes, and long fingers that emerge from the sand. At the point where the belt of coral arrives at the vast sandy expanse of the open sea, the depth reaches 60 to 70 feet (17 to 20 meters).

Due to the distance of the coral bank from the coast, it is not possible to enter the water from the shore, so all dives have to be made from a boat. All boats used for diving in the Keys are purpose-built and tested by the Coast Guards. Safety on board is of primary importance, and all d.ive spots are described in great detail.

The area around Key Largo is part of Pennekamp Coral Reef State Park. Opened in 1960,

this was the first underwater park in the United States, named after John D. Pennekamp, a Florida citizen strongly committed to the protection of the coral banks and the natural environment. This area extends for 3.4 miles (5.5 kilometers) from the last coral bank and reaches a depth of 300 feet (90 meters).

If you ask any diver who has visited Key Largo for his favorite dive spot, it will be Molasses Reef. This stretch of external coral lies on the southern boundary of the park and is the most varied. Not far from here lies the famous wreck of the *Duane,* which was sunk for divers. Nearby, many other ships have foundered involuntarily on the dangerous coral reef, and today Molasses Reef is marked by a light tower.

*30-31 The tips of the
tentacles of a giant anemone
(Condylactis gigantea) are
swollen and colored a brilliant
pink; this is where the
creature's stings are kept.*

*31 bottom A cleaner shrimp
(Periclimens yucatanicus) pauses
on the tentacle of an anemone;
the symbiotic relationship means
that the anemone gets cleaned
and the shrimp is protected.*

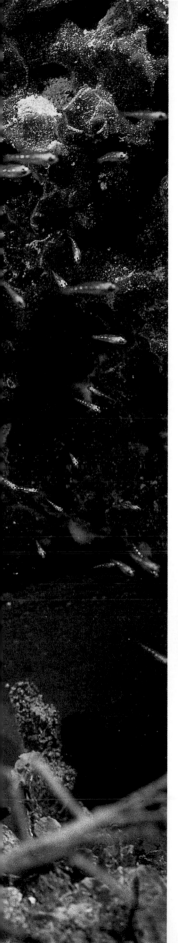

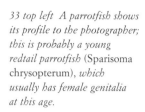

32-33 A green moray (Gymnothorax funebris) *sticks its head out of a crack in the reef and shows its teeth; this is not threatening behavior but simply fulfills the moray's need to take water into its gills.*

33 top left A parrotfish shows its profile to the photographer; this is probably a young redtail parrotfish (Sparisoma chrysopterum), *which usually has female genitalia at this age.*

The Gulf Stream passes across the coral bank, bringing fresh healthy water that has a positive effect on flora and fauna; this explains why you often see large pelagic fish in these waters. The topography of the coral bank is very interesting, even when you do not have especially deep water to explore. The coral bank is crossed by canyons and stretches of sand. The plateau starts near the surface and then slopes quickly to the vertical to a maximum depth of 60 feet (17 meters). At some points the Miniwall is very prominent. Below, the fish mass in a manner rarely seen. Divers can explore a large number of hollows and galleries.

Molasses Reef is interesting at all points; it

does not matter if you enter the water at Fire Coral Cave, Miniwall, or Wellwood Side. On the flat bottom of a place called Hole in the Wall, you will see a large anchor known as Spanish Anchor.

Wherever you look, gigantic fingers of elkhorn coral grow on the edge of the interruption and the surface of the coral bank. These corals are typical of the Caribbean and west Atlantic.

Besides the coral, you will see small groups of fish all around—for example, French grunts, bluestriped grunts, and white grunts. Trumpetfish lurk unmoving among the branches of coral; their similarity to the coral branches means that their prey may swim close enough to be caught unawares. Large French angelfish and other members of the same family are everywhere. The gray and queen angelfish are brightly colored.

As in an aquarium, everywhere you look you see the vivid colors of fish, morays, and sea bass, but in the open sea you will also find interesting sights. Near the shoals of yellowtails there are at least eight Atlantic spadefish (*Chateodipterus faber*) lined up on the coral. Reaching 20 inches (50 centimeters) in height, these resemble tropical batfish but are no relation.

When visiting Molasses Reef, remember one thing—time flies, and your air will be used up in no time!

33 bottom left A schoolmaster snapper (Lutjanus apodus) *has taken shelter below an overhang in the reef; this species normally lives in large groups but is reluctant to be approached.*

33 top right A nurse shark (Ginglymostoma cirratum) *rests in a hollow in the reef with a sharksucker attached to its head; the roughness of the shark's skin is quite apparent, rather like sandpaper.*

33 center right Two groupers (probably Epinephelus itajara) *face one another threateningly; given their size, they are probably two males arguing over territory using characteristic shakes of the body and holding their mouths open.*

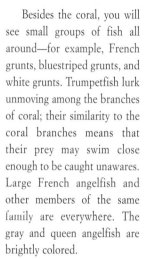

N

ISLA DE LA
JUVENTUD

Cabo
Francés

Caribbean Sea

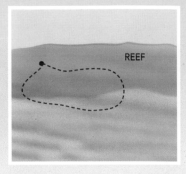

REEF

PRACTICAL TIPS

MAXIMUM DEPTH:
66 ft (20 m)

RECOMMENDED PERIOD:
May—November

LEVEL OF DIFFICULTY:
Easy

SPECIAL FEATURES:
schools of tarpon

VISIBILITY:
over 99 ft (30 m)

STRENGTH OF CURRENT:
Variable

Text and photographs by Eleonora De Sabata – Illustrations by Domitilla Müller

Atlantic Ocean

Gulf of Mexico

CUBA

Cabo Francés

Caribbean Sea

CUBA—ISLA DE LA JUVENTUD
CABO FRANCÉS

The wall that skims Cabo Francés on the Isla de la Juventud is highly impressive. It coincides with the edge of the continental platform and descends to over 1,300 feet (1,000 meters) in leaps and bounds. A very famous dive point, for decades it has been a meeting point for divers from all over the world, attracted by its clear waters, its depths, and its gigantic sponges. The edge of the drop begins at 70 feet (20 meters) and disappears down into the blue, where it meets the bottom several hundred feet farther down. The wall is very long, with an infinite number of entry points, whether along the wall or in the shallows behind. Sponges are everywhere, of every shape and size, from the invisible, minuscule ones that live by excavating complicated tunnels inside the coral to the gigantic elephant-ear sponges that can reach up to 10 feet (3 meters) in diameter. Don't just look at them from afar or for their size: sponges are not inert but living creatures that grow, reproduce, and fight among themselves; you can see them engaged in silent but cruel battles for space and light all along the wall. It is worth watching

35 left The vegetation reaches right down to the edge of the beach, which is composed of fine white particles of coral.

35 right The walls of Cabo Francés often plunge vertically into the deep, and the clarity of the water means that sometimes it is easy to miscalculate depth. The photograph shows a barrel sponge in the foreground; although the diver is on the bottom, the weak light suggests he is at a substantial depth.

15 m
50 ft

20 m
66 ft

50 m
165 ft

35

36-37 *A diver meets a school of tarpon* (Megalops atlanticus) *in an underwater cave; these fish are so territorial that a single shoal may remain in the same area for years.*

37 top left The perspective makes it look as if the diver is coming out of the tube sponge; gorgonians and sponges of this type are typical of the Caribbean.

37 bòttom left A tangle of branched sponges occupies a ledge on the reef; this type of growth allows maximum absorption by offering a large surface area to the current.

37 top right Sea fans always
grow at right angles to the reef
to offer the maximum possible
surface area to the current.

them with attention because they are a key feature of this sea. Their colonies are formed of thousands of cells that assume different shapes and characteristics, even within the same species, depending on the environment and depth at which they live. They breathe the surrounding water through thousands of tiny holes, then filter it and pump it out again through the large central aperture known as the osculum. One hundred and fifty gallons (200 liters) of water pass through a medium-size sponge in twenty-four hours.

There are several grottoes along the wall, one very large one stretches down as far as 160 feet (50 meters). The top of the fissure is open: against the luminous background of the surface, you can see tarpons with large silver scales, the typical fish of the Caribbean, swimming slowly.

A deep vertical cut in the wall has a poetic name, the Tunnel of Love; you can swim through between large sponges that grow on the walls inside.

Behind the wall, the coral platform does not drop below 50 feet (15 meters). Formations of madrepore rise from the sandy bottom, where expert divers will find much of interest. A large coral arch 10 or 13 feet (3 or 4 meters) high is the meeting place for a school of ceaselessly moving tarpons. Groupers abound everywhere and can be approached with ease, as divers often take food with them. No species of fish will turn its nose up at a snack between meals, and often guides take advantage of this weakness to take their divers up close.

El Cabezo Solitario, as the name suggests, is an isolated reef that is home to many crustacean cleaning stations. Look for the anemones with the twisted tentacles in the cracks; it is here that the transparent and violet shrimps whose task it is to clean fish of parasites hide. Nearby, the groupers with their open mouths seem surprised as they are subjected to careful cleaning. And if you are looking for lovely violet sea fans, you will find plenty on the walls of the gullies in the reef. Look carefully on the branches to catch sight of "flamingo tongues," mollusks that live only in the Caribbean; when left undisturbed, they camouflage their shell with a square pattern to hide against the background of the gorgonia branches.

Even the least promising place of all, under the platform supporting the restaurant where you might rest between dives, is worth a visit, even if only with a mask and fins, for you will find a dense bank of tropical umbrines between the poles. Visibility is often mediocre, but it is worth a plunge. The best period here is from May to November but avoid September and October, when the rains are heaviest.

37 bottom right A shoal of small
silver fish lurk so compactly in a
ravine that the flashlight hardly
penetrates; swimming together in
large shoals reduces the risk to
individual small fish of being eaten.

Text and photographs by Eleonora De Sabata

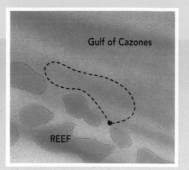

PRACTICAL TIPS

MAXIMUM DEPTH:
53 ft (16 m)

RECOMMENDED PERIOD:
June — December

LEVEL OF DIFFICULTY:
Expert

SPECIAL FEATURES:
many large fish

VISIBILITY:
over 99 ft (30 m)

STRENGTH OF CURRENT:
Strong

Illustrations by Domitilla Müller

Gulf of
Mexico

CUBA

Cabezeria de
Cayo Blanco

Caribbean
Sea

CUBA—CAYO LARGO
CABEZERIA
DE CAYO BLANCO

A deep underwater canyon snakes between Cuba and Cayo Largo. It is along the walls of this gigantic ravine—the Cabezeria de Cayo Blanco, which falls steeply to over 650 feet (200 meters) before descending slowly to greater depths—that some of the most wonderful dives in the Caribbean are to be made. The setting could not be more dramatic. The canyon opens into a vast bank that rings Cayo Largo to the north; this is

10 m
33 ft

16 m
53 ft

39 top One of the many coralline islets that ring Cayo Largo is surrounded by white sand and a turquoise sea; this is the typical landscape of this area.

39 bottom An aerial view of Cayo Largo; the clear water allows the bottom to be seen clearly.

40 top left The outline of a spotted eagle ray (Aetobatus narinari) can be seen against the light. These animals are difficult to approach; they have a spotted body and large eyes on a pointed head.

40 center left A large southern stingray (Dasyatis americana) swims over the bottom formed by a mixture of sand and coral; stingrays haunt sandy areas, on the lookout for invertebrates that they dig out of the sediment.

40 bottom left A giant grouper (Epinephelus itajara) pokes its head out of its lair; a live sharksucker (Echeneis naucrates) is attached to the great fish, which can exceed 7 feet (2 meters) in length.

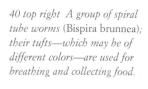

Jardines Bank, a long trail of reefs and white sandbanks that appear and disappear with the tides.

This vast area, part sea, part land, comes to a sudden halt with the dramatic drop of the rock wall to a depth of 650 feet (200 meters). This transition point generates and is often subject to strong currents that encourage the proliferation of benthonic life and reef fish; this abundance of life is an irresistible attraction to all pelagic fish that cross the area on their migrations. Large hammerhead and tiger sharks frequent these waters during the early months of the year.

It is difficult to pinpoint a single dive along the Cabezeria. The wall is largely unexplored, and rich with benthonic life: corals, sponges, gorgonians, and fish of all kinds—gigantic dentex, tropical groupers, and nurse sharks. Then comes the territory of the great pelagic creatures: sharks (including the whale shark), manta and eagle rays, carangids, and migratory fish. Keep one eye on the wall and one on the open sea and, above all, watch for the fish in constant motion along the wall. Truly unusual is the descent in the local "blue hole;" this immense black chasm in the reef has very little "blue" about it. You enter it via a well-hidden, relatively shallow passage. Twisting galleries unravel below the reef to significant depths. The smooth walls harbor no life, but the descent into the darkness of this grotto is very exciting. The whole of the Cabezeria is equally interesting, especially suited to expert divers, not because it is necessary to reach extreme depths to see the large ocean fish, which in fact swim close to the surface, but because the current is so strong, and many dives end up as "drifts." However, there is something for everyone; even the beginner who cannot risk going too deep will enjoy encounters with the lords of the sea, and everyone will take pleasure in the sensation of diving in almost unknown sites. The sheer numbers of fish—groupers, dentex, sea rays, and stingrays—show how this area of sea has only been skimmed by man. The best period to visit the Gulf of Cazones is from June to December, when the dominating wind is from east-southeast.

40 top right A group of spiral tube worms (Bispira brunnea); their tufts—which may be of different colors—are used for breathing and collecting food.

40 bottom right A shoal of schoolmaster snappers (Lutjanus apodus) swims on the reef; these fish always remain in a group and often stop below large coral formations in the shelter of gorgonians.

41 A gray angelfish (Pomacanthus arcuatus) swims on the reef; they normally move in pairs and do not take fright at the approach of a diver, often coming close themselves.

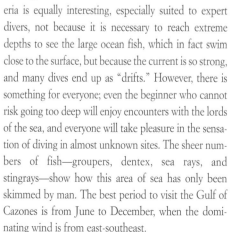

Text and photographs by Kurt Amsler

COZUMEL

N

◆ *Santa Rosas Wall*

Caribbean Sea

lighthouse

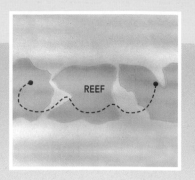

REEF

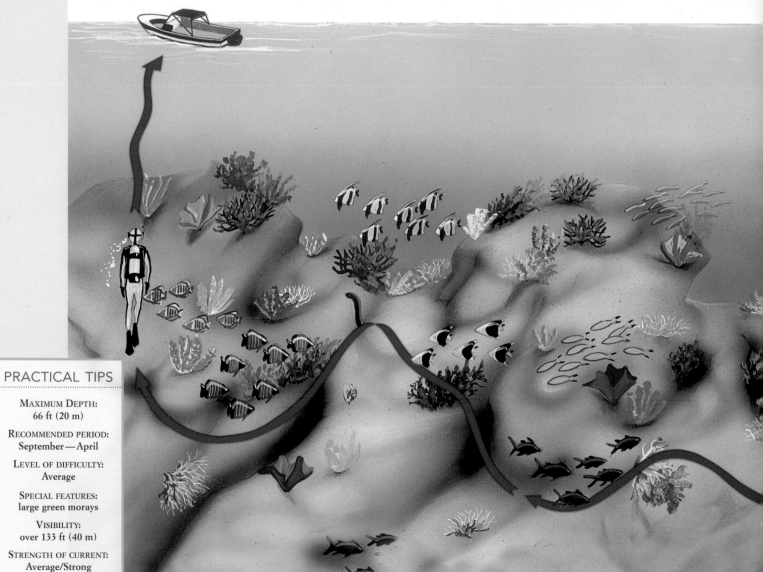

PRACTICAL TIPS

MAXIMUM DEPTH:
66 ft (20 m)

RECOMMENDED PERIOD:
September — April

LEVEL OF DIFFICULTY:
Average

SPECIAL FEATURES:
large green morays

VISIBILITY:
over 133 ft (40 m)

STRENGTH OF CURRENT:
Average/Strong

Illustrations by Domitilla Müller

Mexico—Cozumel
SANTA ROSAS WALL

he Mexican island of Cozumel lies 8 miles (12 kilometers) from the northeast coast of the Yucatán peninsula. It is a small island 30 miles (47 kilometers) long and 9 miles (15 kilometers) wide, and its highest point is only 50 feet (14 meters) above sea level. Cozumel is the largest of the three islands that lie off the coast, the other two being Mujeres and Contoy.

The underwater world of Cozumel is part of the

10 m
33 ft

15 m
50 ft

20 m
66 ft

43 top *A school of grunts (*Haemulon album*) swims along the reef; they eat both by day and by night, grubbing in the sand for benthonic invertebrates.*

43 bottom *A large gorgonian flexes with the current that is vital to its growth.*

43

second-largest coral bank in the world, the Belize reef, which stretches 200 miles (320 kilometers) from the southern tip of Isla Mujeres to the bay of Honduras.

Nearly all diving on Cozumel takes place out of the wind on the west coast. Coral banks almost surround the island, making diving on the east side impossible due to high tide. It is possible to enter the water from the shore, and where the coral comes close to the shore, you can reach the

dropoff point with just a few strokes. After presenting your credit card, you can rent your diving equipment and drive along the coast in a rental car. Every one of the twenty dive shops will provide you with a list of entry points.

Respect for the underwater environment must be observed at Cozumel, and proper buoyancy control is one of the necessary conditions for joining a dive expedition.

The underwater world of Cozumel is typical of the northeast area of the Caribbean. The coral banks are divided into three categories:

• shallow reef;
• medium reef;
• dropoff.

Everywhere the underwater landscape, especially on the shallow and medium reefs, is interrupted by rectangular gullies called sandshuts that run all the way to the shore. During the Ice Age, these gullies were created by fast-running water, as with all the land above sea level. Today the entire area has been covered by hard corals, white coral, and sponges; it presents a world of spectacular beauty. The constant currents mean that the water off Cozumel is always crystal clear; visibility of up to 160 feet (50 meters) is not unheard of! The water temperature is almost constant all year round, too, at about 77°F (25°C) in winter and even over 84°F (29°C) in summer!

The quantity of fish is extraordinary. Even when the large pelagic fish are not to be seen, anyone entering the water at the dropoff points or medium reefs will continually see spotted eagle rays, barracudas, jacks, gray reef sharks,

45 bottom Hundreds of great barracuda (Sphyraena barracuda) *swim in a group; they tend to remain together when young but are solitary as adults. .*

and blacktip sharks. You will often also see southern stingrays on the sandy bed and, below overhangs along the entire reef, huge nurse sharks.

The range of colorful reef fish includes all Caribbean species. The most common is the angelfish; also numerous are the schools of snappers, seen mostly on the medium reefs. Cozumel also boasts an endemic fish that can only be seen in this location: this is the coral toadfish *(Sanopus splendidus),* which spends its days below overhangs and comes out at night to swim over the reef. As they can bite very quickly, it is best not to touch them. You will hear their noise during any night dive, as they grind their teeth.

The Santa Rosas Wall is on this coral plateau at about 30 to 40 feet (10 to 12 meters), and descending vertically into the depths. It is possible to cross the wall through tunnels and look out into the deep sea on the other side. The steep wall is covered with deep-water gorgonians, wipecorals, and sponges, including the orange elephant-ear sponge and the yellow tube sponge, which is over a yard long.

If you look around the black corals or on the branches of dead gorgonians, you may see some

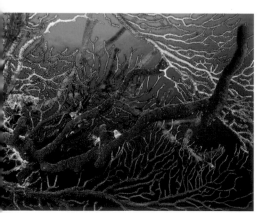

46 top Large sponges are a constant feature of the flora, their presence indicating that sufficient organic material is suspended in the water to enable their enormous growth.

46 center A forest of gorgonians covers an outcrop of the reef where yellow sponges

and stalked lettuce leaves (Halimeda *sp.), unusual green algae, also grow.*

46 bottom Different animals use similar strategies to capture planktonic material from the currents; gorgonians capture the particles using their tiny polyps, whereas

sponges, like this red one, collect the nutrients by filtering water.

46-47 A coral toadfish (Sanopus splendidus) *peeks out from its lair; this species seems to be endemic to Cozumel, where it is very common.*

Dives are generally begun behind the coral bank and continued by swimming over the slightly sloping sand to reach the reef itself. The coral bank is interrupted by a number of gullies, which all lead down to the steep slope. The bottom of these gullies is covered with white sand, and the coral bank overhangs are in turn covered with white corals and sponges. The highly colored robe sponges make a lovely contrast to the blue water. The current doesn't really make itself felt in the gullies, but once you reach the slope in the open sea, you will find yourself tugged along by it slowly but constantly. It is a wonderful feeling to let yourself be pulled along the coral bank as you simply take it all in.

If you see something interesting, with just a few flaps of your fins you will arrive close to the bank, where the current is so weak that you will easily keep your place. The water is so clear that you can see well beyond the permitted depth, and the temptation to go deeper is very strong.

47 top right A longspine squirrelfish (Holocentrus rufus) *pauses to be photographed among the madrepore; it can be distinguished from similar species by the triangular marks on the tip of its dorsal fin.*

47 bottom right A nurse shark (Ginglymostoma cirratum) *rests in a sandy area, hiding its head below a crack in the coral; a sharksucker is attached to its caudal zone.*

marvelous tunicates *(Ascidiacei)*. The level of 70-foot (20-meter) depth separates the world of fish above from the world of vegetation below. Among the fish are the enormous black groupers *(Mycteroperca bonaci)* and green morays *(Gymnothorax funebris)* that slide their long bodies through the cracks. Below overhangs in the canyon you will often find whole groups of spiny lobsters.

47

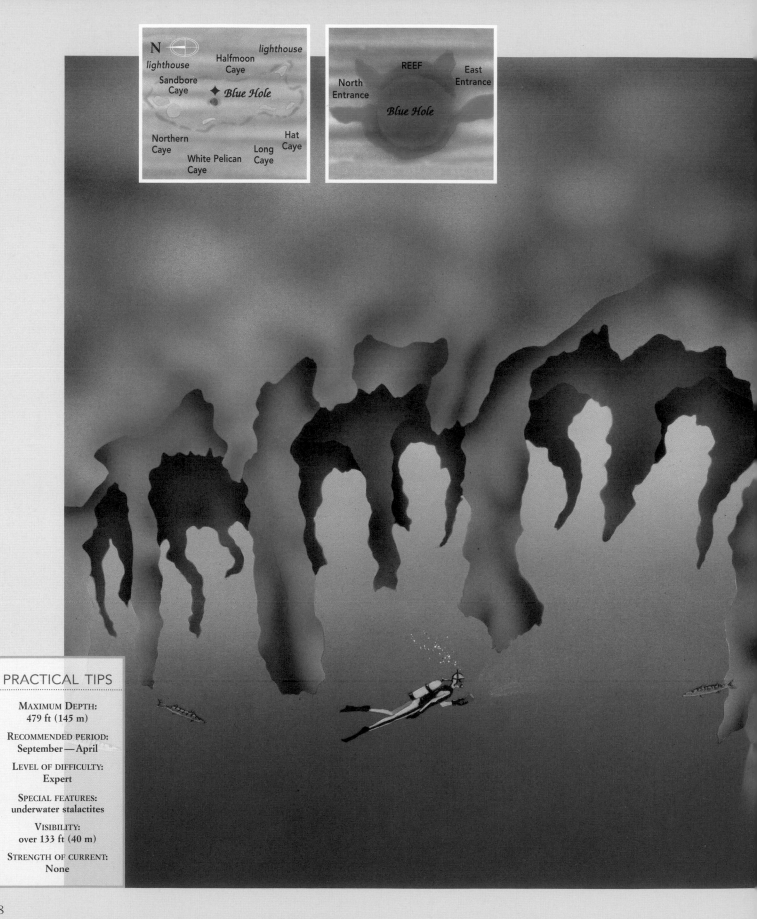

N lighthouse

lighthouse

Halfmoon Caye

Sandbore Caye

◆ *Blue Hole*

Northern Caye

White Pelican Caye

Long Caye

Hat Caye

REEF

North Entrance

East Entrance

Blue Hole

PRACTICAL TIPS

MAXIMUM DEPTH:
479 ft (145 m)

RECOMMENDED PERIOD:
September — April

LEVEL OF DIFFICULTY:
Expert

SPECIAL FEATURES:
underwater stalactites

VISIBILITY:
over 133 ft (40 m)

STRENGTH OF CURRENT:
None

Text and photographs by Kurt Amsler – Illustrations by Domitilla Müller

Atlantic Ocean

Gulf of
Mexico

BELIZE

◆ *Blue Hole*

Gulf of Mexico

BELIZE—LIGHTHOUSE REEF
BLUE HOLE

The Belize Barrier Reef is the second biggest in the world after Australia, extending 175 miles (280 kilometers) along the coast. The reef is a wall that runs parallel to the coast, 8 to 15 miles (13 to 24 kilometers) from the mainland, and offers an almost untouched underwater world. Between the reef and the mainland the seabed is flat and sandy, with tiny islands where mangroves grow—the so-called Cayes. To the east a deep depression in the ocean defines three separate atolls: Turneffe Islands, Glovers Reef,

49 top The blue holes are hollows formed by the collapse of the vault of underwater grottoes; the color of the deep water inside the blue hole contrasts with the pale colors of the seabed around it.

49 bottom The wall of the chasm drops into darkness; the clarity of the water means you have to keep a close eye on the depth meter, as it is easy to go too deep without realizing it.

40 m
133 ft

and Lighthouse Reef, where the best diving is to be found.

The flora and fauna in the waters around Belize is typical of the Caribbean, but richer in color and variety. There are places where once a year thousands of perch mate, thornbacks gather for the wedding journey, or dolphins welcome visits from with divers. The reef area, extensive in an ocean full of currents, is reflected in a rich growth of coral and

145 m

479 ft

sponge. When you dive at the external atoll reefs, sheer drops, the so-called dropoffs, plunge over 3,000 feet (1,000 meters) to the depths below. Water temperatures are constant throughout the year, ranging from 73° to 77°F (23° to 25°C) in the winter and 77° to 82°F (25 to 28°C) in the summer. At all tourist resorts on the islands along the barrier reef and on the atolls, diving centers transport their guests to dive sites. Diving ships, the so-called Liveaboards, cruise the waters as well.

There are many blue holes in the Caribbean, such as at Andros Island or Grand Bahamas Island. The largest lies almost in the center of Lighthouse Reef. These karst caves were formed in the Ice Age, when great volumes of water hollowed out the sandstone rocks and the sea level lay a few hundred yards lower. That these caves must once have been dry is evidenced by the stalagmites and stalactites. When later the sea flooded the area, the ceiling caved in, leaving the circular opening, typical of a sinkhole. In 1972 the ocean explorer Jacques Cousteau unveiled the secret of the blue hole, bringing his vessel *Calypso* into it and exploring it with minisubmarines to the bottom. The blue hole has two entrances through which the smaller submarines could reach the inside.

The blue hole has a diameter of 1,300 feet (400 meters) and is 480 feet (145 meters) deep. The walls drop sheer, and below the overhangs the diver can find stalactites, some over 10 feet (3 meters) long. As regards living creatures, the blue hole has nothing

special to offer, but this is not what makes the dive fascinating. It is a return to the past, which leaves the visitor with an unforgettable impression. The fact that the dive can take you to a depth of over 130 feet (40 meters) and is carried out in water 480 feet (145 meters) deep puts great demands on the diver. Before the dive, the start, duration, and depth level are clearly defined; as a rule, diving masters accompany the dives.

Not much light penetrates the hole. A flashlight should be taken along, not only to observe the stalactites but also for safety.

Photographers might best use 200 ASA/ISO films to capture something of the background brightness; video films will need artificial lighting.

The largest stalactites are located at the northwestern side of the blue hole, not far from the northern entrance. Here, where the slightly dropping sandy floor of this channel is covered with sticks of coral, the dive can finish. At the spot where the diving takes place there is, as a rule, a small buoy whose lines go down as far as the precipice. From that point the descent into deep water starts. Much attention must be paid to perfect buoyancy, for you are hovering over an abyss over 490 feet (150 meters) deep. In contrast to the open-water reef, here the walls are smooth and covered by brown and green seaweed. Even when there is sunshine above, after 100 feet (30 meters) it is already dark, and the use of a flashlight is encouraged. At a depth of 130 feet (40 meters) the black line of the overhangs can be seen where the stalactite scenery starts. The rays of the flashlights throw a ghostly light on the pinecone shapes hanging from the roof: some are twisted like corkscrews. It is a fantastic sight! Time here below flies, and attention to instruments is therefore very important. The dive ends where it started, on the sloping sandy bottom. At a depth of 20 to 13 feet (6 to 4 meters) you might spend some time looking at the fish, but above all taking in the tremendous impression that the great Blue Hole of Belize has left behind.

50 top left A small group of great barracuda (Sphyraena barracuda) patrols the sandy seabed; they are only considered dangerous to man when visibility is poor.

50 bottom left Gorgonians grow haphazardly on the coralline concretions on the seabed around the chasm.

50 right A diver at the entrance to the hole shines a flashlight on the enormous stalactites; these structures were formed by the deposit of carbonates before the cavern was submerged by water.

50-51 A diver swims between the stalactites in the darkness of the grotto; the lack of light and limited hydrodynamism means that the living conditions are unfavorable to most marine organisms.

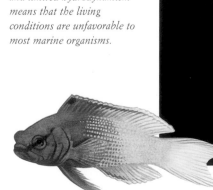

East End Channel

N

GRAND CAYMAN

Three Sisters

Caribbean Sea

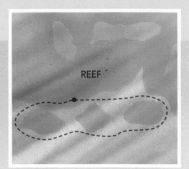

REEF

Text and photographs by Kurt Amsler

PRACTICAL TIPS

MAXIMUM DEPTH:
133 ft (40 m)

RECOMMENDED PERIOD:
September—April

LEVEL OF DIFFICULTY:
Expert

SPECIAL FEATURES:
large gorgonias

VISIBILITY:
over 99 ft (30 m)

STRENGTH OF CURRENT:
None

Atlantic Ocean

Gulf of Mexico

Three Sisters ◆

Caribbean Sea

GRAND CAYMAN—NORTH WEST WALL
THREE SISTERS

5 m
17 ft

22 m
73 ft

40 m
133 ft

The Grand Cayman Islands lie 480 miles (770 kilometers) south of Miami, between Cuba and Central America. Christopher Columbus discovered the islands by chance during his fourth journey in 1503. More precisely, he landed on "Little Cayman," which he named Las Tortugas because of the large number of turtles. Later ocean maps show the islands with the name "Lagatargos," and in 1530 they are mentioned as "Las Cayman," deriving from an Indian word meaning "little crocodile."

Diving activities take place all around the island, though the west side, which offers the most tranquil waters and permits problem-free diving throughout the year, is most frequented. More demanding diving spots are on the north coast on the so-called Northwest Wall. It is a long trip to these locations, so they are dependent on good weather. Strong winds and waves

*53 top A view of the reef gives an idea of its variety; green algae, hard corals, gorgonians, and sponges share space. In the foreground is an elephant-ear sponge (*probably Agelas clathrodes*).*

*53 bottom A pair of gray angelfish (*Pomacanthus arcuatus*) swims slowly through a dense tangle of gorgonians on the coral; the young of this species are colored black, with yellow stripes and edging on their blue fins.*

53

54-55 *A characteristic feature of the Caribbean reefs is the sponges that are present in many different shapes and* colors, often quite bright; the photograph shows tube sponges around a black ball sponge (Ircinia strobilina).

55 left *This large barrel sponge* (Xestospongia muta) *is typical of the reef; it can reach 7 feet (2 meters) in height and an age of over 100 years.*

55 top right
A great barracuda (Sphyraena barracuda) *approaches to within a few inches of the camera lens.*

55 center right The impression
of size is increased by the disc
of the sun and by the effect of
the wide-angle lens; the
gorgonian (probably Gorgonia
ventalina) in the center is
indeed large and can reach 7
feet (2 meters) in height.

55 bottom right
A diver shines a flashlight on a
sponge that has reached an
enormous size.

can limit diving or even render this impossible. The north side of the island definitely offers the most spectacular places; far from any hotel or diving center, they must be reached with larger diving boats. This is also where our chosen diving spot, Three Sisters, is to be found.

This dive site lies almost at the end of the south coast, not far from the corner of East End Channel. Noticeably, on this side of the island the dropoffs are much deeper than those, for example, on the west coast. The reef at the Three Sisters only reaches to within 70 feet (22 meters) of the surface. The Sisters consist of three enormous plinths of rock that stand before the wall of the reef as if they had been placed there. They lie completely apart, and it is possible to swim through the canyons. These are rank with

growth; it is advisable to swim carefully so not to damage the plant life. If the diver wishes to explore fully all the Sisters, he must plan his dive exactly, as they are spread over a distance of about 250 feet (80 meters). The route from the boat to the side of the reef has to be included as well in the calculation. To save air, we recommend that you snorkel on the surface toward the dropoff, which will also give you a good impression of the seabed's topography and enable you more easily to find your way around.

Another way to dive here is to strike a direct route through the canyon. This is naturally more spectacular, but it takes you deep down through the reef. Here again it is a question of diving time and air supply, since as a rule this is insufficient to swim the whole area.

The Sisters are rich in growth, sparkling with many deep-water gorgonians and various sponges. Everywhere the orange elephant-ear sponges shine, and tube sponges stand

erect in the open water like gun barrels. As for marine life, the visitor can find the whole range of fish and lesser animals, which are no different from those of other locations. There is still the chance of sighting here, in the East End Channel, larger fish such as spotted eagle rays, sharks, or other sea predators, but above all it is the strange underwater scenery that fascinates the visitor, together with the marine growth and the crystal-clear water that is almost standard for this part of the island.

Because of the depth and the need to keep exactly to the diving plan, visits to Three Sisters are reserved only for experienced divers. Briefing by the divemaster is therefore an important part of the dive. An underwater map showing the run of the reef is a fundamental aid to mark the boat's location and the quickest way to reach the best spots. For a sample dive that will give as comprehensive an experience of the Three Sisters as possible, the first objective is to dive to the Sister lying to the west, then along the dropoff to the second, and then to the third, striking off in an easterly direction—all in accordance with the current, which must naturally be considered in the plan.

From a long way off the colossal cliff can be seen growing out of the depths. It is almost square, separated from the actual wall of the reef by a deep canyon. What strikes you immediately are the great swarms of Creole wrasse, and the many overhanging sheet corals, under which the ever respectable groups of perch with their large eyes size up the trespassers curiously. Passing along the dropoff, richly decorated with soft coral, you reach the second Sister. It is thinner and rises sharply upward like a giant finger. Here too gorgons grow, one after the other; set against the sun above us are fantastic silhouettes. To the left and right the sea plunges down

bottomlessly. Here you could stay for hours, were it not for the time that always brings us divers back to reality. The distance to the third cliff is, however, farther than expected. This Sister is somewhat bigger but no less attractive. At this point the diving time only permits an observation of the top side, 70 feet (22 meters) distant.

56 bottom right Horse-eye jacks can reach a length of 30 inches (75 centimeters); the young adapt well to changes in salinity and are sometimes seen in fresh water.

56 left The branches of this sponge (Aplysina fistularis) are raised against the background of the sun; vertical growth offers the sponge a large surface area for feeding without requiring a large area of the reef to attach to.

56 top right A gray reef shark (Carcharhinus amblyrhynchos) swims closer to the photographer on a sandy expanse; sharks have achieved a perfection of form perfectly adapted to their life as predators.

56 center right This shoal of horse-eye jacks (Caranx latus) numbers hundreds of members; they are predators at the top of the food chain, and on occasion their flesh contains a concentrate of a toxin dangerous to man called ciguatera.

57 left The photograph shows the richness and variety of underwater life at Three Sisters.

57 right A huge group of snappers (Lutjanus sp.) *remains undisturbed by the presence of divers; there are at least five species of silver-colored snappers in the Caribbean, impossible to distinguish from one another at a distance.*

Text and photographs by Egidio Trainito

Atlantic Ocean

Gulf of Mexico

SANTO DOMINGO

Isla Catalina

Caribbean Sea

DOMINICAN REP.—PARQUE NATURAL DE ESTE
ISLA CATALINA

Т he eastern section of the Dominican Republic is one of the most heavily exploited tourist areas in the world. An area covering 106,000 acres (43,000 hectares), including the island of Saona, forms the Parque Natural del Este, but unfortunately it does not include the seabed of one of the most interesting diving areas in the Caribbean. To the east of the park, not far from the shore, the Isla Catalina boasts the best dives. Close to the north shore of the island, a plateau 23 to 26 feet (7 to 8 meters) deep leads to an edge that drops almost vertically to 80 feet (25 meters). From this depth, the seabed slopes gently, becoming less interesting.

58 top The ramifications of this gorgonian are densely packed to form a filter; this is not just to catch the particles on which it feeds but also for light, a flashlight in this case, which is greatly dimmed.

58 bottom A tube sponge rises from a hard coral reef; the sponge is one of the most characteristic elements of this area. The osculum at the tip of the tubes is where the water absorbed by the sponge is squirted out.

The dive takes place along the section 70 feet (20 meters) deep in a varied and colorful environment.

A series of channels crosses the edge at regular distances, creating fissures where the current washes in and encourages large sponges to establish themselves. Sponges and gorgonians are the two most characteristic organisms in this seascape. The yellow, violet, and brown tube

8 m
26 ft

25 m
83 ft

58

Atlantic Ocean

N

SANTO
DOMINGO

Isla Catalina

Caribbean Sea

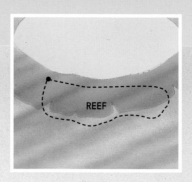

REEF

PRACTICAL TIPS

MAXIMUM DEPTH:
83 ft (25 m)

RECOMMENDED PERIOD:
September—April

LEVEL OF DIFFICULTY:
Average

SPECIAL FEATURES:
large tube-shaped sponges

VISIBILITY:
over 99 ft (30 m)

STRENGTH OF CURRENT:
Weak

60 top left
An American whitespotted filefish (Cantherhines macrocerus) *swims indolently over coral concretions where sponges and gorgonias grow; filefish will approach easily, and you can note how their spots appear or disappear as they change color.*

60 bottom left
A great barracuda swims alone over the reef; this fearsome predator is known to have made attacks on humans in the Caribbean, though always in particular situations, generally in murky waters.

sponges are slender in shape, and often their ramifications radiate from a common base, at times resembling large trombones with a flared tip. There are also large barrel sponges inhabited by small fish and crustaceans. The gorgonians grow between the sponges and other soft and hard corals, forming large, light blue fans with ramifications woven together to almost form a net. This development increases the ability of the innumerable small polyps in the colony to gather food.

In deeper water you will find orange gorgonians with long stems. The sponges and gorgonians give the scene a rather untidy appearance, typical of the Caribbean seabed. Here there is very little open space on the seafloor, and rarely will you find patches of sand.

The dive is a simple return journey made at the same depth. If there is a current, however,

follow it; then there is more chance of large barracuda approaching you from the open sea in the clear water, which often offers visibility of more than 100 feet (30 meters). Given the moderate depth, the dive is a long one, and its final section provides great interest; a great many discoveries may be made among the organisms that thrive on the shallow seabed. You will find large crabs *(Mitrax spinosissimus)* in the cracks, and porcupinefish with their unusual green eyes, moving slowly over the coral. The sea fans seem to form a separate world, numerous invertebrates populating their elaborate ramifications. Some, like the cleaner shrimps, simply take shelter there, while others, like the flamingo tongue *(Cyphoma gibbosum),* are predators that feed on the gorgonians' polyps. The flamingo tongue's shiny shell, swollen in the center, appears to be made of porcelain. Its shine comes from the creature's habit of covering it with slime, also patterned like the gorgonians for camouflage.

You will commonly find small families of crayfish with their long antennae on the sponges or anemones; they act as cleaners, providing an important service for the reef fish. Among the many that occupy the scene, you will see the American whitespotted filefish *(Cantherhines macrocerus),* which can make large round white patches appear and disappear from its yellow-and-brown coloring. It swims slowly between the corals and sponges and will not easily take fright if approached.

Among the algae that cover the seabed in shallower water, you may come across a lovely sea snail *(Tridachia crispata)* whose shell seems to be a piece of lace, and sharp-eyed divers may catch sight of a shrimp *(Gnathophyllum americanum)* among the red bumps on its host, a large starfish.

60 top right
The diver shines a flashlight onto a giant barrel sponge (Xestospongia muta) *surrounded by gorgonians; often fish or small crustaceans hide in the central cavity of the sponge.*

60 bottom right *A large southern stingray* (Dasyatis americana) *has just emerged from his hiding place under the sand and flaps away over the reef; stingrays search for their prey in the sand, concealing themselves with a layer of sediment.*

61 left Long stems of a sea whip (Ellisella elongata) *trail from the almost vertical reef; this species is typical of this sea and generally found below 70 feet (20 meters) depth.*

61 right Tube sponges (Aplysina fistularia) *are easily seen, with their distinctive shape and color, among the hard corals and various species of gorgonians atop the reef; one in particular seems to have taken the shape of a saxophone.*

MARTINIQUE

N

Caribbean
Sea

La Faille

Diamond Rock

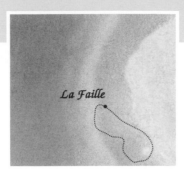

La Faille

Text and photographs by James Treter

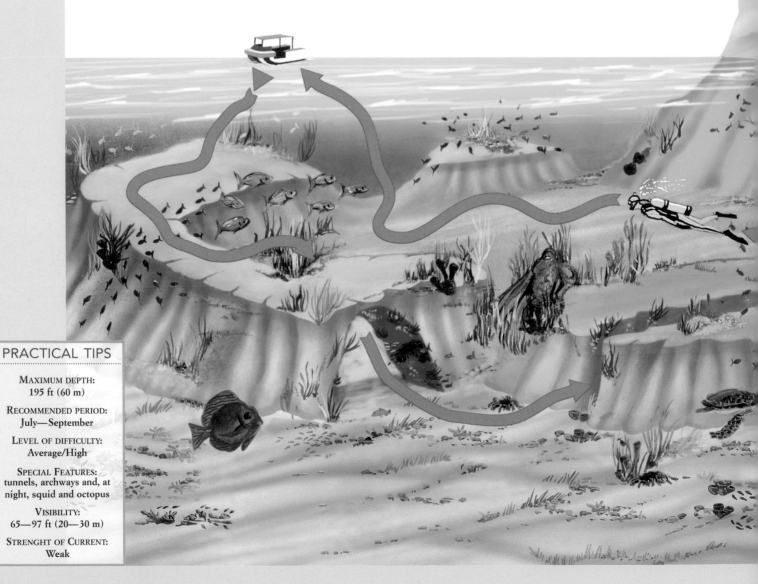

PRACTICAL TIPS

MAXIMUM DEPTH:
195 ft (60 m)

RECOMMENDED PERIOD:
July—September

LEVEL OF DIFFICULTY:
Average/High

SPECIAL FEATURES:
tunnels, archways and, at
night, squid and octopus

VISIBILITY:
65—97 ft (20—30 m)

STRENGHT OF CURRENT:
Weak

15 m
49 ft

30 m
98 ft

40 m
131 ft

MARTINIQUE—DIAMOND ROCK
LA FAILLE

Thehe island of Martinique has many amazingly beautiful dive sites for all divers, from the novice to advanced. The varied dive sites of this island offer ideal water temperatures. Probably the best dives are on the southern tip and southwest coast of Martinique. These sites offer opportunities to explore reefs, caves, tunnels, arches, walls, and, of course,

63 top An Atlantic blue tang (Acanthurus caeruleus) patrols the waters off La Faille.

63 bottom In La Faille, the sea polyp can be found even at a depth of 65 feet (20 meters), the depth favored by the largest members of this species.

63

64 top left A Platychthys flesus, *a relative of the sole, swims in the depths where it gets its nourishment.*

64 center left One of La Faille's most interesting inhabitants is the Balistes vetula, *which is always famished and which has very poisonous flesh.*

shipwrecks. The flora and fauna of each site is abundant, ranging from corals, sponges, and crinoids, to many species of tropical fish, turtles, and invertebrates.

Without doubt, the most popular and amazing dive sites are around Rocher du Diamant or Diamond Rock. These dives are located at the southwest end of Martinique, thus sheltering them, for the most part, from the strong currents of the open ocean. A short boat ride will take you approximately a mile from shore. At this point, a huge diamond-shaped rock about 250 feet (176 meters) in height rises from the ocean.

On the northwest side of the rock is a wonderful dive site known as La Faille. This dive ranges from 50 to 200 feet (15 to 60 meters) in depth, with a visibility of about 65 feet (20 meters), and consists of an underwater breach in the rock, a tunnel, and an archway with an abundance of marine plant and animal life. The dive boat will most likely anchor in the sand over the top of a ledge that is about 68 feet (21 meters) deep. Upon entering the water, and submerging to the rocks and sandy bottom, you will encounter a large field of sargassum. With a keen eye, a diver will be able to observe camouflaged trumpet fish floating vertically with their heads pointing downward. Further down the sargassum clears and the scenery unfolds to a brilliantly colorful vision of various sponges and

corals. Beautiful and delicate crinoids with their arms flowing blend in with the anemones and species of hydroids. At the entrance of the tunnel there are numerous sea fans with flamingo tongues feeding on them. On exiting the tunnel, divers enjoy a vision of various species of hard corals, yellow tube sponges, and gorgonians. To return to the boat anchor, veer right, after the tunnel. At this point, you will be making your way along a slope of interesting plant and animal life. The slope has brain corals, flower corals, colorful sponges, and anemones. There are also various spectacular tropical fish, such as sergeant majors, blue tangs, and triggerfish which swim in and around the corals and sponges. If you look closely, you should be able to find spotted drums hiding under the many ledges. Other rewarding sights might be finding

crustaceans such as lobsters and crabs hiding in the cracks and crevices with only their antennae showing. Anemone cleaner shrimp can most always be found flirtatiously dancing amidst the stinging tentacles of the colorful anemones.

There is never enough time or air to observe everything that waits for you on this dive. Night dives on this site are breathtaking and several dive shops will accommodate the experienced diver. During such a dive you should look out for turtles, octopuses, and feeding corals.

64 bottom left Sea lilies, which are echinodermata *related to starfish, share the waters with a sponge.*

64 right A Lima scabra *uses its tentacles like arms to bring food to its interior; it also uses them as feelers.*

65 Coral polyps stretch out in the current. Their structure is diaphanous and covered with a layer of living organism.

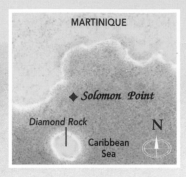

MARTINIQUE

◆ *Solomon Point*

Diamond Rock

Caribbean
Sea

N

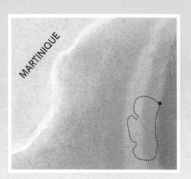

MARTINIQUE

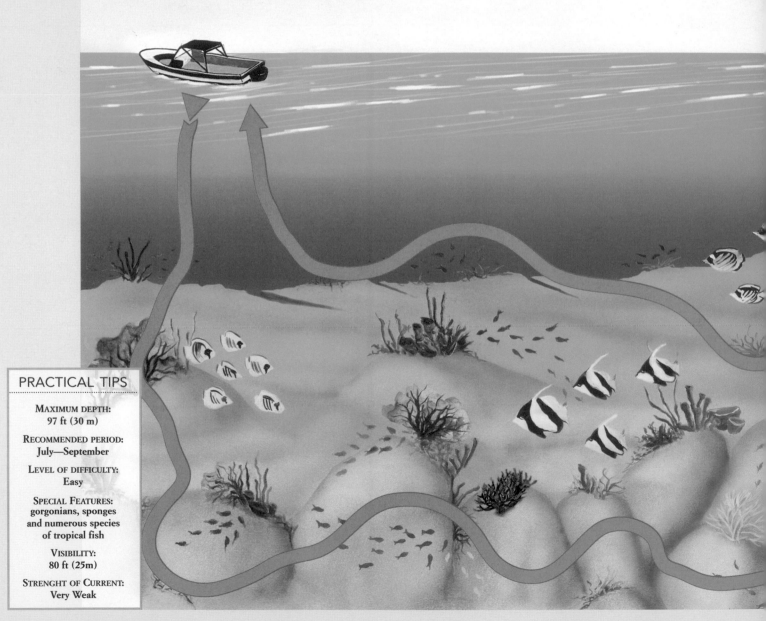

PRACTICAL TIPS

MAXIMUM DEPTH:
97 ft (30 m)

RECOMMENDED PERIOD:
July—September

LEVEL OF DIFFICULTY:
Easy

SPECIAL FEATURES:
gorgonians, sponges
and numerous species
of tropical fish

VISIBILITY:
80 ft (25m)

STRENGHT OF CURRENT:
Very Weak

Text and photographs by James Treter – Illustrations by Aurora Antico

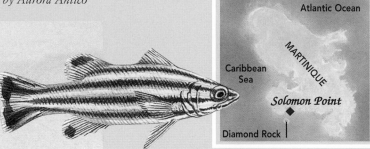

MARTINIQUE—PASSE DES FOURS
SOLOMON POINT

Solomon Point is another fantastic dive that is very different than Diamond Rock, especially in the variation of the terrain. There are several sites at and around this location, but Solomon Point is the most alluring. This site is actually a small yet very beautiful reef that is located to the north of Diamond Rock, which is not very far away. The dive is on the point of the large north cove and not far from the shoreline. The dive begins at about 50 feet (15 meters) and slopes downward to about 80 to 100 feet

67 top The most colorful denizen of Solomon Point is the parrot fish (Scarus vetula), which feeds on the vegetation growing on the coral.

67 bottom Solomon Point is a very lively diving site where you'll meet the Holocanthus ciliaris, *which feeds on sponges, algae and tunicates.*

22 m
72 ft

30 m
98 ft

40 m
131 ft

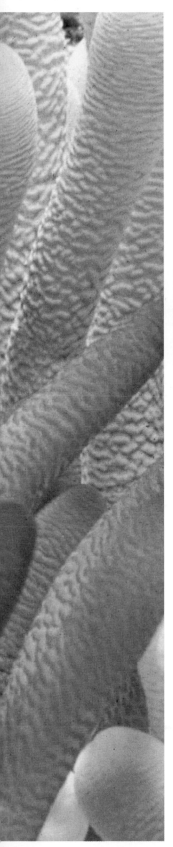

68-69 *A "cleaner" shrimp at work among the tentacles of an anemone.*

69 *top A Pomacanths paru explores the reef at Solomon Point. It's rather easy to get close to this fish, which isn't shy when facing divers.*

69 *center A* Hermodice carunculata *crosses fan-shaped coral. The voracious predator feeds on coral and jellyfish.*

69 *bottom The delicate color of this sponge is one of many hues seen in the crystal clear waters off Solomon Point.*

(25 to 30 meters) deep. As you submerge into the water you can see the reef. The dive gradually winds down a coral-covered platform of steps. The fantastic visibility of about 80 feet (25 meters) allows a panoramic vision for all divers to anticipate an expedition filled with wonder and amazement.

This reef dive is remarkable for the slopes covered with gorgonians and sponges in all sizes, shapes, and colors. This site has an abundance of majestic colorful flora and fauna. Many different corals, both hard and soft, have anchored themselves here and present dazzling formations of color and textures. Among the hard corals, bristle worms can easily be found crawling slowly to their destination. You can look but do not touch, because the bristle worm has hundreds of tiny fur-like stingers that will sting and burn. Marine snails, such as the flamingo tongue with its mantle of camouflage, can be found feeding on the soft corals. Looking among the flowing tentacles of the colorful anemones, you can see the tiny anemone cleaner shrimp as they flit back and forth through those stinging tentacles. You will most likely find arrowhead crabs or even a hermit crab or two, making their way over the corals.

On the rocks and corals, many spirographs, the technical name for them is Christmas tree worms, will amaze you with their colorful plumes until they quickly disappear as they feel the difference in the water pressure caused by your approach. Divers will be amazed as they observe the abundance of colorful tropical fish of many significant species, such as angelfish, butterfly fish, puffers, and trumpet fish, as they swim carefree in and among the flora.

More often than not, most species of the angelfish and the butterfly fish will be observed swimming in pairs.

This is because many of them are generally known to mate with one another for life. The brilliantly colored male parrot fish will hold your attention as he nibbles through the coral, while depositing clouds of white sand to add to the ocean floor.

Although this dive is suited for novice divers, it will also appeal to the more advanced diver, especially if you want to take photographs. Be sure to make this a leisurely dive since at every turn the view is breathtakingly beautiful and every nook and crevice holds different attractions.

Each time you visit this dive site, you will find and observe species of fish, mollusks, crustaceans, and invertebrates that you did not notice in the dive before.

Text and photographs by Giorgio Mesturini – Illustrations by Domitilla Müller

BRAZIL—FERNANDO DE NORONHA
PONTA DA SAPATA

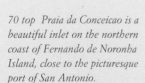

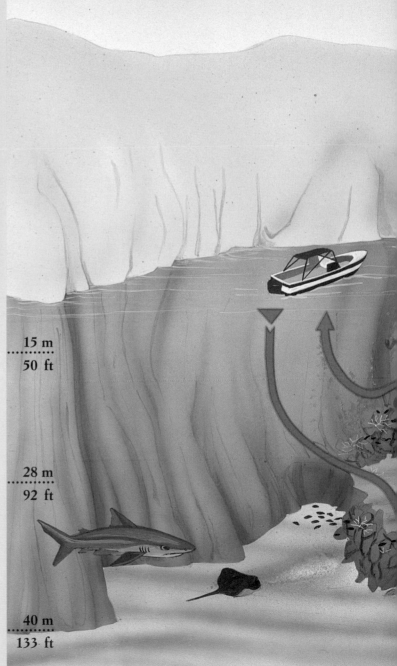

15 m
50 ft

28 m
92 ft

40 m
133 ft

70 top Praia da Conceicao is a beautiful inlet on the northern coast of Fernando de Noronha Island, close to the picturesque port of San Antonio.

70 bottom The coast of Fernando de Noronha is a continuous contrast of colors as a result of the alternation of black volcanic rock with the blue of the ocean and the long beaches of white sand.

F ernando de Noronha lies in the Atlantic Ocean 1,200 miles (350 kilometers) off the northeast coast of Brazil. It is the largest in a small archipelago of twenty-one islands discovered by Amerigo Vespucci in 1503 during a series of expeditions financed by the rich Portuguese merchant Fernando de Noronha.

After being a strategic military base for many years, in 1988 the archipelago was declared a national park, covering 70 square miles (112 square kilometers), to preserve the immense biological wealth both above and below water.

Strict but necessary rules protect the natural life of the archipelago from anything that might alter its natural balance; for example, underwater fishing, the collection of shells, and the capture of animals are prohibited, and the beaches may not be visited during the season when the turtles

Ponta da
Sapata

FERNANDO DE
NORONHA

N

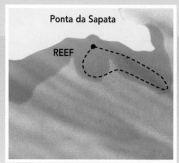

Ponta da Sapata

REEF

PRACTICAL TIPS

MAXIMUM DEPTH:
133 ft (40 m)

RECOMMENDED PERIOD:
August—April

LEVEL OF DIFFICULTY:
Average

SPECIAL FEATURES:
schools of jacks, barracuda
and snappers

VISIBILITY:
over 99 ft (30 m)

STRENGTH OF CURRENT:
Weak

lay their eggs. As a result, these islands remain a small fragment of paradise lost in the ocean.

One of the most extraordinary aspects of Fernando can be admired in the Baia Dos Dolfinhos, where hundreds of dolphins *(Stenella longirostris)* enter the peaceful waters of the inlet at dawn each day. Here they remain until dusk, when they return to the open sea.

The underwater world of Fernando de Noronha is also extraordinary. The volcanic origins of the island form a spectacular foundation, in which black volcanic rock alternates with areas covered with madrepore, and from the first moments underwater the diver is given the impression of a unique environment, with scenery that more resembles the Mediterranean than the tropics.

One of the loveliest areas to explore is Ponta da Sapata, on the extreme west of the island. The dive begins on the north side of the promontory, where you descend an attractive wall of rocks and gullies that comes to an end 130 feet (40 meters) down on the sandy bed. Being exposed to the ocean, the bed may display signs of the action of the large Atlantic waves, which together with the currents make their effects felt at a

depth of more than 30 feet (10 meters).

The black rocks of the seabed have interesting formations of madrepore with low but solid bases, best able to resist the impetus of the waves. At a depth of 50 feet (15 meters), a large flat section appears where expanses of lava pebbles alternate with large rocky spurs. This is the kingdom of the parrotfish, which attempts to break off bits of coral with its teeth, and of the sparkling blue surgeonfish, which moves around the rocks, indifferent to the diver's presence. The clarity of the water is incredible, thanks to the rocky bottom and the lack of phytoplankton; visibility is between 70 and 100 feet (20 and 30 meters).

Moving farther out, at about 90 feet (28 meters) deep, you will find the edge of a rock fall that drops to 130 feet (40 meters), where a vast expanse of sand stretches out to sea, the ideal habitat for rays and sole.

Every nook in the rocks hosts communities of lobsters, eels, shoals of squirrelfish, and especially grunts *(Anisotremus surinamensis)*, while silvery walls of carangids, barracuda, and snappers can be seen out to sea, and maybe the occasional black flash of a large shark.

Returning to the surface, if the current is not too strong head west, where you will come across a lovely wall covered with numerous multicolored sponges and inhabited by curious angel- and surgeonfish.

Rising along the cliff edge, at about 50 feet (15 meters) deep, you will find an area of huge rocks. Swim south, and you will find yourself back at the diving boat.

72 top left Silvery grunts (Anisotremus surinamensis) are one of the most common fish in these waters, both in the shallows and in deeper water.

72 bottom left The green moray (Gymnothorax funebris) may seem aggressive but will let you approach without difficulty.

72 top right The hard coral formations that cover the volcanic rocks of the seabed are neither high nor voluminous, making this seem more like the Mediterranean than a tropical sea.

72 bottom right Schools of striped snappers swim in water where visibility can exceed 100 feet (30 meters); in such conditions a dive is made much more interesting.

72-73 *Large lobsters are abundant in the waters of Fernando de Noronha, as the rough, creviced volcanic bed provides them with an ideal habitat.*

73 bottom *A silvery barracuda (Sphyraena sp.) swims undisturbed across the infinite blue depths of the Atlantic Ocean.*

73

France

Portofino the Mount

The Pampelonne Shallows

Grand Conglue

Ile Verte

Spain

LIGURIAN SEA

The Gabinière

Corsica

Carall Bernat

Mérouville

Balearic Islands

Sardinia

Secca
del Papa

Italy

ADRIATIC SEA

TYRRHENIAN SEA

Ustica

Colombara
Bank

Sicily

The Mountain
of Scilla

Corfù

Colovri
Island

Greece

IONIAN SEA

AEGEAN
SEA

Crete

Africa

Mediterranean

N

BLACK SEA

Turkey

Sea

Africa

THE MEDITERRANEAN:

INTRODUCTION

BY EGIDIO TRAINITO

The most enclosed sea in the world, the Mediterranean is connected to the Atlantic by the narrow Straits of Gibraltar—only 9 miles (14 kilometers) wide—across which only surface-level waters can flow. Even narrower is the Suez Canal, built by man in 1869, through which the exchange of water with the Red Sea, impeded by the difference in salinity of the bodies of water within the canal, is minimal and very recent. The Mediterranean is unique among the world's seas, not only as a result of its natural isolation but above all because of its variety of climatic conditions: the sea itself is relatively cold, with the temperature varying from 54–56°F (12–13°C) in the coldest season to 76–79°F (25–26°C) in summer. It is a relatively infertile sea—as defined by biologists—as overall its waters are less rich in organic materials than those of other seas. Here sunlight seems to have a contrary effect: although the light is a source of life and fundamental to the growth of vegetation, and thanks to the clarity of the water in many areas it penetrates to a good depth, it seems to drive away natural colors. The sections that receive the most sunlight—the expanses of sand along the coast, the fields of posidonia, the well-lit rocks—seem wrapped in a uniform blue, the complete opposite of the colors that attract the gaze of divers in tropical waters from just a few yards down. But this is the first element in the attraction of the Mediterranean; color does exist—just look through the pictures here—but you have to search for it in the shadows of the large rocks, in grottoes, in crevices, and in the depths. All the most brightly colored organisms—the sponges, gorgonians, and even the fish—seem to hide from the light, almost as if playing at hide-and-seek with the observer.

And here is the second reason the Mediterranean is intriguing: it does not show its cards all at once. It needs exploration, knowledge, attention, and patience. Perhaps it is also ancient in this, not just in its human history: its aesthetics belong to the past, in contrast to the rapidly moving phantasmagoria of the younger barrier reefs where you seem to be flicking through Internet screens rather than the pages of a book.

The Mediterranean is at first most striking in its underwater landscape, so difficult to reproduce in photography yet so important when diving. Vertical walls, pinnacles, great masses of rock, grottoes, and tunnels often reproduce scenes from the land, but the blue transforms them, wrapping them round with myriad life forms.

And this is the third reason for the beauty of the Mediterranean: it teems with large and small organisms that do not immediately offer themselves to the diver but require a knowledgeable search. Close examination reveals intricate relationships between organisms of all sizes and colors and exposes the extent of endemic species to the Mediterranean: a full 20 percent of the total from the forests of posidonia (*Posidonia oceanica*) to the omnipresent dotted sea slug (*Discodoris atromaculata*)—has evolved within this isolated body of water. Of the remainder of Mediterranean life forms, 75 percent are of Atlantic or northern origin, and 5 percent are tropical. This is the result of the sea's geological history; in perpetual change, it seems destined to become completely isolated if its geological evolution continues in the same way. Despite its small size (only 1.8 million square miles [3 million square kilometers], with a total length of 2,500 miles [4,000 kilometers]), from the point of view of its ecosystems, the Mediterranean can be divided into distinctly different geographical areas. A hypothetical dive from west to east would reveal a clear drop in the quantity of Atlantic organisms and a corresponding rise in tropical species, until eventually you met species from the Red Sea, which are slowly colonizing the eastern basin.

In the Mediterranean, the equation "protected area = environmental quality" is immediately evident. Close encounters with large groupers, and swirls of fish of all types around the diver, are spectacles exclusive to marine parks. In the protected areas of Spain, France, Sardinia, Tunisia, and elsewhere, you can see how the sea used to be long before diving became a common sport. To be sure, even outside the protected areas it is possible to make memorable dives—as the pages that follow show—but these marine parks demonstrate that a correct policy of protection of underwater environments (not just prohibitions) creates exceptional conditions compared to the norm.

Text and photographs by Giorgio Mesturini – Illustrations by Domitilla Müller

Carall Bernat
Rock

SPAIN

Balearic
Islands

Mediterranean Sea

AFRICA

SPAIN—MEDAS ISLANDS
CARALL BERNAT

The Medas Islands lie approximately a mile from the port of Estartit, and make up the geological extension of the Montgrì limestone massif. The sea around this archipelago holds a concentration of marine life rarely found in other Mediterranean areas. Its richness is due to a combination of various elements, one of the most significant of which is the nutritive contribution of the river Ter, which joins the sea on the west side of the archipelago. In

76 top Small Medas Island lies to the south of Large Medas, the rocky nesting home of many species of birds.

76 bottom This seagull forms one of the largest colonies in the Mediterranean on the Medas Islands in April and May.

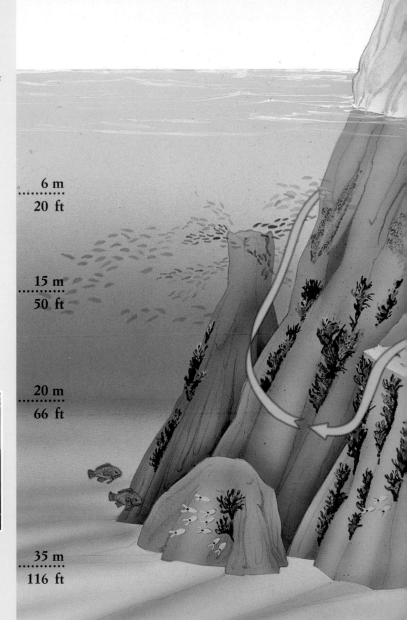

6 m
20 ft

15 m
50 ft

20 m
66 ft

35 m
116 ft

addition, currents guarantee a continual movement and exchange of water, even in the deepest stretches around the islands. With the further advantage presented by certain morphological aspects of these waters, the Medas Islands boast a remarkable variety of natural habitats. Adding to these favorable conditions for marine life, for several years the islands have been protected by strict environmental laws; since 1983, in fact, the independent Catalan government

Large Medas

Small Medas

Carall Bernat Rock

N

Tascons Grossos

CARALL BERNAT

Roca De L' Escrivana

PRACTICAL TIPS

MAXIMUM DEPTH:
116 ft (35 m)

RECOMMENDED PERIOD:
April—November

LEVEL OF DIFFICULTY:
Average

SPECIAL FEATURES:
red gorgonias and many fish

VISIBILITY:
in summer up to 99 ft (30 m)

STRENGTH OF CURRENT:
Weak

has prohibited all forms of fishing in the island area, and in 1990 a law was issued enforcing the conservation of wildlife. Consequently, the Medas Islands have become the largest marine park in Catalonia, as well as one of the most important in the Mediterranean.

Among the many great possibilities for underwater diving offered by the Medas Islands, the best location is Carall Bernat, a small island situated at the southernmost point of the archipelago, near the larger island of Tascons Grossos. Diving may begin in the narrow passage separating the two islands, where the sea reaches a depth of around 20 feet (6 meters). As you keep the rockface of Carall on the right, the seabed slopes gently forward. The underwater landscape is char-

78 top left Thanks to its exceptional ability to change color, the octopus (Octopus vulgaris) *is one of the most mimetic of creatures and is often difficult to see.*

acterized by large, clefted rocks and deep gorges; in areas less exposed to the light the diver is presented with an endless display of brightly colored organisms, such as sponges, madrepores, calcareous algae, and nudibranchs, which cover the whole seabed. Drawn by curiosity, Mediterranean morays *(Muraena helena),* sea eels *(Conger conger),* and forkbeard *(Phycis phycis)* can be seen now and again peering out from the safety of the deeper gorges. Still descending, after you pass several wide "steps," at a depth of 50 feet (15 meters) several small underwater caves appear along the northern slope of Carall. From 70 feet (20 meters)

onward, the seabed slopes rapidly, displaying a steep rockface that descends as far as a depth of 115 feet (35 meters). At this point the dive becomes quite exciting, thanks to the enormous quantity of sea fans *(Paramuricea clavata)* that entirely cover the seabed and, once caught in the flashlight, are revealed in all their graceful beauty, an intense red color streaked with yellow. Without reaching the bottom of the rockface, it is possible to stay at a depth of 80–100 feet (25–30 meters), where we can marvel at the silver carousels formed by shoals of large twoband bream *(Diplodus vulgaris),* saddled seabream *(Oblada melanura),* and dentex *(Dentex dentex).* Curious groupers *(Epinephelus guaza)* appear from among the rocks, not in the least intimidated by the presence of divers, who can get close enough to take spectacular photographs. Still keeping the rockface of Carall Bernat on the right and ascending to around 70 feet (20 meters), we pass through a magnificent gully and then follow the southern side of the rock, where the seabed at around 50 feet (15 meters) becomes less steep and is made up of large boulders and rocks. In spite of the reduced depth this slope is especially interesting, thanks to numerous rock fish, such as the scorpionfish, twoband bream, and damselfish gobies that inhabit every gorge. Moving on, we ascend to around 35 feet (10 meters), reaching the area that forms the strait between Carall Bernat and the little island of Tascons Grossos, where we began the dive.

78 bottom left The Mediterranean moray (Muraena helena) *can be seen during the day poking its head out of dark lairs.*

78 top right The gorgonians (Paramuricea clavata) *off the Medas Islands have a distinctive coloring; at the base of the fan they are a reddish-purple, tinged with yellow at the tip.*

78 bottom right The waters around the Medas Islands are filled with fish, divers here are constantly ringed by twoband bream (Diplodus vulgaris) *and black seabream* (Spondyliosoma cantharus).

78-79 *The painted comber* (Serranus scriba) *belongs to the family of Serranidae (sea basses); it has blue and red stripes on each side of its head.*

79 bottom *One thing that makes the Medas Islands unforgettable is the possibility of seeing brown groupers* (Epinephelus guaza), *immobile outside their lairs.*

79

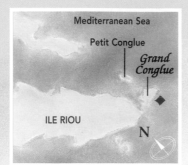

Mediterranean Sea

Petit Conglue

Grand Conglue

ILE RIOU

N

Grand Conglue

Mediterranean Sea

PRACTICAL TIPS

MAXIMUM DEPTH:
260 ft (80 m)

RECOMMENDED PERIOD:
May to October

LEVEL OF DIFFICULTY:
Average to difficult

SPECIAL FEATURES:
gorgonians, mullet

VISIBILITY:
in summer up to 162 ft (50 m)

STRENGTH OF CURRENT:
Average to Very Strong

Text and photographs by Kurt Amsler – Illustrations by Aurora Antico

FRANCE—MARSEILLE
GRAND CONGLUE

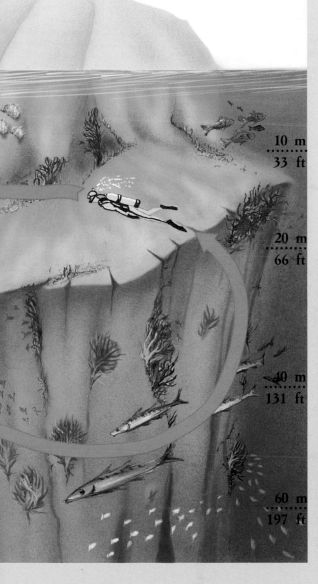

G rand Conglue is the last of a series of uninhabited islands about 10 miles (16 kilometers) east of Marseille. Wild and rugged, windswept and beaten by waves, with storms of seagulls surrounding them, these giant rocks have a truly unique allure. A visitor to Grand Conglue's steep, plunging bluffs will feel miniscule and cut off from the rest of the world.

For extraordinary diving in the waters around Grand Conglue, Petit Conglue, and the interesting Sec des Impériaux, set off from either the west or east. The fastest way to reach the immersion sites is to set sail from the port of Pointe Rouge,

81 The Paramuricea clavata *prefers the shade and it is usually found at a depth of 65-100 feet (20-30 meters), but in Grand Conglue it's found even at 32 feet (10 meters).*

10 m
33 ft

20 m
66 ft

40 m
131 ft

60 m
197 ft

Marseille, where there are various diving stations that offer boats heading towards the most spectacular underwater destinations in the area.

To the east there are the ports of Cassis, La Ciotat, and Les Lecques. Despite the greater distance (about 15 miles/25 kilometers), boats also sail to the diving sites from here.

Grand Conglue is an exceptional underwater destination and a paradise for undersea photography enthusiasts, thanks to the site's unique features, which give excellent results with wide-angle lenses and panoramic filming.

Access to the seabeds northwest of the gigantic mass is closed to diving and fishing, and no anchoring is allowed here either, whereas the waters to the southeast of the island are open to divers. The most spectacular seabeds are in the northern corner of this area, where it is possible to admire a fantastic underwater world of sheer rock faces, canyons, and plateaus.

Depending on wind and weather conditions, this nook will almost always offer a safe mooring for a boat. Nevertheless, some care will be required, as the region east of Marseille is

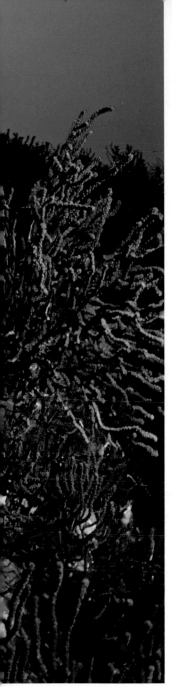

82 bottom It's easy to see large schools of fish hunting their prey when looking into the waters off Grand Conglue.

83 top An Axinella cannabina *sponge, with its characteristically branched structure which gives it a greater surface area for the absorption of nutrients, thrives on underwater reefs.*

83 center A Scyliorhinus sp. *egg on a* Paramuricea clavata.

83 bottom A starfish is bizarrely striking on a Paramuricea clavata.

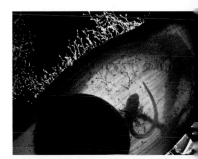

82-83 The Paramuricea clavata *thrive in the waters off Grand Conglue because of the strong sea currents that guarantee the colony an abundant flow of nourishing particles.*

renowned for its very unstable weather conditions. It only takes a few minutes for currents to change and the wind can make life very difficult for any sailor. The violent, gusty mistral can create some dangerous turbulence and spin a boat around its anchor, so when the "east wind" blows up, seek refuge behind Conglue as quickly as possible. In any case, it is recommended that at least one person always stays aboard, which is a suggestion that applies to all who arrive at this marvelous undersea destination with their own boats. The rest of us can blissfully rely on the diving center's skipper.

Here we dive directly alongside the rock face, which plunges sheer into the water and remains vertical for about 65 feet (20 meters) beneath the surface. Since the island's southern side is sunlit only in the mornings and for the rest of the day there is shade, from just a few centimeters below the surface, the walls are covered with yellow sea anemones and sponges of all shapes and colors. A few meters further down it is worth looking upwards to the surface. Where the waves beat against the rocks, shoals of mullet and other predatory fish hunt out their prey. On the open sea, not far from the rock face, there are resident barracuda – once rare in the Mediterranean – that settled in the waters around Grand Conglue some years ago.

The site is famous for the luxuriant forest of gorgonians, whose growth is fostered by the intense currents that are so typical of the island. The wall of *Paramuricea clavata* sea fans starts just 30 feet (10 meters) under sea level and descends to over 260 feet (80 m). Before the wall becomes perpendicular we swim just above a small, slightly sloping plateau. Here, too, the branches of massive specimens of gorgonian

stretch upwards. A close observation of them will reveal white basket stars of the *Astrospartus mediterraneus* species. These starfish are extremely rare in the Mediterranean and are more typical of tropical waters.

As we swim along the plateau it is not unusual to encounter shoals of comber (Serranus), which is a species that has been protected for years along the French coast. If we are lucky, we may spot moray eels (*Muraena helena*) peeking out of their lairs.

A dive at Grand Conglue can only be considered complete if it includes passing the edge of the cliff – never exceeding your level of experience – and swimming down the astonishing sheer face completely coated in gorgonians. It is interesting to note the behavior of the cuttlefish, concealed amongst the red gorgonians, as they change color to merge into the background. In spring, the odd nursehound (*Scyliorhinus stellaris*) maybe encountered, which is sadly increasingly rare in the Mediterranean. These small sharks are never more than a three feet in length and live mainly on the seabed, swimming smoothly amongst the labyrinthine gorgonians, laying their eggs in its branches.

When the time in deep water is up, return to the plateau, and here it is worth exploring the countless reefs, crevasses, and tiny grottoes. There are lobsters (*Palinurus vulgaris*) and mantis-shrimp, and those lucky enough to have good eyesight and a good underwater torch, will find sea snails, flatworms, and other multicolored sea creatures.

The required safety stop or decompression can be comfortably organized near the wall. The boat can come and pick divers up at just a few yards from the island.

Text and photographs by Kurt Amsler – Illustrations by Aurora Antico

FRANCE, LA CIOTAT

FRANCE—LA CIOTAT
ILE VERTE

84 top A scorpion fish waiting in ambush in the Sec de Rosiers, just southeast of Ile Verte.

84 bottom A forest of Paramuricea clavata awaits divers in the Sec des Rosiers. In 2005, a prohibition was issued against anchoring in this area to safeguard its fragile ecosystem.

Ile Verte (the Green Isle), whose name comes from the pines and other luxuriant vegetation that cover it, is located in the northwest part of Les Lecques Bay. The Bec de l'Aigle, or Eagle's Beak, promontory soars to the northwest of the island, dominating the former shipyard at La Ciotat, which has been in disuse for many years now.

To the north the arm of sea that separates Ile Verte from the mainland is 50 feet (15 meters) at its deepest point, and in the center there is an interesting sandbank called Le Cannonier, whose tip reaches 13 feet (4 meters) below the water's surface. The shallow is crossed by a natural and accessible tunnel, about 32 feet (10 meters) long. From northwest to southeast of the island the seabeds slope more sharply and reach greater depths, with two underwater plateaux hallmarking the topography of the floor.

The first shallow, Sec des Rosiers, stretches to the southeast of the island and starts at about 330 feet (100 meters) from the shore. Again, this is a place where divers can enjoy some interesting bluffs and a jagged, undersea world, crammed with crevices down to about 100 feet (30 meters), where the sandbank slopes down to a flat, sandy bottom.

The sandy bed continues as far as the second shallow, called La Pierre du Levant, about 980–1300 feet (300–400 meters) from the island, and continues as far as a depth of 50 feet (15 meters) below sea level. For divers the most interesting side of the sandbank is that opposite

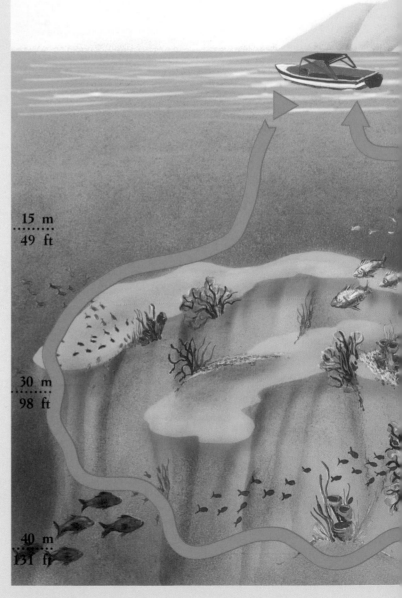

15 m
....
49 ft

30 m
....
98 ft

40 m
....
131 ft

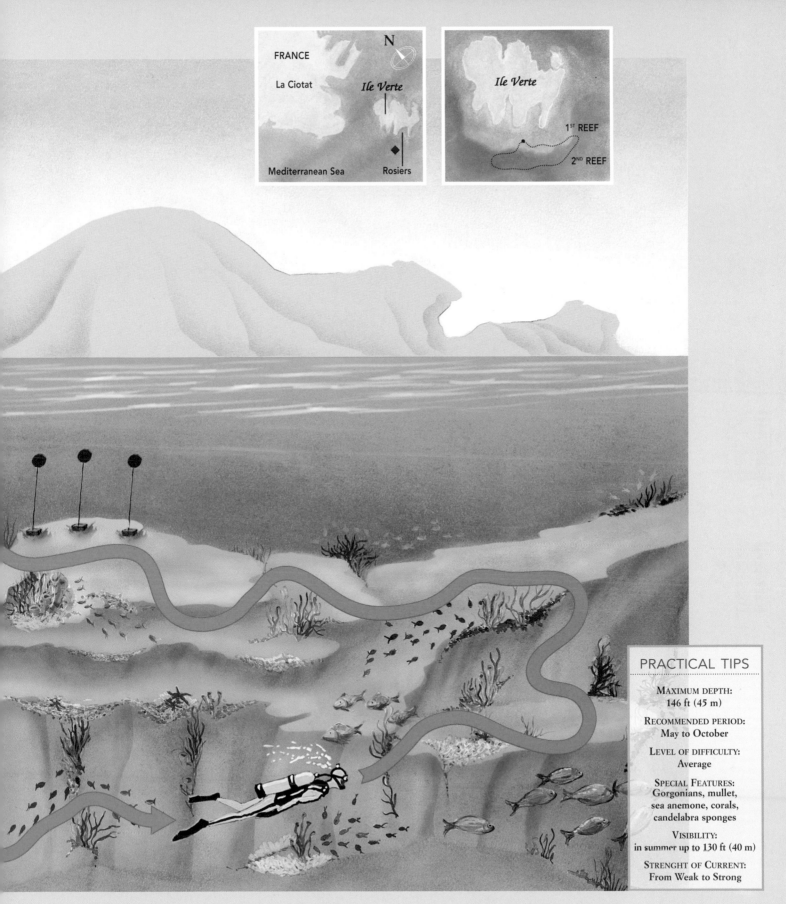

FRANCE

La Ciotat

Ile Verte

Mediterranean Sea

Rosiers

N

Ile Verte

1ST REEF

2ND REEF

PRACTICAL TIPS

MAXIMUM DEPTH:
146 ft (45 m)

RECOMMENDED PERIOD:
May to October

LEVEL OF DIFFICULTY:
Average

SPECIAL FEATURES:
Gorgonians, mullet,
sea anemone, corals,
candelabra sponges

VISIBILITY:
in summer up to 130 ft (40 m)

STRENGHT OF CURRENT:
From Weak to Strong

the island. Here the rocks are covered in red gorgonians and, unlike the other side, yellow "candelabra" sponges proliferate (Axinella sp.).

The most spectacular part, of course, is the southeast, where the shallows drop sheer and in some areas reach 200 feet (60 meters) in depth. Thanks to the current, the mantle of sea fans is truly sumptuous and fish abound. Depending on the season and weather conditions, there is quite often excellent visibility, even over 130 feet (40 meters) horizontal.

The two diving sites, Le Sec des Rosiers (the Rose Garden Shallows) and La Pierre du Levant (the Levant Stone), are certainly amongst the 10 best underwater venues of the Côte d'Azur. We must bear in mind, however, that La Pierre du Levant is strictly for very experienced divers, since the rock formations do not start until about 100 feet (30 meters) down, then plunge very deep, while Le Sec des Rosiers is perfect for divers of all standards. The diving stations at La Ciotat, Les Lecques, and La Madrague are excel-

86-87 A large colony of anemones thriving in the Sec des Rosiers.

lent set-off points for some memorable dives.

From 2005 it is no longer possible to cast anchor near the Rosiers shallow. This decision has been made to safeguard the seabed. Boats can moor at several boas attached to the seabed. A dive from this point will take you directly to the bluff's highest point, 50 feet (15 meters) in depth. You can enjoy the strange rocky peaks, completely covered in yellow snakelocks anemones *(Anemonia viridis)*. Around the reef's highest point there are shoals of Mediterranean blacktails (Diplodus) and dense clouds of damselfish (Chromis). Depending on the weather, the currents vary from light to strong. The dive begins, as usual, against the current, following the classic course and dropping immediately down to the envisaged depth.

The best feature of this site is certainly the cloak of red sea fans. The Paramuricea type of gorgonian is a coral with a soft, flexible skeleton, and is made up of colonies of billions of minuscule animals, so-called coral polyps. They vary in color from dark red to light red and several colonies may even have a changing hue that fades from red to a splendid glowing yellow. For most of the day, the vertical face is in shadow and exposed to currents, which naturally encourages the growth of these gorgonians.

A swim above the edge of the cliff is breathtaking, as the seabed drops away down into the blue. At several points small grottoes open up in the rock face. As you proceed in your exploration of the sheer face you should always take an underwater torch. If you light up the grotto ceiling you will observe whole stretches of splendid red coral, *Corallium rubrum*. Here a short pause is worthwhile, to enjoy the sight at close quarters. Red coral was considered a priceless underwater treasure even in ancient Roman times, and it was cut like a gemstone, polished and set into jewelry. In the Middle Ages, trade in coral ornaments flourished to the point that even Buddhist monks and other important prelates wore jewels made from this material.

The sheer rock faces at Sec des Rosiers are

the secret home of several nudibranchs, more commonly known as sea snails. With luck, you may sight the Mediterranean's largest sea slugs, part of the Hypselodoris class, which can grow to 8 inches (20 cm) in length and are easy to recognize because of the deep yellow stripe on their bodies.

At the base of the bluff, you will find yourself at 115–150 feet (35–45 meters) below sea level, depending on where you began the dive. Here the sandy bed slopes gently out to the open sea. It is not worth going any further here because at these depths there is never much time, and the seabed is not very interesting in any case.

Beginning a slow ascent to the surface, you should gaze upwards and enjoy the vertical face from the bottom. Only now can you see the entire view of the lavish mantle of gorgonians that covers the reef. Small pink anthias dart around the coral branches. These fish are totally similar to their tropical cousins and can be recognized by the three pale stripes on its head and for its long, multicolored pectoral fin. During the dive, you will also meet many wreckfish (Polyprion americanum), now repopulating the French coast thanks to a successful protection scheme. At Rosiers these fish are especially curious and follow divers, although they keep a safe distance.

When you reach the top of the bluff, you should be about 65 feet (20 meters) under the surface of the water. If you have enough air left, you can continue exploring the other slope of the cliff, where the wall slopes at about 40 degrees. The layer of sea fans also dominates this side, but the most eye-catching feature is the large number of yellow "candelabra" sponges, Axinella sp., which can grow to a 3 feet in height here.

After the Rosiers dive you must take a 3–5-minute safety stop, at 16 feet (5 meters) below sea level, and this is easily and safely done along the boa chain, before returning aboard the boat, still glowing from the wonderful experience you have just enjoyed.

87 top Notwithstanding the clarity of the waters (130 feet/40 meters horizontally), sea creatures capable of camouflage are able to escape observation, like this octopus does.

87 bottom A magnificent Antedon mediterranea *is at ease on the rocky seabed, rich in algae, in the Sec des Rosiers.*

PORT CROS ISLAND

Gabinière Bank

Hyères Islands

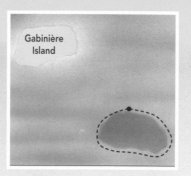

Gabinière Island

PRACTICAL TIPS

Maximum Depth:
149 ft (45 m)

Recommended period:
April—November

Level of difficulty:
Average

Special features:
groupers and corvine

Visibility:
in summer up to 99 ft (30 m)

Strength of current:
Weak

Text and photographs by Giorgio Mesturini – Illustrations by Domitilla Müller

FRANCE
ITALY
Ligurian Sea
◆ *Gabinière Bank*
Hyères Islands
CORSICA

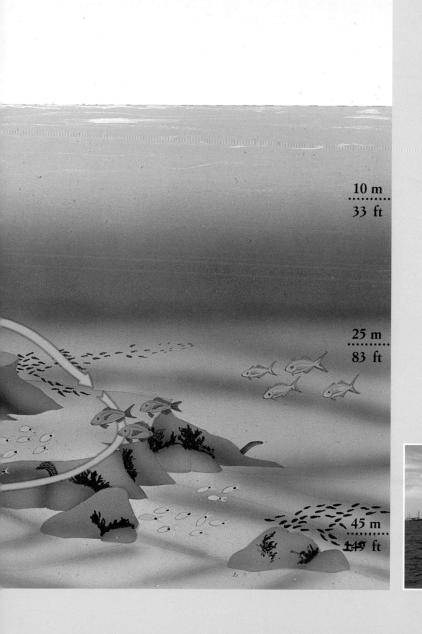

10 m
33 ft

25 m
83 ft

45 m
149 ft

FRANCE — HYÈRES ISLANDS
THE GABINIÈRE SANDBANK

The Hyères are a group of three small islands, Porquerolles, Port Cros, and Ile du Levant, that lie off the Côte d'Azur, a few miles from the port of Lavandou.

This archipelago is protected from exploitation through tourism, thanks to a specific law issued by the French government. In 1963, in fact, the island of Port Cros with its surrounding waters was declared a national park, and in 1971 the government bought a large part

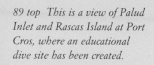

89 top This is a view of Palud Inlet and Rascas Island at Port Cros, where an educational dive site has been created.

89 bottom Gabinière Island still has lively, unpolluted seabeds.

89

90 top left Exploring the depths of the spire to the south of Gabinière Island, you will often come face to face with large groupers (Epinephelus guaza) that may exceed 3 feet (1 meter) in length.

90 center left Off the Gabinière bank, you will certainly find lairs inhabited by schools of brown meagre (Sciaena umbra) that are not bothered at all by the presence of divers and which will let you observe them at short range.

90 bottom left You will often find shoals of small poor cod (Trisopterus minutus), recognizable by their silvery color and long barbels.

of the island of Porquerolles, thus safeguarding its valuable natural environment.

Port Cros appears today as an island consecrated to nature, totally covered by dense woodland, where in the course of time man has left only faint signs of his passage.

In keeping with the reserve's present management policies, the National Park of Port Cros, besides guaranteeing the protection of fauna and flora, has a distinct educational component. Only certain areas, in fact, are closed to the public; the rest of the park is visited by numerous tourists who come to admire its wealth of nature.

To the south of Port Cros lies the little island of Gabinière, which boasts one of the most impressive underwater landscapes of the archipelago. An even more precious treasure, however, is found just off shore. At a few hundred yards south of Gabinière, in fact, we come across the sandbank from which the island takes its name, which reaches a height of 35 feet (10 meters); on a calm day this sandbank can be seen easily from the surface.

Beginning the dive on the southern side of the island, we descend in a southwesterly direction. Once submerged in the crystal-clear water, we are immediately struck by the lunar appearance of the seabed, due to the light-colored rocks that seem to form an immense staircase, descending gently to a depth of around 150 feet (45 meters), where large boulders form a spectacular labyrinth.

Exploring the inside of the numerous inhabited holes, we are amazed to see that every cleft in the rock is a refuge for lobsters (*Palinurus elephas*), Mediterranean morays (*Muraena helena*), brown meagre (*Sciaena umbra*), and many twoband bream (*Diplodus vulgaris*). As we look toward the surface the scene is indeed dreamlike, with a continual passage of sea urchins (*Seriola dumerini*), dentex (*Dentex dentex*), and shoals of saddled seabream (*Oblada melanura*) and bogues (*Boops boops*), which swim peacefully around our air bub-

90 top right The octopus (Octopus vulgaris), *a curious creature, is happy to come out of its lair to greet divers.*

90 bottom right Young Mediterranean groupers (Epinephelus guaza) *are recognizable from adults by their paler colors.*

91 The coloring of the black scorpionfish (Scorpaena porcus) *enables it to hide on the seabed. Its dorsal spines secrete a powerful poison, and a prick from one of them can cause intense pain.*

92 *The elegant* Alicia mirabilis *can only be seen in all its beauty by night as it lengthens its transparent tentacles in the dark; during the day, it holds them in and resembles a small chestnut-colored cone.*

93 top *Diving in from the top of the Gabinière spire, you are surrounded by dense shoals of saddled seabream* (Oblada melanura) *and bogues* (Boops boops).

93 center left *Among the many species of sponge in the Mediterranean, the most gaudy is certainly* Axinella cannabina.

bles. Moving on, we head westward, ascending to around 100 feet (30 meters), and come eventually to the westernmost point of the sandbank, where we begin to follow the northern slope. This side presents a different type of morphology; the rock, in fact, descends more steeply, forming tall rocky ramparts, up to around 80 feet (25 meters). The whole of this slope is characterized by an explosion of brightly colored coral—bryozoa, serpulids, annelids, sponges, and large red sea fans line the smallest crevices in the seabed. Swimming among the Paramuricae are thick shoals of anthias, the males of which sport a magnificent red plumage delicately streaked with yellow and lilac. And finally we are honored by the appearance of the undisputed queens of this underwater landscape—the groupers *(Epinephelus guaza)*, who, completely undisturbed by the presence of divers, float immobile in a classic "candle" position, far from their refuge. A little farther on, we are greeted by another surprise—magnificent shoals of brown meagre *(Sciaena umbra)* swimming freely among innumerable twoband bream, which make this sandbank one of the most valuable in the Mediterranean. Rising toward the surface, we might pause briefly on the top of the sandbank to admire the throng of twoband bream, zebra seabream, and black seabream *(Spondyliosoma cantharus)* that swim undisturbed around the divers' masks.

93 bottom left *On occasion, the branches of red gorgonians* (Paramuricea clavata) *form an excellent support for various species of sessile animals such as the delicate hydrozoans, which form irregularly ramified arborescent colonies.*

93 center right *The nudibranch* Cratena peregrina *is an elegant translucid white with bright violet dorsal papillae; it also has two orange marks in front of its nose.*

93 bottom right *The large fans of the red gorgonians can reach up to 3 feet (1 meter) in length and cover the north side of Gabinière bank with color.*

Text and photographs by Kurt Amsler – Illustrations by Aurora Antico

FRANCE
• St. Tropez

The Pampelonne Shallows

CORSICA

Mediterranean Sea

FRANCE—ST. TROPEZ
THE PAMPELONNE SHALLOWS

18 m
59 ft

25 m
82 ft

44 m
144 ft

St. Tropez, the little town of the "rich and beautiful," is world renowned for the many film stars, musicians, and celebrities who own a villa or, at least, have a big yacht moored there. St. Tropez also boasts the famous Pampelonne Beach, 4 miles (6 kilometers) of white sand, ideal for swimming and sunbathing, but also for a whole range of water sports. Pampelonne has no villas or hotels, just a few holiday villages, campsites, and restaurants of all standards, including some very exclusive venues, amidst the unspoilt landscape. Since the bay of

94 left Hanging perpendicular to the wall, the Paramuricea clavata *tint the waters off Pampelonne all shades of red.*

94 right A moray eel waiting in ambush among the rocks in the waters off Pampelonne.

the same name faces east, the beach is sheltered from the mistral, a gusty wind that blows from the northwest and often makes it impossible to dive off this shore. One of the loveliest diving sites here is called the Pampelonne Shallows, which is exactly opposite the beach, about 3 miles (5 kilometers) away. The highest part of the shallows reaches 50 feet (15 meters) below sea level and that is why it is quite difficult to spot the diving site from the surface unless the water is

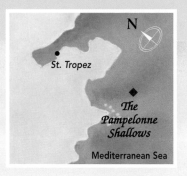

St. Tropez

The
Pampelonne
Shallows

Mediterranean Sea

N

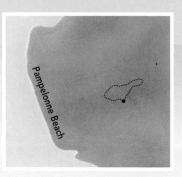

Pampelonne Beach

PRACTICAL TIPS

MAXIMUM DEPTH:
143 ft (44 m)

RECOMMENDED PERIOD:
May to October

LEVEL OF DIFFICULTY:
Average

SPECIAL FEATURES:
gorgonians, wreckfish,
corals, lobsters, blennies

VISIBILITY:
in summer up to 130 ft (40 m)

STRENGHT OF CURRENT:
From Weak to Strong

96 top *A school of salpa searches for algae and small crustaceans in the waters off Pampelonne.*

96 bottom *Pampelonne Shallows are a real paradise of red gorgonians, whose colonies cover the reef and grow out towards the open waters.*

96-97 *Schools of* Paramuricea clavata, *perpendicular to the current in order to better filter the nutrient-laden water, thrive throughout the waters off Pampelonne.*

very clear and still. Naturally, the problem can be resolved using an echo-sounder. In any case, the handiest and easiest solution is to reach the site with one of the excursions organized by local diving centers. The European Diving Center, located directly on the beach, has daily trips out the Pampelonne Shallows. From the St. Tropez station it takes about 45 minutes.

The shallows stretch from northwest to southeast and the most spectacular undersea destination, with three grottoes and mullet rocks, is about 330 feet (100 meters) from the mooring point. Never forget we are on the open sea. The site's exposure makes it liable to very strong currents at times. For that same reason the visibility is great (often up to 165 feet/50 meters), because the water is never cloudy even when the current is truly strong.

To dive from the point described above, the boat pilot will have to anchor at one of the highest points of the shallows, which descend to about 60 feet (18 meters) below the surface. Given that the depth is not excessive, this is a suitable spot for less experienced divers. At the top of the shallows the rocks are bare, so there are no risks of damaging an anchor on gorgonians and corals. From the

instant you dive to the instant you reach the rock formations, you will be surrounded by hundreds of damselfish *(Chromis chromis)*, which is a small species of fish very common in the Mediterranean. The top of the shallows comprises a plateau that slopes gently down a few yards, to then drop sheer to the depths. As usual, you swim directly beyond the edge and descend along the vertical face to reach the greatest depth envisaged.

The most evident feature of these beds is the luxuriant carpet of gorgonians whose branches stretch perpendicular out towards the open sea, dancing in the current. If you light up these animals with an underwater torch, you can admire their wonderful bright colors, ranging through all shades of red, from the darkest to the lightest. Several gorgonians of the *Paramuricea clavata* species have yellow tips.

The vertical face continues for about 65 feet (20 meters), then the cliff slopes down to a flat, sandy seabed at about 130 feet (40 meters). At about 50 feet (15 meters) ahead of the rock face we find a tall mass, also covered in sea fans. Its unique feature is the large number of wreckfish that can be encountered here. It is worth exploring the nooks in the rock and, if in luck, you may meet up with one or two moray eels.

After reaching a depth of 144 feet (44 meters) at this point, it is a good idea to turn back to the shallows. Continue, ascending the cliff diagonally, heading southeast. You will soon note a large mass, not far from the rock face. Between this and the cliff there is a small canyon. As you enter and continue to swim upwards, it will be easy to find the entrance to a grotto (13–16 feet/4–5 meters in size), completely covered in sponges and precious red coral *(Corallium rubrum)*. If you look carefully, you will notice the long antennae of lobsters who spend the day holed up in the rocky nooks and only leave their lairs at night to explore the reef in search of food.

Several yards further on to the southeast you will find another two, smaller grottoes, equally lavish with gorgonians and teeming with small sea creatures. The creatures who prefer the shadowy grottoes more than any other are the nudibranchs or sea snails. These tiny animals do not have a shell to protect them and are totally "nude," with external branchiae that jut out in tufts from their

lower third back area. They may appear vulnerable, but sea snails are no one's prey, since they are inedible for fish and some are even poisonous.

Several types of blenny, small fish of the Blennidi family, live at the entrance to the grottoes. The finest species are definitely the ocellated blenny and the black-headed blenny. During the mating season the head and body of the male blenny change color. These fish are unique as they make their comic "bouncing" way across the seabed:

because they have no air bladder they keep to the rocks and we will never find them on the open sea. Also at the entrance of the three grottoes, you may find a few wreckfish (*Polyprion americanus*), but they are quite shy and difficult to approach. Even the tiniest gesture can frighten them off and we recommend moving as little as possible, breathing slowly and evenly. Eye contact is also important. It is more likely that an animal will stay where it is, if it sees what is approaching, whereas

there is a strong chance it will flee if caught from the rear.

Now you are quite near the top of the sand bank. When you reach the surface you can head for the boat. Depending on the time and air available, you can go straight back along the reef or explore the seabed further. It is advisable to use the anchor chain when returning to the surface. At 16 feet (5 meters) you must undertake the compulsory three-minute safety stop.

LIGURIA

Genoa

Portofino
Promontory

Chiappa Point

N

Portofino ◆
The Mount

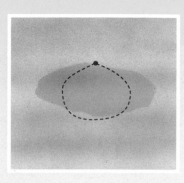

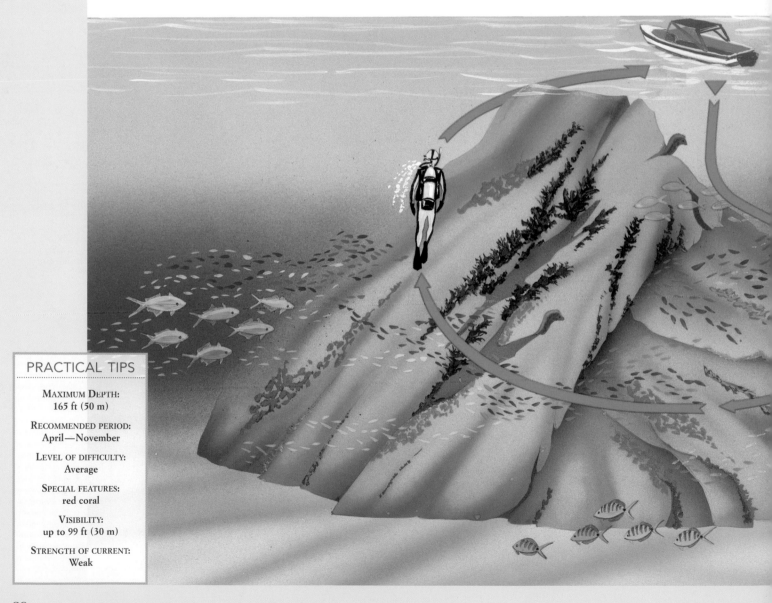

PRACTICAL TIPS

MAXIMUM DEPTH:
165 ft (50 m)

RECOMMENDED PERIOD:
April—November

LEVEL OF DIFFICULTY:
Average

SPECIAL FEATURES:
red coral

VISIBILITY:
up to 99 ft (30 m)

STRENGTH OF CURRENT:
Weak

Text and photographs by Vincenzo Paolillo – Illustrations by Domitilla Müller

13 m
....
43 ft

50 m
....
165 ft

ITALY—PORTOFINO
THE MOUNT

There are many dives that can be made off the headland of Portofino, known as Il Monte ("The Mount") by the locals. All are interesting for the environment, the varied colors, and encounters with interesting fish, but the loveliest, most complete, but also most demanding dives are those from the Isuela bank.

In front of the strip of granite that forms the

99 The photos show the enchanting gulf of Portofino. In the aerial views, in particular, one can see the point of Portofino, with the boats at anchor in the small bay. Photograph by Marcello Bertinetti (top) and Anne Conway (bottom)/Archivio White Star).

northeast corner of the headland, Punta Chiappa, the bed rises to almost 45 feet (13 meters) in depth about 650 feet (200 meters) from the tip of the point. This is the "cappella of the secca," (chapel of the shoal), which rests on a plateau of mud about 160–200 feet (50-60 meters) down.

To dive here, it is convenient to anchor on the shoal, though the new Park Authority will soon

fix a mooring buoy in place. You can then dive in any direction you like.

All sides of the shoal offer interesting sights: what you do depends on the current and your own ability, bearing in mind that if you descend on the side toward the land, the depth does not exceed 130 feet (40 meters), while on the west side, which faces out to sea, the base of the shoal reaches 160–180 feet (50–55 meters). This is the more attractive of the two.

Descend heading south, but slowly turn toward the west as you go down, and you will come across a sloping shelf slashed by crevices where you may well find eels, lobsters, or many types of octopus and scorpionfish. If you dive ear-

100 top *Meetings with large ocean sunfish* (Mola mola) *are common on Isuela.*

100 bottom *Packed schools of salema* (Sarpa salpa) *meander among the algae in search of food.*

100-101 *The stupendous fans of the red gorgonians* (Paramuricea clavata) *characterize the seabeds of The Mount at Portofino.*

101 top *A small Mediterranean moray* (Muraena helena) *peeps out of its hole.*

101 bottom *Often clouds of barbier* (Anthias anthias) *move among the sea fans.*

101

102 top left A wonderful example of a sea slug (Coryphella lineata) *moving among the hydrozoa on which it feeds.*

102 center left The striped galathea (Galathea strigosa) *hide against the rocky dropoff.*

ly in the day, you may find decently sized groupers, conger eels, or martens.

First you will see the yellow branches of *Eunicella verrucosa,* then increasingly dense populations of splendid giant red sea fans and stupendous purple gorgonians surrounded by swarms of barbier *(Anthias anthias),* as well as scorpionfish and some lovely examples of *Hypselodoris webbi,* a wonderful yellow nudibranch that climbs over the branches of the gorgonians. There are also sea lilies *(Antedon mediterranea).*

In the cracks between the rocks you will find red coral all around The Mount, behind which a red scorpionfish *(Scorpaena scrofa* or *Scorpaena notata)* might have camouflaged itself. On the steps in the middle of the algae on some sandy terrace, you are sure to come across sea anemones, shellfish *(Galatea strigosa,* among others), and squills.

At this point you should make a proper ascent and safety stop. Take a look around: besides jellyfish you will see sea urchins, schools of twoband bream and salema milling around the shoal, ocean sunfish *(Mola mola),* nudibranchs—dotted sea slugs *(Peltodoris atromaculata)* and pink flabellina *(Flabellina* sp.)—and lots of nonmigratory fish. If you dive at night (be careful of the depth) you will also come across squid and *Alicia mirabilis.*

102 top right A large red scorpionfish (Scorpaena notata) *was surprised amid the yellow sea daisies* (Parazoanthus axinellae).

102 bottom The sea lily (Antedon mediterranea) *is anything but rare on Isuela.*

102-103 A largescale scorpionfish (Scorpaena scrofa), *the same color as the red coral* (Corallium rubrum), *tries to camouflage itself.*

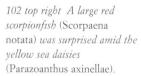

N

Cavallo Island

Lavezzi Island

✦ *Merouville*

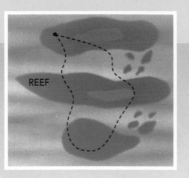

REEF

PRACTICAL TIPS

MAXIMUM DEPTH:
99 ft (30 m)

RECOMMENDED PERIOD:
April—November

LEVEL OF DIFFICULTY:
Average

UNUSUAL FEATURES:
large groupers

VISIBILITY:
over 99 ft (30 m)

STRENGTH OF CURRENT:
Sometimes Strong

Text and photographs by Kurt Amsler – Illustrations by Domitilla Müller

CORSICA

Tyrrhenian Sea

Merouville ◆

FRANCE—LAVEZZI ISLAND
MEROUVILLE

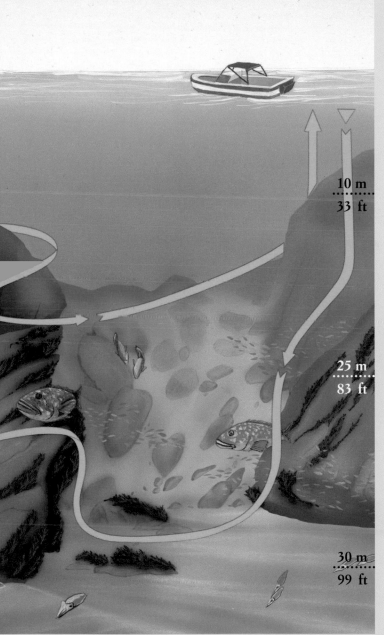

10 m
33 ft

25 m
83 ft

30 m
99 ft

105 top Bonifacio—here can be seen the Madonetta lighthouse— is the port from which diving trips to Merouville leave. Photograph by Marcello Bertinetti/Archivio White Star.

105 bottom The soft limestone of the cliffs of Bonifacio is marked by the action of the sea, and the large boulders at the base are indicative of wave erosion. Photograph by Marcello Bertinetti/Archivio White Star.

Bonifacio, the southern-most town in France, stands on white cretaceous rock 200 feet (60 meters) above the surface of the sea, on a narrow peninsula 1 mile (1.5 kilometers) long. The town was important at the time of the Roman Empire, and during the Middle Ages the citadels along the steep rocky coast were obliged to withstand numerous attacks. The port is a truly picturesque sight, especially at sundown, when the lights come on along the seafront. The old town is a maze of tiny alleys and squares, hemmed in by medieval hous-es. The rock gives a marvelous view of the

106-107 and 107 bottom
Dusky groupers (Epinephelus marginatus) *at Merouville are accustomed to the approach of divers with offerings of food, and even though this practice is much less common today, they continue to approach divers.*

Nowhere else in the Mediterranean do so many and such large serranids (groupers) live. The Mediterranean grouper *(Epinephelus guaza)* was once very common in coastal waters, but because they make such good eating, they have been hunted by divers and fished in a ruthless manner. You used to need a good dose of luck to see one during a dive, and only at a distance and great depth, but since capture of serranids was banned in France some years ago, the population has rapidly increased. The grouper is a splendid creature, its long oval body reaching a length of 5 feet (150 centimeters). Its slightly protruding lower jaw gives the fish, which is able to swallow prey half its own weight, both a fearsome and an engaging appearance.

"Bouches," Bonifacio's road, and the Italian island of Sardinia, just 7 miles (12 kilometers) away. Bonifacio is the ideal departure point for diving in the underwater Lavezzi National Park, where our diving center is located.

Lavezzi Island protrudes from the deep blue sea on the east of the town. This small island just 330 feet (100 meters) across lies in the strait between Corsica and Sardinia. In 1982 the entire area of Lavezzi was declared an underwater national park, and one of the reasons for this was undoubtedly the immense numbers of fish that inhabit the zone. Thanks to the depth of the water and the constant current, the water is crystal clear and full of food for the fish.

Merouville—literally, "Grouper City"—is found on the east slope of Lavezzi Island. The diving point is a heap of three gigantic underwater granite rocks and other, smaller, boulders. They lie on a sandy bottom 100 feet (30 meters) down and cover roughly 160 by 330 feet (50 by 100 meters). The highest point in the tumble of rocks reaches about 50 feet (16 meters) from the surface of the water.

Merouville is indeed a well-chosen name.

107 top *A wall of the spire is entirely covered with golden zoanthids* (Parazoanthus axinellae), *which like to colonize areas that receive little light; the polyps of the plants have no skeletons.*

107 center *Certain colonies of coral* (Corallium rubrum) *have white open polyps that contrast with the red of their skeleton; the coral off the coast of Bonifacio is very widespread, and even today is harvested for sale.*

Groupers are nonmigratory fish and only live around rocky seabeds, where they use the hollows and tunnels as hiding places. Anyone who has attempted to photograph one of these fish will know their intelligent game of hide-and-seek with the diver, but at Lavezzi they are anything but shy. It is also possible to observe their sexual transformation from female to male.

Normally groupers can be found among the three large blocks of rock. They don't keep you waiting long; they arrive one by one and follow the diver on his route. The best dive area is the east slope, where hollows and cracks are entirely covered with vegetation.

108 top left Two small scorpionfish (Scorpaena sp.) trust to their mimetic ability to hide on the rock; it works fine in natural light, but the effect is lost with the use of the flash.

108 bottom left The groupers at Merouville are all especially large and can weigh in excess of 66 pounds (30 kg); they are therefore almost exclusively male, as groupers change sex when they reach about 10 pounds (5 kg).

108-109 The octopus (Octopus vulgaris) is an intelligent predator, but it has a difficult life at Merouville; groupers find it a tasty meal, and it is not rare to see an octopus with raddled tentacles.

Groupers are without doubt the stars of Lavezzi, but its diverse Mediterranean flora and fauna should not be ignored despite one's enthusiasm for the big fish. Large morays and groupers live in perfect harmony and may even be seen together, scorpionfish live on the rocks, and the gray bodies of large conger eels can be seen hiding in the niches. The projections and summits of the rocks are home to yellow anemones that provide a lovely contrast to the blue background of the water. Naturally there is no lack of red gorgonians growing in the shaded sections of the enormous boulders, which form the topography of the seabed here. The diver will also be surrounded by hundreds of barbier and may see, depending on the time of the year, large jellyfish *(Cotyloriza tuberculata)*. In this exposed area between Corsica and Sardinia, not even spotted eagle rays and other pelagic fish are a rarity.

The coral plateau hosts many forms of life. You will see shoals of salemas *(Sarpa salpa)* and seabream *(Diplodus* sp.). They rush to feed on algae on a ledge all together and, in the same way, all move away together. Close to the rocks covered with thick red algae swim variously colored damselfish. Always on the lookout for a nibble, they can be found everywhere there is something to eat.

109 bottom left The John Dory (Zeus faber) *is unmistakable with its long, flat body and extra-long dorsal fin.*

109 top right The large granite rocks at Merouville are covered with gorgonians (Paramuricea clavata) *that enjoy the currents, often strong, on the spire.*

109 bottom right The yellow ramifications of a large sponge (Axinella sp.) *make the surrounding gorgonians seem small; this growth strategy allows the sponge to offer a large surface area for absorption of nutrients while occupying a minimum of space on the seabed.*

Text and photographs by Egidio Trainito – Illustrations by Domitilla Müller

Secca
del Papa

SARDINIA

Tyrrhenian
Sea

ITALY—TAVOLARA
THE SECCA DEL PAPA

Tavolara is a rocky limestone island 4 miles (6 kilometers) long by half a mile (1 kilometers) wide and reaches a height of 1,850 feet (565 meters) above sea level. It lies in the center of a protected marine area, an anomaly in the gentle granite landscape of the northeast coast of Sardinia. Its white cliffs on the southwest side of the island fall vertically into the sea.

To reach Tavolara by boat you have to pass Punta del Papa, the eastern tip of the island, and roughly 1,000 feet (300 meters) farther out the Secca del Papa rises over 130 feet (40 meters)

110 left The north-facing slopes of the spire are covered with large red and yellow sea fans (Paramuricea clavata), surrounded by shoals of barbier (Anthias anthias), twoband bream, and damselfish.

110 right The rainbow seems to grow out of the tall rocks on the island of Tavolara along the east coast of Sardinia; there are many dive sites around the island but the best is at the eastern tip, off the Secca del Papa.

from the bottom. The highest is a limestone tower that stands 50 feet (15 meters) above the water in the center of the spires aligned east-west. You descend 50 feet (15 meters) or so, but you can see the bed 100 feet (30 meters) below you clearly. The upper sections of the spires are cloaked by a dense shoal of damselfish (*Chromis chromis*) that opens to let you pass. There are many routes you may follow, but the most common heads west first, passing the main spire at

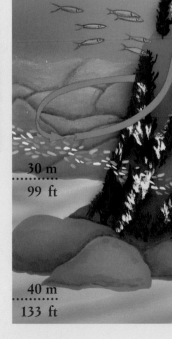

15 m
50 ft

30 m
99 ft

40 m
133 ft

TAVOLARA

Secca del Papa

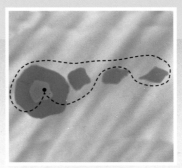

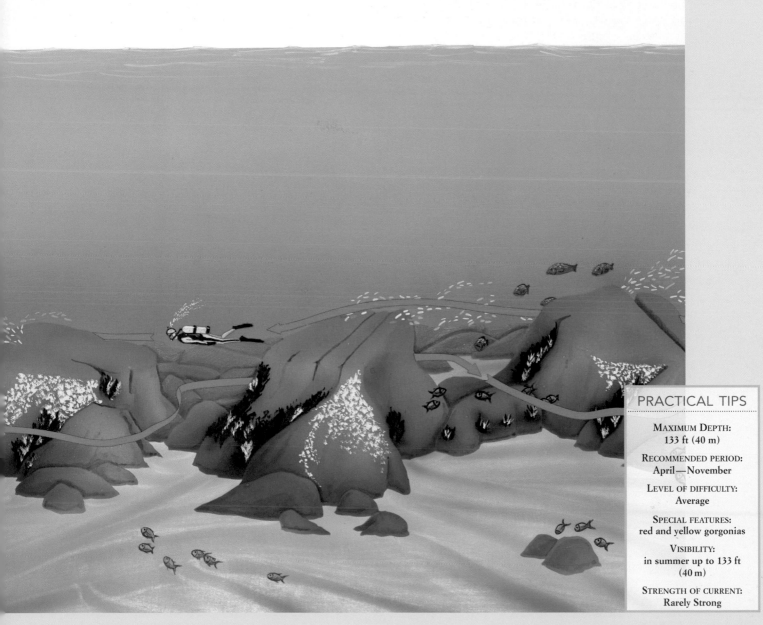

113 *bottom right The bank is formed by outcrops, and from the top of one, you may see the others; at the base of the gorgonians, the rock is covered with green algae typical of zones with weak light, for example, the "coin of the sea" (Halimeda tuna) and the sea fan* Udotea petiolata.

112-113 The gorgonians on the Secca del Papa are yellow-tipped, as in few other areas of the Mediterranean; as yet we have no scientific explanation for this color variation.

113 left As soon as the spire wall becomes vertical, the rock is covered with a carpet of large golden zoanthids (Parazoanthus axinellae).

about 100 feet (30 meters) deep to where an elevation is covered with red gorgonians among swarms of barbier (*Anthias anthias*). As you continue at the same depth toward a second rocky projection, also covered with gorgonians, you will see schools of twoband bream and dentex, often of huge size. Once past this projection, continue toward a rise on the seabed; approach slowly, as sharp eyes will discern a good 35 feet (10 meters) away the numerous dark outlines of dusky groupers (*Epinephelus marginatus*) resting on the rocks or hovering slightly above. The best way to entice them to approach is to rest on the highest part of the rock, about 120 feet (36 meters) deep, and wait. One after the other, six or seven suspicious but curious groupers will begin to approach. Some of them weigh over 55 pounds (25 kilograms) and these are also the boldest. If you make no quick movements they may come as close as 7 feet (2 meters). Often an Alexandrian grouper (*Epinephelus costae*) will also approach, easily identified by its horizontal stripes and straight-edged tail. With an eye on your dive computer, head back along the same route. It is best to remain at around 92 feet (28 meters) so as to have more time to rise up the main spire. Head toward the north wall, which falls vertically 80 feet (25 meters) and is entirely covered with red and-yellow gorgonians, a color variant is only found in a few spots in the Mediterranean. At midday, the colors of the gorgonians contrasted against the dark background of the wall and the bright surface is spectacular. Rising slowly, you will see a multitude of organisms that live between the branches of the gorgonians: annelids, bivalves, small shellfish, and swarms of red damselfish.

113 top right In the deepest part of the spire, about 120 feet (36 meters) from the surface, there is a small population of large dusky groupers (Epinephelus marginatus) who are now accustomed to visits by divers.

Often a lovely soft coral (*Pererythropodium coralloides*) grows on the branches, suffocating a part of the colony; its polyps are dappled with yellow and opaque white. Around a depth of 80 feet (24 meters), the purple gorgonians disappear, replaced by carpets of *Parazoanthus axinellae* in the shadows; a number of morays hide in the cracks, sometimes sharing space with a little grouper.

The upper section of the spires is also interesting for the crustaceans that hide in the cracks and hermit crabs among the weeds, their shells covered with anemones. The bright colors of nudibranchs stand out among the waving hydrozoans, and as you watch the tiny creatures intently, you may be surrounded by a carousel of greater amberjacks (*Seriola dumerili*), swimming among the bubbles before they disappear into the distance.

Tyrrhenian Sea

SICILY

Scilla

CALABRIA

N

Text and photographs by Roberto Rinaldi

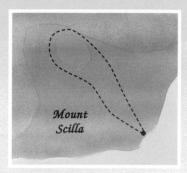

Mount Scilla

PRACTICAL TIPS

MAXIMUM DEPTH:
149 ft (45 m)

RECOMMENDED PERIOD:
April—November

LEVEL OF DIFFICULTY:
Expert

SPECIAL FEATURES:
red and yellow gorgonias
and black coral

VISIBILITY:
in summer up to 133 ft (40 m)

STRENGTH OF CURRENT:
Variable

22 m
73 ft

30 m
99 ft

45 m
149 ft

57 m
188 ft

Italy—Strait of Messina
Mount Scilla

Indubitably the Mediterranean Sea can offer diving at the level of many tropical seas, if not superior to them. A place that represents the treasures that the Romans emphatically called "Mare Nostrum" (Our Sea) is the Strait of Messina, which separates the Italian mainland from Sicily. In the few miles, traveling from the south to the north of the strait, the seabed rises by over 4,260 feet (1,300 meters) to only 230 feet (70 meters). The coasts of Calabria and Sicily approach each other in the space of a mile or so, creating a gigantic funnel, with a wider opening to the south, toward the Ionian Sea, and a narrower one to the north, near the cities of Messina and Villa San Giovanni. The alternation of the tides leads to variations in the level of the two basins—the Tyrrhenian and the Ionian—which, due to the Venturi effect, are great enough to generate strong currents, intensified by the narrowing of of that arm of the sea. This impetuous tidal water flows along the north-south axis of the Strait of Messina, changing direction every six hours. Before diving, given what has been said above, we need to refer to the tide tables published every year by the navy's Istituto Idrografico. Here we find, for each day of the year, the intensity of the currents forecast and times of their maximum intensity and moderation. It is to this guide that we must refer in order to explore the waters of the strait.

Many dives are possible in this section of the sea, but one in particular deserves description because of its overall quality. In the first place, here, in a few hundred square yards, it seems that the sea

115 bottom These gorgonians still have their red color, though their tips are just tinged with yellow.

wishes to offer a summary of everything beautiful found in these waters. Then, this dive can be done directly from the beach. For these reasons this is a well-known site, yet each day, each time that you put your fins back on, it never fails to show you something completely new.

So we go to the village of Scilla, the northern entry to the strait on the Italian peninsula side. We go down to the sea and along the beach until the path passes through the tunnel under the rocks. Here, having checked the tide tables, we enter the water and swim for about 650 feet (200 meters) toward the point, which looks out on the open sea. Diving near

some partially exposed rocks, we find ourselves on a steep seabed consisting of a landslide of gigantic rocks. This is a spectacular place, rich in rock-dwelling fish along a wall covered with starfish, sponges, and bryozoa. At night, it is a paradise. At about 100 feet (30 meters) the rocks are replaced by very lightly colored, coarse sand, which reflects the light of the environment surrounding it, due in part to the proverbial clarity of the water. In the distance in front of us, we discover the imposing outline of an underwater mountain—in fact, the Mount Scilla for which this dive has been named. We swim toward the outline, which now seems clearer in the crystalline waters. The large rock, an audacious granite steeple, rises from the seabed from around 130 feet (40 meters) to a few more than 65 feet (20 meters). When we get closer, we are breathless. The

walls are covered with red sea fans with yellow shading—a truly marvelous spectacle! A series of large rocks rises from the sand, these too covered with splendid coelenterates. Each rock is cloaked in these supple fans, while schools of black-and-red damselfish swim through the waters. On the sides of the main shoal, the seabed—sandy and studded with large boulders—gradually slopes down until it takes a sharp, rocky drop down for another 35 feet (10 meters). Toward the open sea, instead, the rocks soar again in a spectacular way, rising from a bed that here is even deeper. Now we find ourselves in a spectacular channel, covered with yellow-and-red

sea fans at the bottom and lit up by bright carpets of orange starfish above. The sides of the rocks fall precipitously for some dozens of yards. We observe them as we swim up toward the summit of the external pinnacle. From here, we emerge onto an impressive balcony. Below us the rocks fall compactly, vertically, cloaked in incredible sea fans. One day I was captured by the desire to reach the end of the abyss and, from this point, began a long descent. I let myself fall into the void, descending rapidly, like a parachutist who jumps off a peak in the Alps. In a second, I was at 260 feet (80 meters), and below me the abyss continued, incapable of being sounded, the walls descending unchanged, the yellow of the sea fans standing out against the dark blue. Here and there, above me and below me, shone the brightest yellow branches of black coral.

And this is a clue to the morphology of a site that you never succeed in exploring completely. But let's speak for a moment about the creatures, other than the showy sea fans, that populate these rocks. Since it would take a book to name all the inhabitants of this seabed, we will name only the most extraordinary, beginning with the large cerianthus found on the sandy bottom. We meet a pair of them between 100 and 120 feet (30 and 36 meters), deep among the rocks of the landslide and the slopes of the Mount itself, while another pair are found between the Mount and the lateral drop of an amphitheater of truly suggestive rocks and sea fans. Here it is very common to meet with gigantic examples of John Dory, which rise from the abysses, or with monstrous anglerfish. The John Dory are marvelous at hiding among the branches, offering potential aggressors only a front view so as to appear slim and invisible. The anglerfish, instead, remain immobile on the sand, covered by protuberances resembling the harbor algae that cover the seabed. An enormous grouper has been seen for years on the external side of the Mount, within a deep fissure cut into the large final drop. Also worthy of note are the numerous branches of black coral, which grow from 115 feet (30 meters) in depth. The black Mediterranean coral, *Gerardia savaglia,* grows as a parasite on other sea fans. It attacks the red-and-yellow Paramuricae, kills its polyps, and grows in its place. When the entire colony has been destroyed by the aggressive yellow polyps of the black coral, it begins to transform the skeleton of the sea fan on which it lives into a different, harder and more resistant one, black in color, from which it takes its common name. Naturally this animal only resembles its precious tropical relative; its skeleton, however, is valueless.

After a day of diving at the Mount, don't give in to tiredness. Dive once again in the dark. Apart from all the other fantastic creatures that come out of their hiding places at night, you will also discover the rare *Astropartus,* an echinoderm that opens its arms to the current only at night and closes them a few seconds after light reaches it.

Tyrrhenian Sea

◆ The Colombara Bank

SICILY

Ionian sea

Text and photographs by Roberto Rinaldi – Illustrations by Domitilla Müller

ITALY—ISLAND OF USTICA
THE COLOMBARA BANK

The island of Ustica, which lies off the northern coast of Sicily, is undoubtedly a symbol for Italian divers. And yet it is also more than that, as it is home to the Academy of Underwater Sciences and Techniques, which in its survey of all underwater activities for over forty years, has awarded the honorific "Golden Trident" to the most important figures connected to the life of the sea. Figures of the cal-

118 top A glance over the side of any of the cliffs on the north side of the island will give proof of the clearness of the water.

118 bottom Leaving the port and heading toward the Colombara spire, you round the majestic headland of Falconara, crowned by one of the island's two lighthouses.

5 m
17 ft

15 m
50 ft

45 m
149 ft

The Colombara Bank

Tyrrhenian Sea

Ustica Island

N

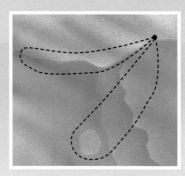

120 in alto Two divers swim over the tip of the bank. The water is crystal clear and the light strong in the summer.

120 center As you rise toward the top of the bank, the rocks become white and clean; beaten by the waves and currents, only the most tenacious forms of life—like sea urchins and acorn barnacles—can survive here.

iber of Jacques Cousteau, Duilio Marcante, Jacques Piccard, and many others have received this prestigious award at Ustica. The island is also the site of Italy's first marine park, created to protect the incomparable beauty of its seabed. It is certainly no exaggeration to say that around Ustica can be found all the most beautiful forms of life that exist in the Mediterranean, nor is it an exaggeration to say that few places in the world offer such clear water.

Of the many dives available, the choice has fallen on one that offers different itineraries, different types of dive, and varying degrees of difficulty to suit divers of all levels of experience. The site lies in the center of the island's northern

coast, to the east of the rock known as "il Medico," which is easily visible from the top of the bank. It is easy to find the Colombara bank, as the green fringe can be seen from far off. It is very large, a plateau of pale rocks that gradually descends from 10 feet (3 meters) toward the west.

The sides we are most interested in are the west and the south, with the latter being the traditional point of entry. From here, swim along the plateau heading south until you meet a clean drop that falls to a depth of 15 to 35 feet (5 to 10 meters). From here you look onto a vertical wall that falls down to a step at about 50 feet (15 meters) depth before it continues down to the sand at 150 feet (45 meters). The water is often so clear that you can see the bottom before beginning your descent. The forms of life existing on the wall are spectacular at all levels (mostly sponges, bryozoa, and astroides), due to the vertical wall, which often harbors deep channels. The fish are abundant, including small groupers that watch curiously from their lair. Expert divers will descend to the seabed, where a splendid spectacle awaits: a huge rock mass covered with huge red gorgonians with open polyps rises out of the sand a short distance from the main part of the bank. A school of barbier swallows you up as soon as you hold your breath for a few seconds.

Swimming west, you will comes across a large number of lovely rose-colored sponges; these are organ-pipe sponges, common in the Caribbean but rare in the Mediterranean. And rare too are the sea-tangle algae that lie on the black volcanic sand. All of a sudden, another series of rocks covered with gorgonians appears. These are smaller rocks than the gigantic mass you have just left, but they offer a pleasant surprise: you cannot help but notice the vivid yellow of various branches of black coral among the forest of red branches. If you have seen all

120 bottom Decompression time on the top of the bank passes quickly as you play with the huge number of ornate wrasse that may be waiting to be offered a sea urchin or other snack.

120-121 One of the large branches of Gerardia savaglia *on the spire at 130 feet (40 meters) down. This animal is called Mediterranean black coral due to its black rigid skeleton. In fact the name is misleading, as it is not even related to real black coral.*

121 bottom The long route along the slope that faces Medico Rock is little visited because of the depth and the long swim required. However, the effort is fully repaid by the view of the bottom, as seen in the photograph.

that has been described so far, this is without doubt the moment to ascend along the steep slopes of the bank to your safety stop. But don't forget to organize a dive on the west slope. This one is more demanding and involves passing beyond the edge to the west and swimming over a large tumble of boulders between 70 and 85 feet (20 and 26 meters). The zone is rich with fish, but don't stop if you want to reach your destination. Keep going over another edge that descends in steps over a succession of massive rocks down to a depth of 160 feet (50 meters). The place is quite spectacular. The density and variety of sponges that cover the rocks are amazing, and the colonies of gorgonians that populate the nooks between the boulders are also truly beautiful. This is an ideal place for encounters with large fish.

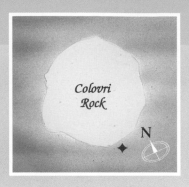

Colovri
Rock

N

Colovri
Island

PRACTICAL TIPS

MAXIMUM DEPTH:
83 ft (25 m)

RECOMMENDED PERIOD:
April—November

LEVEL OF DIFFICULTY:
Average

SPECIAL FEATURES:
grottos and parap≤andali

VISIBILITY:
over 99 ft (30 m)

STRENGTH OF CURRENT:
None

Text and photographs by Giorgio Mesturini – Illustrations by Domitilla Müller

GREECE
CORFÙ ISLAND
Colovri Island
Ionian Sea

20 m
66 ft

25 m
83 ft

GREECE—CORFÙ
THE ISLAND OF COLOVRI

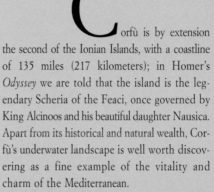

Corfù is by extension the second of the Ionian Islands, with a coastline of 135 miles (217 kilometers); in Homer's *Odyssey* we are told that the island is the legendary Scheria of the Feaci, once governed by King Alcinoos and his beautiful daughter Nausica. Apart from its historical and natural wealth, Corfù's underwater landscape is well worth discovering as a fine example of the vitality and charm of the Mediterranean.

The west side of the island is the most interesting; its northern part is characterized by tall and

jagged cliffs plunging down the sea. To the south the coastline appears more gentle; a succession of wide sandy beaches are punctuated by rocky stretches, and the shoreline descends gradually into the sea.

One of the best diving spots in the area is around the little island of Colovri, at about 1 mile (1.6 kilometers) from the western coast of Corfù. According to legend, this island was once the ship of Ulysses, which was turned to stone by the

123 top The graceful parrotfish (Sparisoma cretense) *can grow to over a foot (30 centimeters) in length; the male is a greenish brown, while the female is decked out in bright reddish colors.*

123 bottom The beach at Aghios Gordis, situated on the west side of the island of Corfù, is an excellent departure point for exploring the depths of Colovri Rock.

123

gods in an effort to prevent the hero from returning to Ithaca.

Colovri is a small island with a perimeter of around 1,300 feet (400 meters); beneath the surface, the side facing Corfù reaches a depth of 160 feet (50 meters), while the part facing the open sea exceeds the 330-foot (100-meter) depth. The monolith is composed of light-colored limestone rock, well eroded by the sea; especially in the first few yards of depth (thanks partly to the transparency of the water), it presents a spectacular scene. The dive may begin on the southeastern side, where, once submerged, we find beneath us the labyrinth of large rocks that form the habitat of golden zoanthids, polychaeta, bryozoa sponges, and numerous other sea creatures, including the pentagon sea star *(Peltaster placenta)*.

Following the rockface westward, we descend, and before us opens an enormous archlike passageway, where in the half-light shoals of twoband bream, saddled seabream, and bogue converge, finding refuge from deep-sea predators. On the other side of the archway, at a depth of 70 feet (20 meters), on our right appears a series of caves, inhabited by thousands of crayfish *(Plesionika narval)*. Apart from admiring the vitality of these little shellfish, inside these clefts we discover by flashlight a species of comber *(Serranus cabrilla)* that remains motionless in the dark, waiting for

the right moment to seize some choice morsel. In the darkness of this cave the catch is somewhat limited, but as soon as the shellfish come into the beam of light, the comber launches a sudden attack, resulting in an unexpected feast.

Continuing the descent, at a depth of 80 feet (25 meters) we come to a rocky spur that stretches out a few dozen yards toward the open sea and

then plunges again into the abyss of the Ionian Sea. This is the ideal environment for watching the passage of deep-sea fish; before long, in fact, out of the intense blue of the sea large shoals of dentex materialize, passing in procession before us. In the spring silver carousels of large sea urchins *(Seriola dumerili)* can be seen, and we may also encounter ocean sunfish. Returning to the coast along the rockface of Colovri, we ascend a few yards, where we can see before us groupers *(Epinephelus guaza)* before their holes. Continuing to follow the southern coast of the island, we pass the top of the archway, where morays peek out from the rocks; from here, through shoals of damselfish and saddled bream, we arrive at the spot where the boat is anchored.

124-125 This crab (Calappa granulata) *seems a bashful creature with its habit of holding its claws close to its shell when it is frightened, thus making itself unassailable.*

125 top left This photograph taken during a night dive shows one of the colorful and strange inhabitants of Colovri Rock, Clathrina clathrus.

125 bottom left The small painted comber (Serranus scriba) *is easily recognized by its bright colors; a very curious fish, it does not hesitate to approach if you should swim into its territory.*

125 top right While exploring the various grottoes off the coast of Corfù, you may well catch sight of magnificent examples of conger eels (Conger conger) *in the most sheltered cracks.*

125 bottom right The anglerfish (Lophius piscatorius) *usually remains hidden in the sediment of the seabed while waiting for its prey; it uses the fleshy protuberances on its head to entice its victims close to its mouth.*

125

RED SEA: INTRODUCTION
BY EGIDIO TRAINITO

The Red Sea is the northernmost section of the enormous fracture that runs through Africa as the Rift Valley and continues as far as the Arabian peninsula. The sea is 1,460 miles (2,350 kilometers) long and at most 217 miles (350 kilometers) wide; at the north end it forks into two fingers, the Gulf of Suez and the Gulf of Aqaba, while to the south it stretches down to the strait of Bab el-Mandeb between Djibouti and the Yemen, only 16 miles (26 kilometers) wide. Like the Mediterranean, it is a closed sea, but it is located below the Tropic of Cancer and has very unusual temperature and salinity levels. The Red Sea lies in a hot, arid climate with high air temperatures. In addition, its moderate exchange of water with the Indian Ocean means that the average temperature of the water is very high, with a minimum of 63°F (17°C) at the northern end and a maximum of 90°F (32°C) in the south, though temperatures in sheltered areas and shallows can exceed 104°F (40°C) and sometimes equal the air temperature. The other climatic consequence is in the salinity, which in areas can reach 42, more than 10 percent more than in other seas. These climatic conditions have encouraged an explosion of madrepore and the formation of extensive barrier reefs along the entire the shoreline. The coasts are rocky and high, created by formations of fossil madrepore that have emerged above the level of the water. The most typical image of the Red Sea is the sharp contrast between the rocky desert that stretches right down to the water's edge and the extraordinary frenzy of life and colors immediately below the surface.

The north is the home of tourist resorts; though recently they occupy large areas of coast, like Eilat and Aqaba at the northern tip of the Gulf of Aqaba, and Sharm el Sheik, Hurghada, Safaga, and El Quseir in Egypt. Farther south and along the Saudi shores of the Red Sea there are no tourist facilities, and some localities have to be reached via cruise ship. Right at the southern end, a huge, shallow basin extends between Eritrea and Yemen, divided down the middle by a trench. Satellite maps that indicate concentrations of chlorophyll in the oceans show the highest levels of phytoplankton in this zone of the Red Sea. Poor water visibility is the consequence; visibility only becomes acceptable at certain times, and is never anything like as clear as the northern end. Hundreds of islands are dotted along both coasts: to the west they form the Dahlak Archipelago, and to the east the Yemeni Islands in the Farasan group, the Kamaran group, and, farther south, the Hanish Islands near the Bab el-Mandeb strait. Zones of great natural interest, these sustain species now very rare, such as the dugong, now almost completely vanished from the northern coasts. Other coral islands rise out of the sea and are the destination of unforgettable cruises; for instance, the Zabargad and the Brothers Islands, where human disturbance is limited to a few fishing boats and even fewer cruise boats bringing divers.

One section of the Red Sea represents the torment of Tantalus to divers; the coast of Sudan, said by many to have some of the most beautiful diving sites in the world, but plagued by the continual uncertainty of the country's political situation, which means that very few boats receive permission to

navigate in those waters, while those that do are sometimes unexpectedly told to leave. Consequently, the waters of Sha'ab Rumi, Sanganeb, Wingate Reef, and the wreck of the *Umbria* remain a pipe dream that very few have been fortunate enough to experience.

The Red Sea also has an important proportion of endemic species in its waters; more than 10 percent of its more than 1,000 species are local. The most easily seen endemic species is the redlined butterflyfish *(Chaetodon semilarvatus)*, which slowly patrols the coral in pairs, wearing its yellow livery with a blue splotch on its eye. Overall, however, most of the underwater flora and fauna of the Red Sea come from the western section of the Indian Ocean.

The extraordinary success of tourism on the northern coasts has brought an increasing flow of divers to the waters of the most well-known resorts; in spite of protected marine areas like Ras Mohammad in the Sinai, the problem of conservation of the coral reefs is ever more acute. Underwater tour operators have risen to the challenge with the creation of an association, HEP-CA, to protect the underwater environment at Hurghada. The association has provided buoys and fixed moorings at all diving points to eliminate the impact of anchoring on the reefs, a small but important first step in the protection of the marvels of the Red Sea.

Jackson Reef

TIRAN ISLAND

N

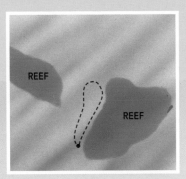

REEF

REEF

PRACTICAL TIPS

MAXIMUM DEPTH:
99 ft (30 m)

RECOMMENDED PERIOD:
All year

LEVEL OF DIFFICULTY:
Average

SPECIAL FEATURES:
turtles and corals

VISIBILITY:
up to 133 ft (40 m)

STRENGTH OF CURRENT:
Strong

Text and photographs by Roberto Rinaldi – Illustrations by Domitilla Müller

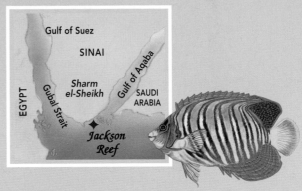

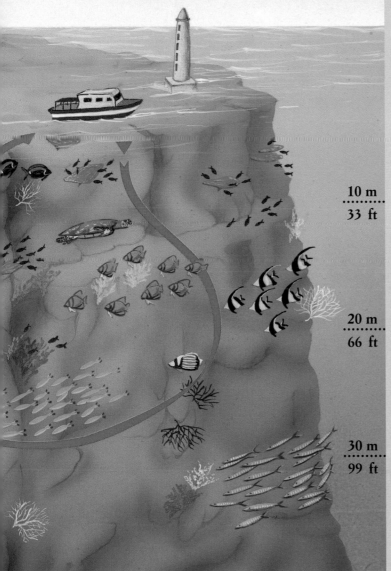

10 m
33 ft

20 m
66 ft

30 m
99 ft

EGYPT—TIRAN ISLAND
JACKSON REEF

The Sinai Peninsula wedges itself into the Red Sea, defining two narrow arms of the sea—the Gulf of Suez and the Gulf of Aqaba. At the entrance to the latter, between the east coast of the Sinai and the island of Tiran, there is a strait that is truly magical for scuba diving but very treacherous for navigation. Here, partially visible above the water, you can spot four extended coral reefs—Gordon, Thomas, Woodhouse, and Jackson. As proof of the navigational hazard that they represent, on the northwestern sides of Gordon and Jackson, approaching from the south, you find the clearly visible wrecks of two ships run aground.

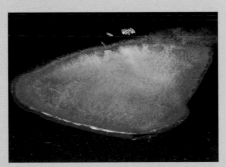

These four coral structures arise from a very deep seabed and grow in waters lapped by strong currents, which is why diving in these places offers some of the most beautiful sights of the entire Red Sea. Also worthy of note is the large lagoon, defined by an extensive coral reef that connects the waters near the eastern end of Jackson to the coast of the island of Tiran. But let's go more specifically to the depths of Jackson Reef.

129 top An aerial view of Jackson Reef; the south side is more beautiful and receives more visitors than the north, and the dive can be enjoyed from right to left or vice versa, depending on the current. Photograph by Itamar Grinberg.

129 bottom This photograph clearly shows the various reefs at Tiran—Jackson, Thomas, Gordon, and Woodhouse. Photograph by Itamar Grinberg.

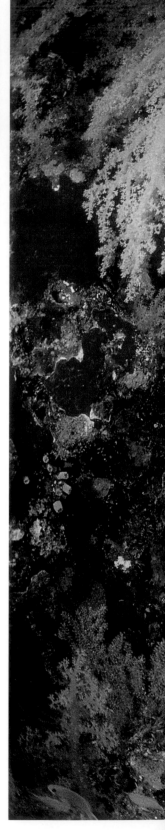

130 top left A longnose hawkfish (Oxycirrhites typus) *hides among the polyps of a large red soft coral. Mimetism is essential to the defense of this fish; its strategy for catching prey is to ambush it.*

130 bottom left A small chromis (Chromis sp.) *seeks refuge for the night in a "bush" of soft coral.*

130 top right Moving westward on the outer edge of the wall, you will find an area filled with soft corals that dangle from the lower wall of the acropore.

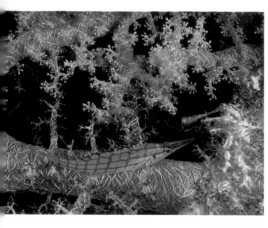

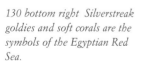

130 bottom right Silverstreak goldies and soft corals are the symbols of the Egyptian Red Sea.

130-131 This enormous group of soft corals can be admired heading east from the anchoring point at Jackson Reef.

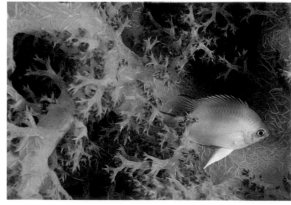

In speaking about this dive, we will also give indications about what you can expect from exploring the beds of the other reefs, especially Gordon, since they have certain characteristics in common. All of them, for example, rise more or less unexpectedly, depending on the area, from a common platform about 200 feet (60 meters) deep. For a few yards, this grows in a weak slope that connects with a second drop, which quickly reaches a depth of 330 feet (100 meters) before losing itself in the abysses of the channel, which reach levels between 1320 and 2640 feet(400 and 800 meters). That's why, in this section of the sea, chances are good of meeting fish passing through these waters. Here, too, you often meet turtles. Almost every time I have dived on the sides of Jackson or the reefs near it, I have seen turtles in the depths, probably swimming around in search of food. Often they moved away with a few, quick flips of their fins. Others, however, allowed me to get very close, letting me swim side by side with them for several minutes.

But let's return to the plan for the wonderful dives at Jackson Reef. You usually enter the water along the southeast side of the flowering reef; the other sides are generally battered by currents that you cannot fight. In the past you could mistake the entry point and jump in a little to the west or east of the best place, taking the risk of running into a strong current or

of swimming in a place that was not as beautiful as you might have expected, but for some years fixed moorings, which also safeguard the coral from damage from anchors, have solved this problem.

The water at Tiran is always clear; immediately below us, we make out the steep decline of the reef. What certainly strikes us most vividly as we begin the dive is the fiery garden of coral found only a few yards down. As far as the eye can see are the audacious, delicate shapes of the green and yellow coral; we could believe that, by some strange spell, we had found ourselves in a garden of petrified plants. The section of wall that goes from 35 to 70 feet (10 to 20 meters) is enchanting. There we find areas literally full of agglomerates of soft corals, amassed one upon the other in the most varied and brilliant colors. Dense schools of orange anthias or, in the darkest ravines, shining pigmy sweepers, are concentrated around these masses. This is an environment rich in life, teeming with colorful, surprising reef fish. We pay attention and scrutinize every ravine. We have no difficulty in discovering red-

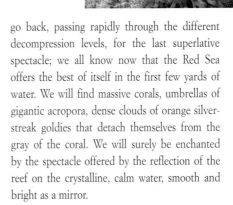

133 bottom right Another common encounter on the reefs of Tiran is with turtles; this one is intent on feeding on the coral.

132 The most notable feature of Jackson Reef is the abundance of fire coral. The picture shows a Pterois twisted around the branches of the greenish coral, which is dangerous to humans.

133 left The deepest zones of the south wall on Jackson Reef are thickly covered with colored soft corals.

133 top right This is a classic sight in the sea off Egypt: a small anemone is inhabited by two twoband anemonefish (Amphiprion bicinctus).

133 center right Fine examples of gorgonians can be admired where the reef wall meets the sandy bottom, as they grow more easily in deep water.

and-black-speckled groupers, scorpionfish perfectly camouflaged among the coral, and elegant pterois chasing glassfish. Diving 80 feet (25 meters) deeper, we enter into the kingdom of the sea fans. Here we find gigantic isolated fans, so immense that they reach 10 feet (3 meters) of width without difficulty. It often happens that a perfect ecosystem made up of coral, small fish, and crustaceans grows on such large branches. At a depth of about 100 feet (30 meters), the incline of the steep slope tends to become a little gentler, forming broad steps, though still decisively inclined toward the open sea. Here branches of black and brown coral prosper. Given the distance that now separates us from the wall and the deeper levels, we begin to feel strong currents and therefore keep an eye open for the powerful shadows of the large marauders that crisscross these waters. In any case, as we are surfacing, we will almost certainly meet up with dense schools of *Idoli moreschi,* the characteristic black-and-white-striped fish with very long dorsal fins. Surfacing is completely enjoyable, since as we have seen, each level offers a magnificent spectacle and an encounter with the extraordinary creatures that populate the Red Sea. During our dive, we will certainly have drifted in one direction or another away from where the boat is anchored. So we stay near the point at which the protection of the reef stops, and find ourselves exposed to the violent currents that batter these waters. We try to go a few yards ahead to where there is more life in the sea, where the probability of meeting large fish or dense schools is higher. There are only a few minutes before we

go back, passing rapidly through the different decompression levels, for the last superlative spectacle; we all know now that the Red Sea offers the best of itself in the first few yards of water. We will find massive corals, umbrellas of gigantic acropora, dense clouds of orange silverstreak goldies that detach themselves from the gray of the coral. We will surely be enchanted by the spectacle offered by the reflection of the reef on the crystalline, calm water, smooth and bright as a mirror.

Naama Bay

Sharm el-Sheikh

lighthouse

Ras Umm Sid

N

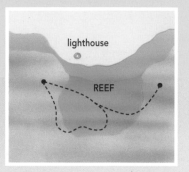

lighthouse

REEF

Text and photographs by Roberto Rinaldi

PRACTICAL TIPS

MAXIMUM DEPTH:
116 ft (35 m)

RECOMMENDED PERIOD:
All year

LEVEL OF DIFFICULTY:
Average

SPECIAL FEATURES:
grottos with soft corals
and glassfish

VISIBILITY:
up to 133 ft (40 m)

STRENGTH OF CURRENT:
Strong in Sections

134

Illustrations by Domitilla Müller

EGYPT—SHARM EL MOYA
RAS UMM SID

It's not always true that the best dives are the farthest from the port, from the routes of the principal cruises, from the base of departure. The case of Ras Umm Sid is a clear example that contradicts this commonly accepted general statement. The great, spectacular wall of Ras Umm Sid is found a few hundred yards from the port of Sharm el Moya, a few miles farther south of the center of Na'ama Bay, on the coast

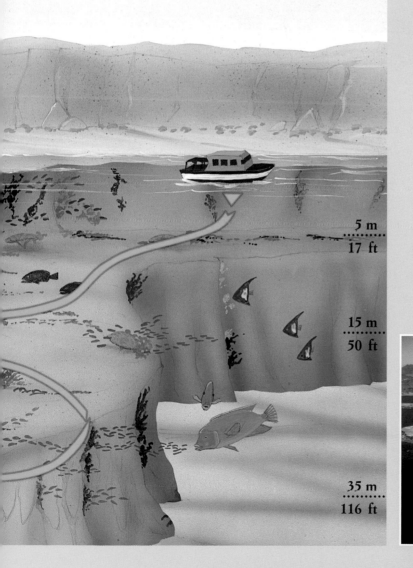

135 top This photo offers a clear view of the dive site at Ras Umm Sid.

135 bottom The aerial photo shows the protected bay of Sharm el Moya, one of the main departure points for diving trips, then the wide Temple Reef and the point of Ras Umm Sid at the end; the dive follows the edge that runs between the reef, the wall, and the shelf.
Photograph by Itamar Grinberg.

5 m
17 ft

15 m
50 ft

35 m
116 ft

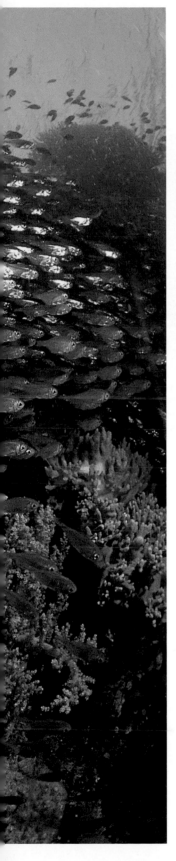

136-137 Here you are on the edge at the point at which the shelf joins the outer wall; a growth of red soft corals is surrounded by a dense shoal of pygmy sweepers.

of the Sinai Peninsula along the Gulf of Aqaba. But that's not all. Diving is done along a vertical wall that ascends from a rather massive point stretching out toward the east, a point at which the desert sandstone rises a few yards above sea level, ensuring some protection against the northerly winds that blow around these parts and providing a kind of shelter. This site is not only a wonderful place to dive but also extremely easy to reach, protected from the waves and close to the base of departure. The point we are going to explore closes the famous Bay of Tempio on the north, where some coral towers appreciated by divers are found, and rises from seabeds between 35 and 70 feet (10 and 20 meters) deep to reach the surface. The buoy to which we are moored is south of the lighthouse at the height of the angle that the coast of the bay forms with the prominent point. Here the coral reef is rather extensive, diminishing a little near the end of the point. We enter along the top, being sure not to follow it to the bottom, but pushing ourselves directly toward the wall that we find approximately 50 feet (15 meters) down. The

strongest currents usually come from the north, so here we should be serenely protected while we leave the surface and swim in the open sea toward the drop. We keep the coral wall on our left and begin to move along it, ready for the first of the splendid sights that this dive promises. We soon find ourselves at a point where the wall of the bay forms an angle with the wall of the point. A mass of enormous sea fans grows here, a splendid spectacle, not only for the sea fans themselves but especially for the beauty of the elegant *Pterois* that permanently live here. The fish move lightly among the branches, hide themselves in the refuge they provide, and come out a little farther ahead. We can go within a few inches of the fish without fear that they will be frightened away while we observe the elegant outline, lit from behind, of the branches of the sea fans against the blinding disk of the sun. The sea-fans accompany us from about 50 to 115 feet (15 to 35 meters). It is in somewhat deeper areas that we see the show offered by dense schools of pygmy sweepers sheltered among the vivid branches of the splendid soft corals, which abundantly colonize that section of the wall as well as the tops of some large fans. The spectacle is certainly superb, but we don't stay there too long, since we still have a lot to see.

The point descends sharply for about 35 feet (10 meters) and then links up with a plateau that dips gently toward the open sea. In these waters, it is possible to meet an incredible number of coral-dwelling fish of every species—large Napoleon wrasse as well as groups of tuna that quickly pass by. The corals that colonize the plateau are

137 left These lovely gorgonians grow at about 120 feet (35 meters) depth at the beginning of the dive, where a corner is formed between the main wall and the offshoot of the reef that heads out to sea.

137 top right The shelf at about 50 feet (15 meters) is rich with acropore, below which colorful colonies of soft corals often grow.

137 bottom right Facing the outer edge of the coral shelf will almost always give you a sight of elegant barracuda (Sphyraena sp.) in deeper water.

splendid and truly spectacular. We find ourselves in front of a large number of highly colorful towers of madrepore and soft coral, populated by glassfish, red and blue groupers, scorpionfish, and elegant *Pterois*. Characteristic of this area are large umbrellas of acropora, colonized on the lower part by a multicolored cascade of soft coral. There is no precise point at which to turn back, no special depth at which to swim. We can feel completely free to go where we want without missing something more beautiful. Even the deeper areas of the point, in addition to the plateau and the rim that, at a certain point, it describes with the wall below are extremely interesting. In particular, we should mention a scenic cave adorned by white soft corals and populated by pygmy sweepers, unfortunately now outside the 100-foot (30-meter) maximum limit allowed by Egyptian law. However, the beauty of the spectacle that we have before our eyes at shallower levels easily compensates what we could have admired in deeper areas. Therefore, arriving at the halfway point of our dive, we go up a little and return via a different route. Turning back, we find other coral structures, colorful and rich. It's certainly worthwhile to stop and observe with attention, as you are sure to discover large numbers of camouflaged fish, small shrimp, sea slugs, and other creatures that populate what can undoubtedly be called ecosystems in themselves. We swim on past the area of the sea fans, passing over them in shallower waters. Finally we can make out the hull of our boat, and the dive has finished. But the surprises are not over. By stopping at this point, we would surely miss a wide area of great interest, though in shallow waters. The coral reef here rises almost to the surface, split into infinite deep fissures through which the strong rays of the sun filter. Peeping within, we discover the walls once again covered with soft corals, the fractures inhabited by dense schools of silver fish. On the outside, hard corals dominate the environment, colonizing it completely. We are in a few yards of water, but the spectacle we are watching is so beautiful that it will always remain with us.

138 top left This photograph gives a good idea of the most notable features of the coral shelf: a shoal of pygmy sweepers swirls around highly colored soft corals and fire corals.

138 bottom left You have reached the bottom, where the coral wall meets the sand; here, a lovely red sponge is fixed to the skeleton of a gorgonian.

138 top right A large red gorgonian sticks out from the coral wall below 100 feet (30 meters), and a cloud of pink anthias enwraps the colony; this is another typical sight in the Red Sea.

138 bottom right Pigmy sweepers inhabit the deepest fissures in the outer wall at Ras Umm Sid.

138-139 Large Pterois volitans *between the branches of the gorgonians are the most typical sight of a dive at Ras Umm Sid.*

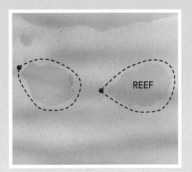

Text and photographs by Vincenzo Paolillo

Ras Mohammed

Jolanda
Reef

Shark
Reef

N

REEF

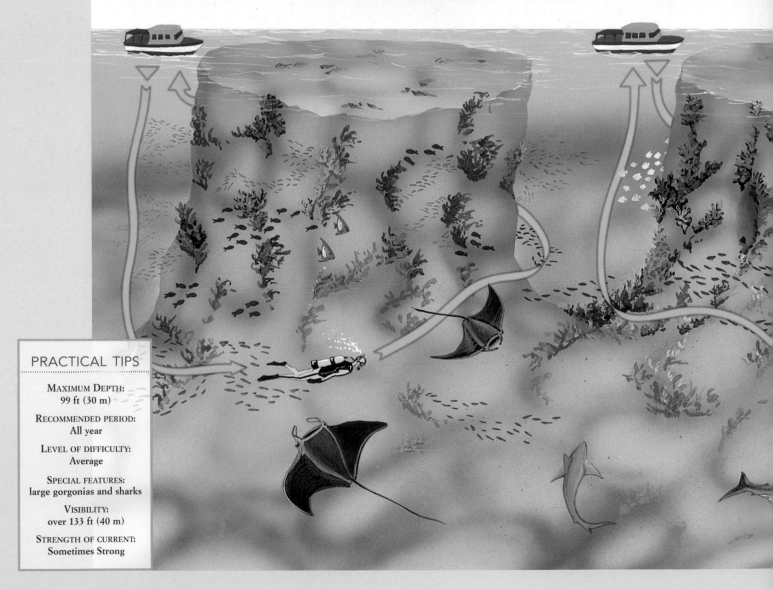

PRACTICAL TIPS

MAXIMUM DEPTH:
99 ft (30 m)

RECOMMENDED PERIOD:
All year

LEVEL OF DIFFICULTY:
Average

SPECIAL FEATURES:
large gorgonias and sharks

VISIBILITY:
over 133 ft (40 m)

STRENGTH OF CURRENT:
Sometimes Strong

Illustrations by Domitilla Müller

Gulf of Suez
SINAI
Gulf of Aqaba
Sharm
el-Sheikh
SAUDI
ARABIA
EGYPT
Gubal Strait
Shark Reef

Egypt—Ras Mohammed
Shark Reef

141 top This aerial view shows Ras Mohammad. The tops of Iolanda and Shark Reefs, which form the classic route for divers, can clearly be seen. Photograph by Itamar Grinberg.

R _as_, in Arabic, means "cape." Ras Mohammad is the southernmost part of the Sinai, after which it opens onto the Red Sea.

The cape is formed from two large rocks. The higher, on the east, is called Shark Observatory; the lower and wider one, on the west, is in the middle of a lagoon in which mangroves grow.

The lagoon continues to the south on a plateau on whose western and eastern sides grow two madreporic towers separated by a saddle

16 m
53 ft

30 m
99 ft

100 m
330 ft

141 bottom A gorgeous example of Napoleon fish (Cheilinus ondulatus) swims undisturbed alongside a scuba-diver.

141

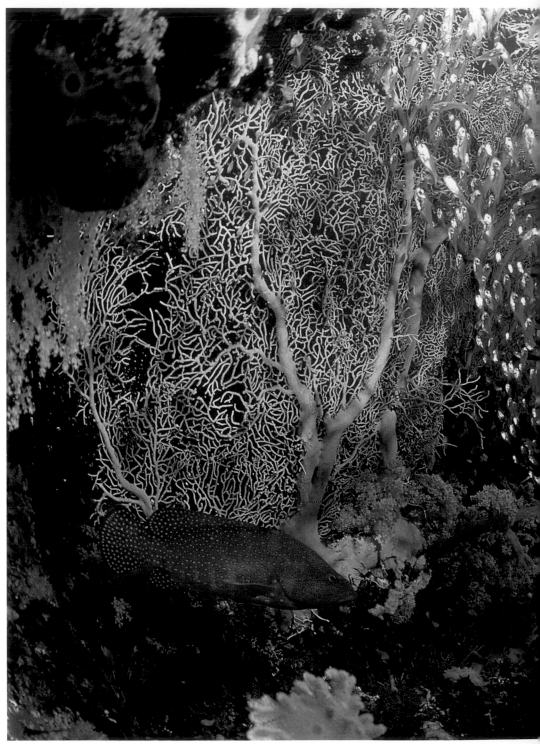

142 top *In the spring, the Red Sea swarms with jellyfish (Aurelia aurita).*

52 feet (16 meters) deep, after which the bottom drops rapidly to a depth of 330 feet (100 meters) and then immediately after to almost 2,600 feet (800 meters).

All this area is now a national park regulated by strict laws that forbid not only leaving or taking anything, but also touching anything or feeding the fish. Until 1989 this was still being done, resulting, among other things, in the death of a splendid Napoleon wrasse.

The eastern tower is called Iolanda Reef because here, in 1981, a violent storm sank a small ship called the *Iolanda* that was transporting, among other items, sinks, bathtubs, and toilets. Another violent storm dragged the wreck to more than 650 feet (200 meters) in depth. On the plateau, at around 40 feet (12 meters), the container structures remain, stupendously colonized by red soft corals (*Dendronepthya* sp.), among a heap of toilets and sinks that, curiously, don't clash with the environment. A buoy has been placed here from which to begin diving or, even better, finish, since the more difficult part is around the other tower, Shark Reef.

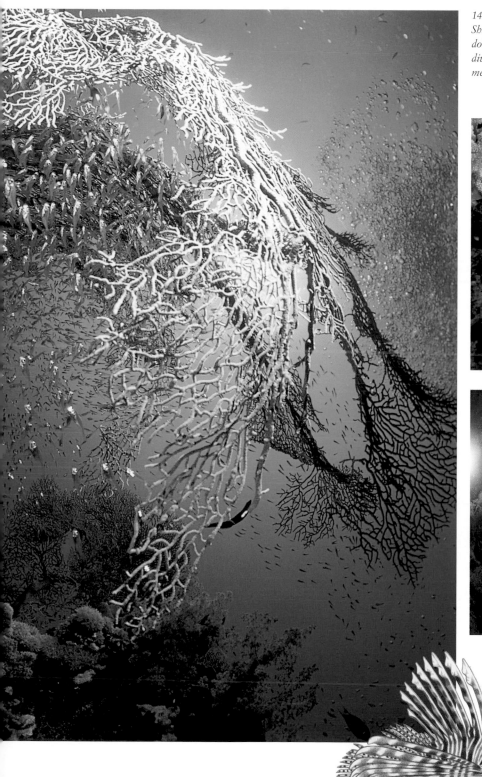

142 bottom *In the waters of Shark Point, the clymene dolphins come closer to the divers, as if they wanted to meet them.*

142-143 *Pygmy sweepers (Parapriacanthus ransonneti) hide among the branches of the sea fans, while coral hinds (Cephalopholis miniata) peek out of the coral.*

143 top *The emperor angelfish (Pomacanthus imperator) is commonly found on the reefs of the Red Sea.*

143 bottom *The swift-moving current favors the growth of rows of sea fans.*

143

144 top left A small reef-dwelling whitetip reef shark (Triaenodon obesus) swims in the waters of Ras Mohammad.

144 bottom left Encounters with large sharks are now rather rare at Ras Mohammad, because of the excessive number of divers.

144 top right In the photo, you can admire one of the numerous coral-dwelling coral hinds (Cephalopholis miniata) encountered at Ras Mohammad.

144 bottom right In the morning and evening the bluefin trevallies (Caranx melampygus) and those with big eyes (Caranx sexfasciatus in the photo) come to hunt on the plateau.

The focus and route of the dive are dictated by the current, which is often quite violent, though its direction is not constant; it usually, but not always, comes from the northeast. Before diving, you need to determine its direction.

If conditions are favorable, you dive in the saddle and pass behind Shark Reef, where the saddle plunges into the sea with an incredible drop. Here truly gigantic sea fans, several yards wide, grow. Visibility is almost always excellent, and the spectacle is impressive. The real risk is to go down too far almost without being aware of it, attracted by the sights.

You continue clockwise around Shark Reef. The sea fans on the outside are smaller, but the spectacle is always breathtaking. The wall is absolutely vertical, and the bottom of the sea is invisible.

This is—or was—the place for emotional encounters. Once whitetip reef sharks, gray sharks, hammerhead sharks, eagle rays, rays, and schools of dentex, trevallies, and tuna were certain companions. Now a meeting, though not impossible, is rare, usually reserved for the early hours of the morning and the seasons with less tourist traffic. But if you are shrewd and lucky, you may very well see a fine school of trevallies, some rays, and—why not?—even dolphins.

The wall in any case remains beautiful, cov-

ered as it is by an exceptional concentration of violet, rose, and white soft corals in the midst of which live the usual reef-dwelling fish, as well as lovely groupers and, on the shelf, even large Napoleon wrasse and isolated batfish.

The diving around Iolanda Reef is less interesting, since there are no sea fans, but it boasts the same coral environment, with a large variety of reef-dwelling fish.

145 The color of the Red Sea is enhanced by branches of soft coral (Dendronephthya sp.).

Bluff Point

SINAI

Gubal Strait

N

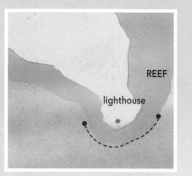

REEF

lighthouse

Text and photographs by Egidio Trainito

PRACTICAL TIPS

Maximum Depth:
83 ft (25 m)

Recommended period:
All year

Level of difficulty:
Average

Special features:
soft corals and scorpionfish

Visibility:
up to 133 ft (40 m)

Strength of current:
From None to Very Strong

146

EGYPT—GUBAL STRAIT
BLUFF POINT

The island of Gubal Kebir (Big Gubal) is separated from Gubal Seghir (Little Gubal) by shallows, at the northeast tip of which a small lighthouse signals the passage in the narrowest point of the Gulf of Suez. An ironic secondary meaning could be assigned to the name Bluff Point, as the movement of the currents is often deceptive here and may change direction unexpectedly during a dive. This is because the dominant current from the strait that washes the reef in a southerly direction meets the current flowing between the two islands, at times generating a change of direction, at others pulling the diver out to sea. In any case, divers should stay close to the reef at all times. Usually the dive starts

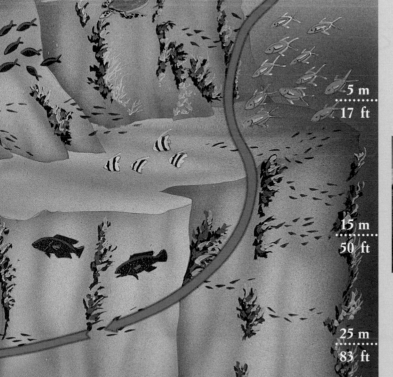

5 m
17 ft

15 m
50 ft

25 m
83 ft

45 m
149 ft

on the outer side of the reef and, following the current, ends soon after the lighthouse where the best anchorage for the boat is. You drop almost 70 feet (20 meters) along the nearly vertical wall, then the seabed slopes more gently for 150 feet (45 meters) or so. Even as you descend, you may encounter a large Napoleon wrasse or moray. It is not worth going very deep, as the best part of the dive is between 50 and 80 feet (15 and 25 meters). Carried by the current, which is at times very

147 top A shoal of small fish and holyfish swim among the ramifications of a gorgonian; two soft corals search for growing space in an advantageous spot, which sticks outward from the reef.

147 bottom The anchorage for diving at Bluff Point lies right below the small lighthouse of Gubal Seghir; the island is completely bare, and the topmost part of the reef can be seen in the clear water.

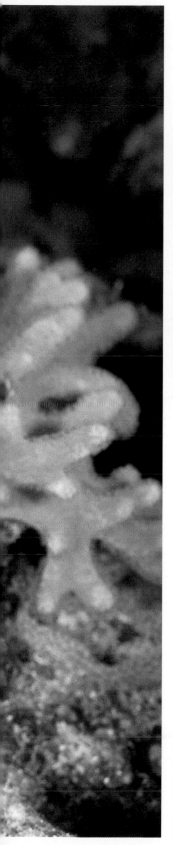

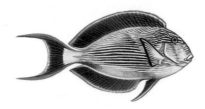

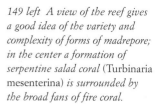

148-149 *A greasy grouper* (Epinephelus tauvina) *allows the photographer a close-up, giving a view of his sharp teeth; his spotted livery helps the fish to remain unseen against his surroundings.*

149 *left A view of the reef gives a good idea of the variety and complexity of forms of madrepore; in the center a formation of serpentine salad coral* (Turbinaria mesenterina) *is surrounded by the broad fans of fire coral.*

149 *top right A colony of fire coral, three soft corals of different hues, and a sea whip form a good summary of the variety and colors at Bluff Point.*

anemones and shrimps, hawkfish, and many other forms of life. Even on the drift you will make interesting discoveries: crocodile flathead fish (*Cociella crocodila*) and scorpionfish displaying their extraordinary skills of mimicry, small groupers, and stinging sea urchins. If you are lucky, you will see some flatworms seemingly wearing black velvet with small yellow spots, or nudibranchs covered with broken ramifications (*Marionopsis cyanobranchiata*). Farther on in the bay, the wreck of a small boat makes a wonderful site for a nighttime dive. Only the skeleton of the boat remains, but it is filled with fish, in particular fusiliers. One part of the boat appears to be the site of a reunion of dozens of large and small scorpionfish. Large yellow-and-blue mullet rummage busily around in the wreck. A white moray with black blotches slips in and out of the sides of the boat, while a crocodile flathead fish attempts to ambush unwary prey. The depth around the wreck is no more than 40 feet (12 meters), and a dive can last more than an hour. The time slips away quickly, with so much to see.

strong, you'll see large sea fans and highly colored soft corals; the effect of the color is heightened by the luminosity of the site. The many fissures are filled with pygmy sweepers and vivid soft corals, and you can even take a little shelter in a large grotto with scorpionfish if the current is particularly strong.

Large ramifications of black coral project from the corals on the wall, and you may well find a turtle swimming slowly in search of food, one of the many that lay their eggs on the beaches of Gubal Island. Every now and then, groups of carangids arrive out of the blue in flashes of silvery light, breaking up shoals of small fish. Pinnacles rise from the coral at intervals, brandishing soft and leatherback corals and gorgonians entwined in ribbons of holyfish, red groupers, or angelfish.

If you do not meet the current at this point, the end of the dive that takes you to the boat winds over a bed between 15 and 50 feet (5 and 15 meters) deep, which is no less interesting than the first section. Numerous coral towers covered with brightly colored soft corals rise against a background of drift and dead coral. Where there is no current, you can stay watching small fish,

149 *center right The crocodile flathead fish* (Papilloculiceps longipes) *has complete trust in his camouflage and allows the diver to approach to just a few inches away.*

149 *bottom A group of yellowspotted trevally* (Carangoides fulvoguttatus) *breaks up a school of small fish pausing on the top of the reef; the lightning attack causes a rapid retreat from the bank.*

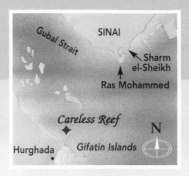

SINAI

Gubal Strait

→ Sharm el-Sheikh

↑ Ras Mohammed

Careless Reef

N

Hurghada   *Gifatin Islands*

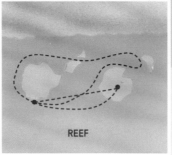

REEF

Text and photographs by Vincenzo Paolillo

PRACTICAL TIPS

MAXIMUM DEPTH:
50 ft (15 m)

RECOMMENDED PERIOD:
All year

LEVEL OF DIFFICULTY:
Average

SPECIAL FEATURES:
large morays
and sharks in transit

VISIBILITY:
up to 133 ft (40 m)

STRENGTH OF CURRENT:
Sometimes Strong

Illustrations by Domitilla Müller

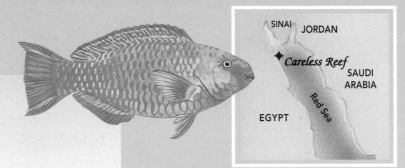

CARELESS REEF

This is one of the three loveliest dive points in the northern section of the Hurghada Archipelago, and probably the most famous. It centers on three madrepore coral towers that rise from a bed 35–50 feet (10–15 meters) down to almost break the surface. They stand on the edge of a wall to the north that descends to a depth of about 230 feet (70 meters) and therefore guarantees a continual

5 m
17 ft

15 m
50 ft

151 top *Two twoband anemonefish* (Amphiprion bicinctus) *in the tentacles of a sea anemone* (Heteractis).

151 bottom *Schools of blackspotted rubberlips* (Plectorhynchus gaterinus) *encountered on the walls of Careless Reef's panettoni.*

151

variety of fish. This is an authentic tropical garden made even more attractive by the exceptional clarity of the water.

There are many fixed anchoring points along the north slope of the shelf; consequently, your itinerary is determined by your point of departure and the current, which, when it is evident, comes from the north.

If you descend in front of the tower to the west, you will move along the west side. Here, on the sandy bottom, you will come across the morays that are the most common visitors to this zone. These are giant morays (*Gymnothorax javanicus*) that peep out from below the acropora or the many holes in the rock with their jaws open and fangs on display. Normally they are not aggressive and do not even defend their territory, but here, unfortunately, they have become accustomed to frequent offerings of food from divers, so they consider anything that moves as something to eat. Therefore be extremely careful if you approach them; do not make any sudden movement, or they may be deceived and bite your hand or arm, which could be very dangerous.

Down on the sand, shoals of masked bluecheek butterflyfish (*Chaetodon semilarvatus*) and Red Sea bannerfish (*Heniocus intermedius*) rest absolutely still around a tower of coral or a rock unless they are disturbed.

Proceeding north, you come across the first gorgonians, which often provide homes to trumpetfish and soldierfish. I was fortunate enough to meet a small but lovely greasy grouper (*Epinephelus tauvina*) hidden among the fans, and a superb scarlet frogfish (*Antennarius coccineus*) that lay immobile on a branch.

You arrive at the edge of the ledge that drops in steps to over 230 feet (70 meters) but continue eastward at a more suitable depth for 70 to 115 feet (20–35 meters). Here you will find interesting fissures, arches of sea fans often mixed with red sea whips, and grottoes filled with glassfish.

At one time a splendid potato grouper (*Epinephelus tukula*) lived here that liked to approach divers and swim with them. You could also be

sure of a sight of reef sharks passing not far below. I was once present when a dozen hammerhead sharks passed; today, with the enormous increase in the number of divers, that spectacle is practically an impossibility.

Continue along the edge, accompanied by Napoleon wrasses and parrotfish perennially engaged in eating the coral, and then, if you have the time, return to the second or third tower; both boast a range of tropical vegetation, shoals of silverstreak goldies, scorpionfish, sweetlips, and squirrelfish.

It is easy to find crocodile flathead fish (*Cociella crocodila*), bluespotted ribbontail rays (*Taeniura lymma*), variegated lizardfish (*Synodus variegatus*), and hundreds of coralfish down on the sand.

152 top left You can admire extraordinary red gorgonian sea fans on the northern drop of Careless Reef.

152 bottom left A grouper (Epinephelus sp.) lies in ambush, waiting for careless prey.

152 top right A fine crab tries to hide among the coral.

152 bottom right A starry toadfish (Arothron stellatus) under a madrepore arch.

153 Madrepore mushrooms shelter bluecheek butterflyfish (Chaetodon semilarvatus).

Text and photographs by Egidio Trainito – Illustrations by Domitilla Müller

EGYPT—HURGHADA
ERG ABU RAMADA

Hurghada, one of the best-known resorts on the Red Sea, was the first of the Egyptian diving resorts. Recent measures taken for the protection of the coral, such as the placement of mooring buoys, and a growing awareness of the need to protect the underwater environment have led to a notable improvement in the state of health of the barrier reefs. Among the high-quality dives to be made at Hurghada, one is quite unfor-

154 top Here is a pair of twoband anemonefish (Amphiprion bicinctus) among the tentacles of their anemone (Heteractis crispa).

154 bottom Soft corals of all colors cover the pinnacles around which thousands of silverstreak goldies and other brightly colored species move frenetically.

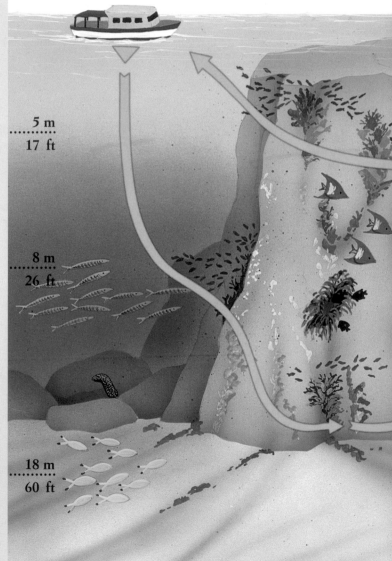

5 m
17 ft

8 m
26 ft

18 m
60 ft

gettable. Abu Ramada is a flat, deserted island surrounded by a wide reef east of Hurghada; 1,300 feet (400 meters) from the southern tip of the island, several coral columns, known as *ergs,* rise from the seabed. Erg Abu Ramada is a wonderful diving site often affected by strong currents, but it is the current that is responsible for the extraordinary explosion of color. You descend the sides of a couple of the larger spires, which are literally covered with red, orange, and yellow alcyonarias. When the current is

154

SINAI

Gubal Strait

Sharm
el-Sheikh

Ras Mohammed

Gifatin Islands

N

Hurghada • ◆ *Erg Abu Ramada*

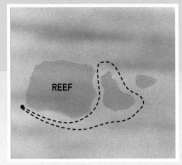

REEF

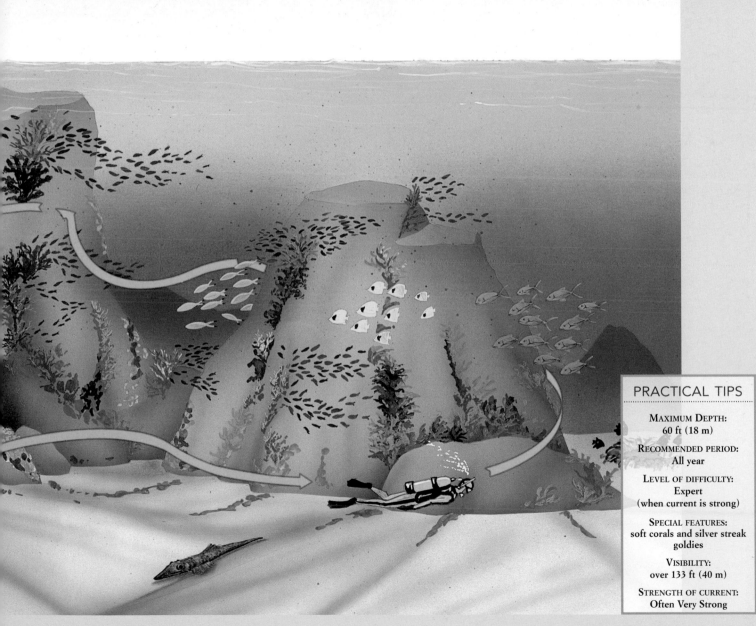

PRACTICAL TIPS

MAXIMUM DEPTH:
60 ft (18 m)

RECOMMENDED PERIOD:
All year

LEVEL OF DIFFICULTY:
Expert
(when current is strong)

SPECIAL FEATURES:
soft corals and silver streak
goldies

VISIBILITY:
over 133 ft (40 m)

STRENGTH OF CURRENT:
Often Very Strong

156-157 *A group of Suez fusiliers* (Caesio suevica), *endemic to the Red Sea, swims among the reef corals, while thousands of fish dance in the weak current behind.*

157 top left *A false stonefish* (Scorpaenopsis diabolus) *camouflages itself among coral concretions.*

zones, and multicolored nudibranchs crawl over the red-and-orange branch sponges; the most common is *Chromodoris quadricolor,* with its black-and-white stripes and orange edging. In the areas around the coral towers dense shoals of Suez fusiliers and angelfish flash about. Groups of jacks occasionally make rapid darts at the top of the *erg* in a hunt for small fish. Deeper down, a whitetip reef shark may cross your field of vision. Crocodile flathead fish, false stonefish *(Scorpaenopsis diabolus),* and stonefish seek camouflage among the coral, and large morays hide in the cracks. Large anemones provide homes for anemonefish in their tentacles in a symbiotic relationship typical of the barrier reefs of the Indian and Pacific Oceans, which extends to ten varieties of anemone and thirty species of anemonefish. The Red Sea has only one endemic species of anemonefish, the twobanded anemonefish, *Amphiprion bicinctus.* Even the diver who has visited all the seas of the world will not be able to resist watching the continual movement of small fish between the tentacles of their host, just as it is impossible not to admire the wonderful shafts of light when the sun is at its height, which make the fish and soft corals into a phantasmagoria of colors.

157 center left *The tips of the coral pinnacles on Erg Abu Ramada nearly reach the surface of the water; the brightness of the light in the clear water makes the carousel of sea goldies* (Pseudanthias squamipinnis) *over the soft corals a swirl of color.*

157 center right *The twoband anemonefish* (Amphiprion bicinctus) *is the only member of the group in the Red Sea, where it lives in the Gulf of Aden and the Chagos Islands; its small mouth is filled with sharp teeth.*

157 bottom right *A bank of hundreds of yellowfin goatfish* (Mulloidichthys vanicolensis) *lets a diver approach as it slowly slides away from the reef; this is where they normally spend the day, but during the night the group breaks up as they look for food in the sand.*

flowing, it is best to let it carry you and then attempt to stop in the lee of the spire, but the other side of the coin is that the number of fish around the coral is always extremely high. The *Dendronephthya* soft corals on the spire all grow up toward the light, but on top of one another, almost suffocating the hard coral underneath. This is the result of the natural competition for the most exposed and therefore most favorable spots, as they allow the small polyps that form the colonies to gather organic material carried on the current. In turn, the soft corals become advantageous habitats for other organisms, such as crustaceans and mollusks that live on their small branches. To increase the color around the coral spires and soft corals, there are dense shoals of sea goldies *(Pseudanthias squamipinnis).* The females, colored orange, are very plentiful, while the red, dominant males, with their long pectoral and dorsal fins, are less numerous. You will also find other soft corals on the spire, like the large roses of leatherback coral *(Sarcophyton).* The coral towers are marked by cracks, cavities, and galleries where you will find pygmy sweepers, squirrelfish, and cardinalfish. *Tubastrea* corals open their tentacles in the darker

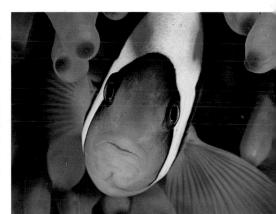

Hurghada
Gifatin Islands
N
Safaga Island
Little Brother

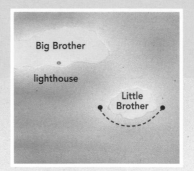

Big Brother
lighthouse
Little Brother

PRACTICAL TIPS

MAXIMUM DEPTH:
133 ft (40 m)

RECOMMENDED PERIOD:
All year

LEVEL OF DIFFICULTY:
Average

SPECIAL FEATURES:
various species of shark

VISIBILITY:
up to 133 ft (40 m)

STRENGTH OF CURRENT:
Strong

Text and photographs by Giorgio Mesturini – Illustrations by Domitilla Müller

SINAI
JORDAN
Little Brother
SAUDI
ARABIA
EGYPT
Red Sea

EGYPT—BROTHERS ISLANDS
LITTLE BROTHER

1 m
3 ft

25 m
83 ft

40 m
133 ft

300 m
990 ft

159 top View of Little Brother; this island is surrounded by a splendid reef that falls vertically to the depths, while in the distance, the larger is home to a lighthouse. Photograph by Massimo Bicciato.

159 bottom In the summer, the Brothers Islands are an important area for birds to rest and nest; for example, the tern, which forms colonies of several hundred pairs.

The two Brothers Islands, or *El Akawein* in Arabic, stand like two solitary columns of abyssal depth in the midst of the Egyptian Red Sea, 33 miles (53 kilometers) northwest of the town of El Quseir. The larger of the two islands, characterized by a flat, uniform profile, is around 980 feet (300 meters) in length and almost 130 feet (40 meters) wide.

In the year 1880, the British built a lighthouse on the island, which up until 1994 was still operated by its original mechanism. This consisted of a paraffin lamp whose light was amplified by means of an effective Fresnel lens system, which made the beam visible up to a distance of 17 miles

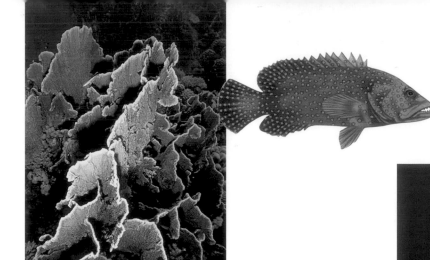

(27 kilometers). The rotation of the heavy lens complex depended on a perfect system of ropes and counterweights that moved up and down inside the lighthouse.

The smaller of the two Brothers Islands lies about a mile (1.6 kilometers) away from the larger, and presents a similarly flat morphology, though slightly smaller and more rounded. Due to the extraordinary position of the Brothers in the open sea, these islands represent a valuable wildlife oasis, inasmuch as they are the only islands present in a very vast stretch of sea. The underwater habitat is exceptional. The rockfaces plunge down into the abyss, displaying an endless succession of gorges and coral that disappear into a deep blue sea populated with sharks, barracudas, and other large deep-sea fish. This rich natural environment is today a national marine park, instituted in May 1998 by the Egyptian government and also including Daedalus Reef and the solitary islands of Zabargad and Rocky.

The waters around the Brothers Islands offer varied and spectacular possibilities for the underwater diver, such as the southern and the northern rockfaces of the larger island, Big Brother, or the two superb wrecks of the *Aida* and the *Namibia,* whose structure appears entirely covered by soft corals.

One of the most beautiful dives around the two Brothers is undoubtedly along the eastern rockface of the smaller island. This stretch of coastline is frequently beaten by wind and waves, making the area at times inaccessible and permitting underwater exploration only in favorable weather conditions.

Diving is organized in drift, beginning off the northern shore of the island and following the current, with the reef on the right, along the whole eastern profile of the barrier as far as the sheltered waters of the south coast, where boats await the divers at the end of their exploration.

160 center left At night it is easy to observe heavybeak parrotfish (Scarus gibbus) wrapped in their protective mucus among the coral.

160 bottom left Crinoids are echinoderms easily identified by their long and slender feathered arms; the purpose of the arms is to catch passing plankton. The slender prehensile structures below the disc at the base of the arms anchor the crinoid to the seabed.

160 right The fan tubeworm (Sabellastarte sanctijosephi) can be recognized by its highly visible white gill, formed by feathery tentacles up to 4 inches (10 centimeters) long, as it lies among the corals.

160-161 Gymnothorax javanicus is the largest moray to be found in the Red Sea; it has a large, solid body and can reach 7 feet (2 meters) in length.

162-163 The most curious characteristic of the redtoothed triggerfish (Odonus niger) is that of hiding in the nearest crack when frightened.

163 top left One of the most attractive sights off the Brothers Islands is the schools of bigeye trevally (Caranx sexfasciatus) that create marvelous ribbons of color in the clear blue water.

163 bottom left The range of jumps, tricks, and twists that a bottlenose dolphin (Tursiops truncatus) is capable of is impressive, but this behavior has a precise purpose: communication within the group.

163 top right The friendly nature of the humphead wrasse (Cheilinus undulatus) results in one of the most enjoyable encounters you can have in the Red Sea.

Diving in these waters is like peering into a deep abyss; just a few dozen yards from the shore, in fact, the bathymetry plunges suddenly into the depths, causing the extraordinary sensation of being suspended in a void.

It is not necessary to descend very far during the dive; at 100 feet (30 meters) it is already possible to see, along the whole length of the precipice, innumerable species of madrepores, huge branches of black coral, soft corals of a multitude of shades, and above all, an enormous quantity of gigantic sea fans (*Subergorgia hicksoni*), which make this one of the most individual underwater landscapes in the whole of the Red Sea. Exploring these rocks is a truly unforgettable experience; the diver, helped along by the current, has the impression of soaring over an endless landscape of coral, while undisturbed at his side swim bigeye trevallies (*Caranx sexfasciatus*), blackfin barracudas (*Sphyraena qenie*), and powerful tunafish.

Another of the most singular aspects of these waters is the constant presence of sharks. In just one dive, in fact, it is possible to see large numbers of gray reef sharks (*Carcharhinus amblyrhynchos*) and whitetip reef sharks (*Triaenodon obesus*), while the less common sight of the scalloped hammerhead shark (*Sphyrna lewini*) or a solitary *Carcharinus longimanus* is certainly cause for excitement.

After the rockface with the sea fans, we come to the southern side of the island, which usually has no currents, making it a good area for anchoring the boats.

It is advisable to dive here in the early hours of the morning, when the sun displays the coral reef in all its colorful beauty.

163 bottom right An encounter with several hundred barracuda (Sphyraena sp.) is one of the most exciting experiences to be had at the Brothers Islands.

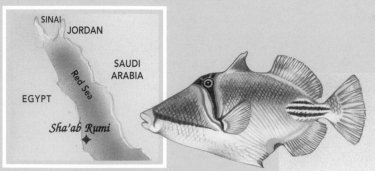

Text and photographs by Giorgio Mesturini

SUDAN—SHA'AB RUMI

PRECONTINENTE II

The Sudanese underwater landscape is—to say the least—exciting, thanks to invariably clear water, frequent encounters with large deep-sea species, and diving spots accessible only by cruise. The touristic infrastructures of the Sudan are very limited on land, but luckily there is a wide choice of cruises, carried out on excellent boats fitted with every comfort, which make it possible to reach unexplored reefs, where diving always has a taste of adventure.

The first underwater pioneers to discover the unequaled riches concealed in the waters off the Sudanese coast were Hans Hass, Jacques Cousteau, Bruno Vailati, Gianni Roghi, Folco Quilici, and many others, who during the 1950s dived in these waters in order to make the marvelous documentaries that

164 top Three hundred feet (100 meters) or so outside the pass of Sha'ab Rumi, you can still see the remains of the expedition Precontinente II, *organized by Cousteau in 1963. You can admire the voluminous structure of the "Urchin" and enter it via an opening in its base.*

164 bottom Striped dolphins are very friendly mammals that live in groups of up to fifty individuals.

were to become the inspiration of whole generations of divers.

If there is one single underwater exploration that alone is worth the journey to the Sudan, this is surely that of Sha'ab Rumi, absolutely one of the most spectacular reefs in the whole of the Red Sea. This reef, situated at around 30 miles (48 kilometers) from Port Sudan, encloses within the barrier a

25 m
83 ft

40 m
133 ft

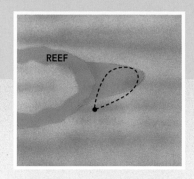

Illustrations by Domitilla Müller

Marsa Fijab

Precontinente II

Port Sudan

Suakin

N

REEF

PRACTICAL TIPS

MAXIMUM DEPTH:
133 ft (40 m)

RECOMMENDED PERIOD:
November—June

LEVEL OF DIFFICULTY:
Average

SPECIAL FEATURES:
sharks and schools of fish

VISIBILITY:
over 99 ft (30 m)

STRENGTH OF CURRENT:
Variable

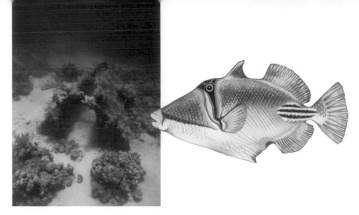

166 top left The "garage," one of the structures belonging to the submerged village of Precontinente II, is still visible.

beautiful lagoon, accessible by boat through a narrow pass.

The outer barrier of Sha'ab Rumi's various diving spots include one that makes the area unique. Outside the lagoon, 300 or so feet (100 meters) south of the entrance and around 50 feet (15 meters) below the surface, it is still possible to see the structures of a settlement created in 1963 by Jacques Cousteau during the expedition *Precontinente II*, in which Cousteau experimented with the possibility of having a group of divers live for several weeks underwater in a specially designed "village."

The first building in this futuristic settlement, placed at a depth of 33 feet (10 meters), was baptized "Urchin" because it was made up of a central body from which radiated a series of cylindrical arms.

On June 15 the five divers taking part in the experiment descended to this underwater home, where they were to remain until July 23! This historical endeavor was recorded in the film *A World Without Sun*, which would eventually receive an Academy Award for its exceptional beauty.

Diving in these waters today, it is still possible to see 35 feet (10 meters) down to parts of this settlement, such as the aquarium used for biological experiments, the "garage" for the small submarine (accessible via an opening at the back), and, at 80 feet (25 meters), one of the antishark cages, now covered with an impressive layer of soft corals.

The most exciting diving spot of the Sha'ab Rumi reef, however, is the southernmost tip. Descending here, we soon arrive at the base of a plateau, situated at 80 feet (25 meters), which stretches out like a balcony toward the open sea, surrounded on three sides by rockfaces that plunge steeply down into the abyss. On our way down, we are aware of the place's unique nature; before us, dancing in a perpetual carousel, are damselfish, barracudas, tunafish, batfish, and above all gray reef sharks, which have taken up residence in the area. At the base of this terrace, home to several species of mushroomlike corals, we move toward the outer edge to enjoy the spectacle of shoals of deep-sea fish drifting with the current. Off these rockfaces, which plunge vertically into the blue, we might see the dark shapes of many scalloped hammerhead sharks (*Sphyrna lewini*), rising as far as the edge of the plateau and then disappearing into the blue. On the southeast slope, not far from the rockface, one of the antishark cages used by Cousteau can still be seen.

166 center left The waters of Sha'ab Rumi are home to several species of shark, like the scalloped hammerhead (Sphyrna lewini) and the silvertip (Carcharhinus albimarginatus), but the largest numbers that swim near to this reef are the gray reef sharks (Carcharhinus wheeleri).

166 center bottom The depths of the south point off Sha'ab Rumi are an extraordinary area where you can see dense banks of bigeye trevally (Caranx sexfasciatus) and barracuda pass.

166 right The coral walls of Sha'ab Rumi are covered by splendidly colored soft corals in which shoals of tiny silver-streak goldies (Pseudanthias squamipinnis) take refuge.

166-167 The spotted coral grouper (Plectropomus maculatus) can be recognized by its red coloring.

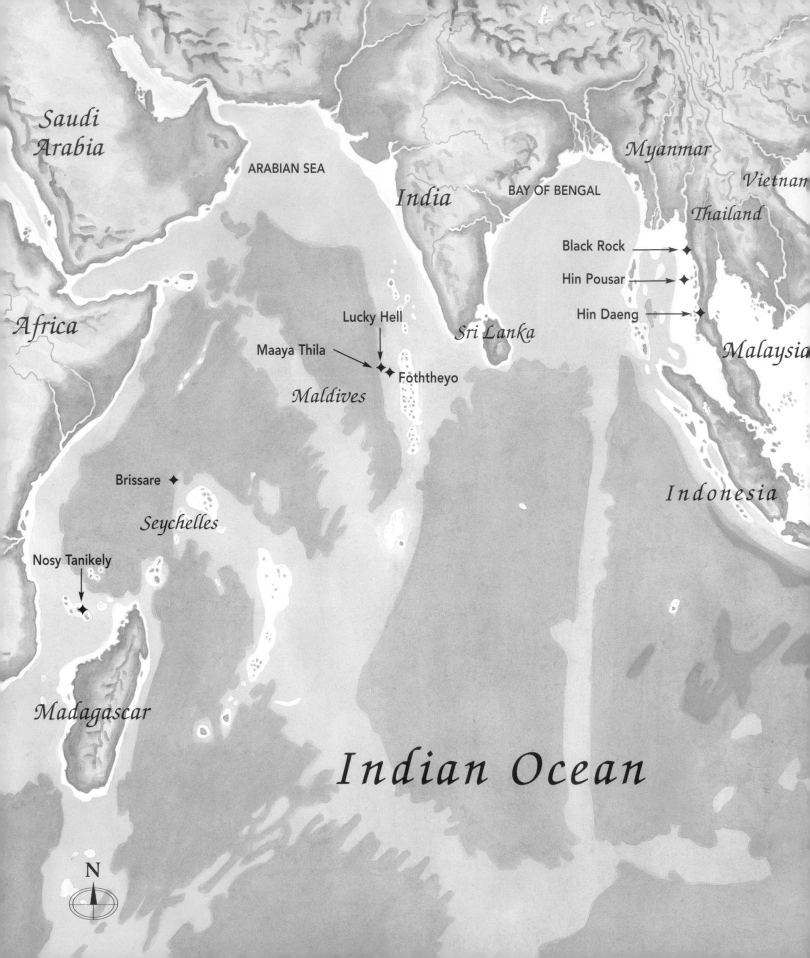

Saudi
Arabia

ARABIAN SEA

India

Myanmar

Vietnam

BAY OF BENGAL

Thailand

Black Rock ✦

Hin Pousar ✦

Africa

Hin Daeng ✦

Lucky Hell

Sri Lanka

Malaysia

Maaya Thila ✦✦ Foththeyo

Maldives

Indonesia

Brissare ✦

Seychelles

Nosy Tanikely

✦

Madagascar

Indian Ocean

N

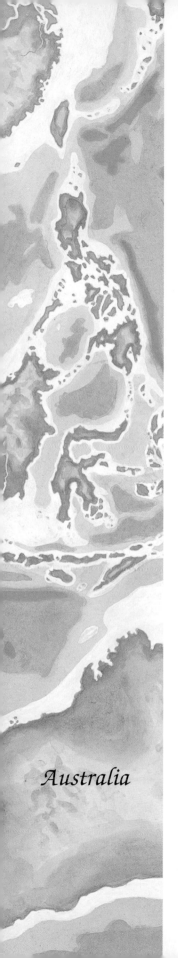

Australia

INDIAN OCEAN:
INTRODUCTION
BY EGIDIO TRAINITO

The Indian Ocean is the smallest of the three main oceans in the world, covering a surface area of about 47 million square miles (75 million square kilometers). It is linked to the Pacific in the southeast through the Malacca Straits, the Sonda Straits, and the Timor Sea, and to the south of Australia through the Bass Straits. Its waters mix with those of the Atlantic in the southwest between South Africa and the Antarctic. In its eastern portion, bounded by Africa, the island of Madagascar is surrounded by the archipelagos of the Comoros, the Seychelles, and the Mascarene Islands of Reunion and Mauritius. A series of parallel underwater elevations running north-south rises from the depths in the western section to form the Laccadives, the Maldives, the Chagos, the Andaman, and the Nicobar archipelagos, which are mostly composed of coral islands. To the south, thousands of miles from any of the continents, small groups of windswept islands herald Antarctica.

Two principal systems of marine current are formed in this immense body of water. The northern system is affected by the circulation that the monsoon season creates, whereas the system to the south includes the Cape current and the Australian current. Average salinity varies between 33° and 36°—low, compared to the Red Sea, which forms its northern offshoot.

Underwater tourists on the African coastline are limited to the islands of Zanzibar and Penba before having to go all the way down to South Africa. In Madagascar, the most developed zones from a tourist point of view are in the north, in the island of Nosy Be and a few other localities. Then, of course, there is the firmament of surrounding islands: the best-known destinations are the Seychelles and Mauritius, where residential tourism has developed. Other famous resorts, such as Aldabra, are only reachable by cruise ship. To the northwest between the Laccadive and the Chagos Islands, the archipelago of the Maldives extends down an area 1,200 miles (2,000 kilometers) long, formed by twenty-six coral atolls, which include over 1,100 islands, often minuscule, that together represent only 0.5% of a surface area of 56,000 square miles (90,000 square kilometers). The Maldives, one of the capitals of world diving, offer hundreds of sites, a large number of tourist facilities on land, and many underwater charters. Recently, more than twenty-five protected areas have been set up in the most frequently visited diving zones, and shark fishing has been prohibited in many atolls.

Farther east, Sri Lanka has several areas of barrier reefs around its coasts. The most visited area is to the south in the marine sanctuary of Hikkaduwa. Off the Indian peninsula, the Andaman and Nicobar Islands enclose the Andaman Sea, but they are difficult to reach, and only sporadically visited by diving cruise ships.

Finally, another important area is formed by the islands to the north and south of Phuket in the Andaman Sea, off the coast of Thailand between the borders with Myanmar (Burma) and Malaysia. Practically all these islands have been declared a marine park, and almost every dive site has mooring buoys. The most heavily visited archipelago, which offers the best dives, comprises the nine granite Similan Islands. Their good visibility, rich underwater life, and well-organized facilities ensure a continuous flow of tourists from Asia and the United States in particular. The Surin Islands, Phee Phee Don Archipelago, and the southern islands are also all popular destinations. Few cruise ships reach the islands of Myanmar.

With few exceptions, all the coasts of the Indian Ocean enjoy a minimum water temperature of 68°F (20°C) and are surrounded by barrier reefs. The variety of species is very great; many range widely throughout the ocean, with a smaller number of endemic species restricted even to a single group of islands or atoll. The classic example of diversification is once more the anemonefish: some species are widely distributed throughout the Indian and Pacific Oceans, while others are limited to tiny areas: for example, the twobar anemonefish (*Amphiprion allardi*), only seen on the east coast of Africa; the Chagos anemonefish (*Amphiprion chagoensis*), which only lives among the anemones of that archipelago; and the Mauritian anemonefish (*Amphiprion chrysogaster*), which is exclusive to the Mascarene Islands. Likewise, Aldabra and the Seychelles have their own species (*Amphiprion fuscocaudatus*), as do Madagascar (*Amphiprion latifasciatus*), Oman (*Amphiprion omanensis*), and the Maldives and Sri Lanka (*Amphiprion nigripes*).

NOSY BE

NOSY KOMBA

N

Nosy Tanikely

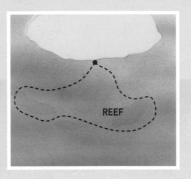

REEF

5 m
·········
17 ft

20 m
·········
66 ft

Text and photographs by Egidio Trainito – Illustrations by Domitilla Müller

MADAGASCAR—NOSY BE
NOSY TANIKELY

Nosy Be, situated on the north side of Madagascar, is one of the most well-known and best-equipped tourist resorts in the country. It is itself an island (*nosy* means "island") and is surrounded by many others, both large and small which can be reached in one day, and also by several archipelagos that require several days cruising to visit. Nosy Tanikely is just a few minutes by boat from the main island and at the center of a small, protected area. Originally formed by coral, the island is covered with thick vegetation and encircled by white beaches. In front of the main beach, where chameleons live on the plants and the boats berth, an excellent dive point offers interesting sights.

171 top Nosy Tanikely marine park includes the small island and sea that surrounds it; the island is covered with dense growth and the west side is rocky, whereas the eastern side, where the dives take place, has a lovely white beach.

171 bottom A group of starfish (Protoreaster sp.) display their characteristic pattern and red spines. Starfish find their prey in areas of sand and detritus among the coral formations; it is probable that their main source of food is sponges.

You can enter the water from the beach. After a few yards of sand, you swim out over a wide expanse of coral at a depth of 13 to 16 feet (4–5 meters), which drops to 70 feet (20 meters) and then returns to another sandy stretch of seabed. Follow the edge of the barrier, aiming at the deepest zone and then rise onto the shoal, where you are certain to come into contact with something interesting. You may find a male and female giant

171

172 top left A dense bank of snappers (probably Lutjanus lutjanus) *surrounds the base of a large bush of black coral* (Antipathes sp.); *colonies of black coral always appear bushy and can reach 7 feet (2 meters) in height.*

172 bottom left A group of snappers swims quietly above a male giant guitarfish (Rhyncobatus djiddensis) *around Nosy Tanikely; giant guitarfish are often present in the sandy areas between the reefs and can be approached when they rest on the bottom.*

172 top right A painted sweetlips (Plectorhynchus pictum) *allows itself to be approached between the corals; its typical environment is the sandy areas between coral formations, where it feeds on invertebrates.*

172 center right A turtle swims on the reef between sea whips; a sharksucker attached to its plastron is carried along by the large reptile, which nests on the sandy shores of the islands around Nosy Be.

guitarfish *(Rhyncobatus djiddensis)* lying together on the sandy patches between the coral or catch sight of one as it moves along just above the sand, looking for a suitable spot to rest. When you find one lying still on the bottom, approach it slowly without making any rapid movements, and you will get close enough almost to touch it. Observe its strange form and the various parts of its body: its nose is very pointed, and the two large, mobile white eyes are set well back, for the greatest field of view. The apertures that take water to the gills lie just behind the eyes. The pectoral fins are no more than a continuation of the triangle of the nose, while the two fins on the back are typical shark fins, with the front one larger than the one behind. The tail is moderately curved, and the gray body is speckled with round, light-colored spots, while the belly area is pale. You can remain close to a giant guitarfish for a remarkably long time, and this encounter alone makes this dive unique; but after spending half an hour together, given the shallowness of the seabed, you still have plenty of time to visit the barrier reef, which is filled with surprises.

You are also sure of another special encounter, this time with the turtles, which, none too confident, swim among the coral but lay their eggs on the beaches of the island during the breeding season. At times, a school of large twospot red snappers *(Lutjanus bohar)* may approach; these large silver fish move together as if choreographed, changing direction frequently. Dense clouds of smaller snappers with yellow-striped bodies swim among the ramifications of the black coral. Painted or lemon sweetlips *(Plectorhincus pictum* and *P. flavomaculatus)* hide in the fissures, while scorpionfish dart among the large sea fans. You can also examine mini-environments such as anemones that coexist with anemonefish *(Amphiprion akallopisos)*. Narrowing your field of research further, you will see various species of nudibranchs, crabs, and other crustaceans.

One last curiosity should not be missed—beautiful starfish *(Protoreaster lincki)* lie in the darker areas between the coral or on the sand, sometimes in groups, covered with tubercles and fire-red stripes. This species is characteristic of eastern Africa, Madagascar, and western Australia, and probably feeds on sponges.

172 bottom right Surprised by the fall of night, a swimming crab (family Portunidae) waves its claws threateningly in front; it probably has not had a quiet life, to judge by the broken claw on the right.

173 Surrounded by hard corals and sea fans, a devil firefish (Pterois miles) *extends all the rays of its long pectoral and dorsal fins; this species feeds on fish and crustaceans, which it entraps with its elaborate fins.*

Text and photographs by Vincenzo Paolillo

Seychelles—Mahe
Brissare

174 top *Characteristic of this part of the Seychelles are granite rocks surrounded by resplendent vegetation.*

174 bottom *Over the course of millennia, atmospheric agents have suggestively shaped white-sand beaches and granite rocks.*

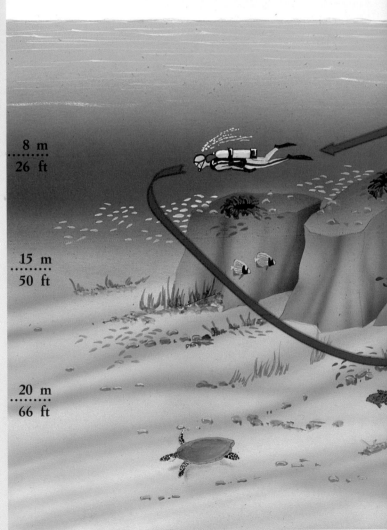

T he Seychelles lie on an extensive underwater plateau that rises from the depths of the ocean to about 100–115 feet (30–35 meters) below the surface of the sea. Consequently, dives are not very deep, often not exceeding 70 feet (20 meters), and therefore not very demanding. Nevertheless, there is a good deal of life beneath the waves, and the underwater environment is unique to the area.

The islands are volcanic in origin, formed of enormous outcrops of granite covered with coral and populated by tropical wildlife. This is a strange world; it seems as though a part of the Mediterranean (for example, Ventotene or Santo Stefano) had been transferred to a tropical sea and colonized by the local inhabitants. To my mind, one of the most characteristic dives is off the rock named

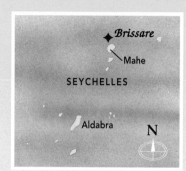

Brissare
Mahe
SEYCHELLES
Aldabra
N

REEF

Illustrations by Domitilla Müller

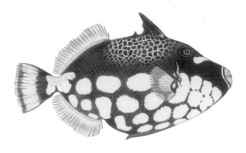

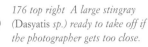

Brissare (derived from the French word *bizarre*). The rock lies in the middle of the sea, about 30 minutes by fast boat from the northern tip of Mahe, the main island in the Seychelles archipelago.

The dive is not deep, about 60 to 70 feet (18 to 20 meters), and the rock itself is fairly small, so there is no difficulty in making a tour of it, especially as the current is not usually very strong.

Entering the water on the south side, you soon come up against a large rock at the base of which a shoal of Tiera batfish (*Platax teira*) lie. If you look up toward the surface, you may seem some timid spotted eagle rays.

Continue along the west flank, where cracks in the large rocks are home to clouds of pigmy sweepers (*Parapriacanthus guentheri*), groupers, enormous morays, and splendid striped cowries. Below one of the rocks, a shoal of about 30 striped eel catfish (*Plotosus lineatus*) inhabit a cavity no larger than 5 feet (1.5 meters) long.

At the northern tip, enormous yellow clouds hover around large rounded rocks: these are schools of mullet and snappers, the most common sight in this area. There are no gorgonians or soft corals, but the lovely algae are the favorite meal of hawksbill turtles.

The rocks suddenly end, leaving the seabed covered with coral as it slopes down and away to the deeps.

It is best to return along the east side of Brissare, the most interesting part of the dive. The shelf, covered with elkshorn coral is like a meadow, in the middle of which it is not unusual to see turtles grazing and coral fish of all species.

But it is around the rocks that rise to the surface that most life is to be seen, most of all in the incredible quantity of rainbow-hued anemones, all of the species *Heteractis magnifica*, as well as anemonefish and porcelain crabs (*Neopetrolisthes maculatus*). A curious phenomenon related to anemonefish is that they all carry one or more parasites on their skin, small and large ticks.

More shoals of yellow and blue coral fish are rocked by the current or make way as you approach: there are yellowfin goatfish (*Mulloidichthys vanicolensis*), bigeye snappers (*Lutjanus lutjanus*), bluestripe snappers (*Lutjanus kasmira*), yellowback fusiliers (*Caesio xantonola*), yellowbanded sweetlips (*Plectorhynchus lineatus*), moontail bullseye (*Priacanthus hamrur*), pinecone soldierfish (*Myripristis murdjan*), bigeyes, small groupers, parrotfish, pufferfish with pointed noses, scorpionfish, and angelfish. In short, a complete catalog of tropical fish, and in exceptional quantities.

Before returning to the boat, it is worth a glance at a curious phenomenon: a small tunnel formed by two absolutely vertical rocks, a sandy bed and a square roof. It is only about 35 feet (10 meters) long, but even if all around the water is gentle, inside there is a strong current where large jacks let themselves be literally sucked in.

INNER
ATOLL

Lily Beach
Resort

Ranvelli
Resort

Vilamendoo
Resort

Kuda-Rah Resort

N

◆ *Lucky Hell*

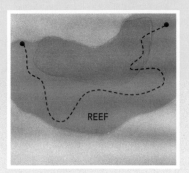

REEF

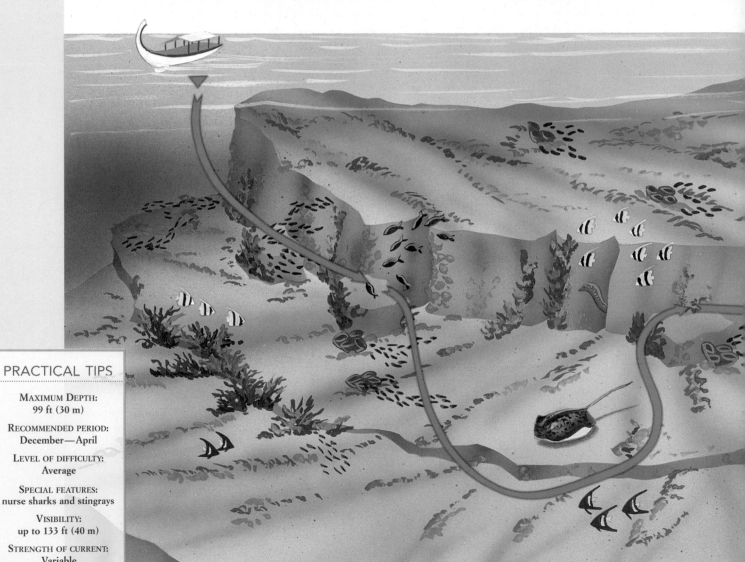

PRACTICAL TIPS

MAXIMUM DEPTH:
99 ft (30 m)

RECOMMENDED PERIOD:
December—April

LEVEL OF DIFFICULTY:
Average

SPECIAL FEATURES:
nurse sharks and stingrays

VISIBILITY:
up to 133 ft (40 m)

STRENGTH OF CURRENT:
Variable

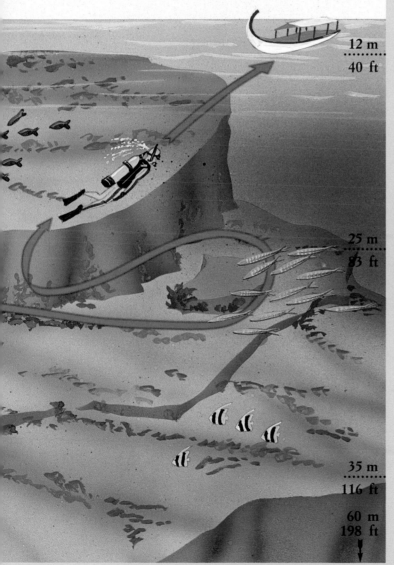

Text and photographs by Kurt Amsler – Illustrations by Domitilla Müller

12 m
40 ft

25 m
83 ft

35 m
116 ft

60 m
198 ft

Indian Ocean

ARI ATOLL

Lucky Hell

MALDIVES—ARI ATOLL
LUCKY HELL

"Lucky Hell" is in the southernmost part of the Ari Atoll, not far from the tourist islands of Vilamendoo, Lily Beach, Ranvelli, Machafushi, Vakarufali, and Kuda-Rah.

This dive spot is very central, and therefore visited by groups of divers from the surrounding area as well as by pleasure boats. At the south, Ari

179 top Innumerable soft corals of all shades of yellow and violet grow on the ledges of the reef, which falls vertically before overhanging; the colonies are not very extensive, probably because of the lack of current.

Atoll boasts a high concentration of soft corals, almost unequaled elsewhere in the Maldives. In particular, the coral platforms known as *thilas,* which rise from a depth of 130 feet (40 meters) nearly to the surface, are a favorite destination of divers.

"Lucky Hell" is one of these *thilas* and therefore sensational, not just because of its steep walls and overhangs but also because the blocks of coral that lie in front of it are completely covered with soft corals.

The gigantic *thila* in the shape of the letter *b* grows from a depth of 200 feet (60 meters) on the outer coral to just 40 feet (12 meters) below the surface, and some branches of the coral reach even higher. All around the *thila* are interesting

179 bottom More than twenty-five areas visited by divers in the Maldives have recently been protected, four in Ari Atoll. Expanses of coral sand, dotted with outcrops of coral, lie between the rich areas of the reef.

179

dives. The area on the west side is called Lucky Hell 2 and has the most to see. The steep walls of the coral create projections and small grottoes whose surfaces are entirely covered with pink, orange, and yellow soft corals. At a certain distance from the reef, various sizable blocks of coral with cracks and fissures lie on the bottom, three of which emerge from the water like knotty branches completely covered with soft corals.

The reef is populated by enormous shoals of silverstreak goldies at a depth that only allows you to see them in the distance. Those inhabitants of the reef that prefer to avoid sunlight, such as hussar fish, morays, bigeye jacks, and groups of sweetlips, live below the projections.

Here you may encounter the large deep-sea fish. Nurse sharks rest in the horizontal cracks

during the day, as they are one of the few families of shark able to aerate their gills by force of their muscles. Their relatives that live in the open sea, unable to enjoy these moments of peace, are forced to spend their entire lives swimming in order to breathe.

Stingrays lying on the seabed and covered by a fine layer of sand are often difficult to recognize despite sometimes being over 3 feet (1 meter) in length. They too like to rest in grottoes and below

projections in the reef during the day.

You may well find all the species that are typical of the Maldives living around this reef—the multicolored and variously shaped coral fish, jacks, barracuda, and other predators that move around the *tilas* in large shoals.

The dive site can be reached when the current is running from either the north or the south. This does not have a great effect on the dive itself, as the boats do not remain in a single place, and the divers can enjoy sights and experiences wherever they emerge. As has been standard in the Maldive Islands for many years, divers are attached to inflatable buoys so that if they wander away, the boat crew can tell their position even at a distance.

When the tide comes in, visibility is better, and conditions of extremely good visibility are predominant at certain times of the year. The topography of the seabed allows various types of dive, but experience has shown that it is possible to descend to the end of the deepest shelf (around 120 feet [35 meters]) or to swim at mid-depth (around 70–80 feet [22–25 meters]) along the first steep wall. Here the bright sunlight allows you to see most of the fish and to admire their splendid colors.

Across the whole area, the most interesting sites are around the large coral blocks, where you will find branches of coral several yards in length, some of which rise out of the sea. At one time they were flowered black coral, but now the skeletons that remain have been completely replaced by soft corals.

At the end of the site known as "Bottom Time" it is still possible to dive along the high shelf of the reef. In this area, where most of the corals died in 1998 due to coral bleaching, the fish teem. The number of herbivorous fish has

180 top left A giant moray (Gymonothorax javanicus) is enjoying a clean-up; four cleaner shrimps (Urocardidella antonbruunii) give it a once-over, immune from being eaten.

180 bottom left A group of yellowback fusilier (Caesio xanthonota) swims over the reef; capable of changing their coloring to red, these fish rest in the cracks in the reef during the night.

180 top right A group of bluestripe snappers (Lutjanus kasmira) occupies a crack in the reef; this species belongs to a family of over 100 different members, twenty-eight of which are present in the Maldives.

180 bottom right Here a view of the reef is dominated by the yellow of a large gorgonian; a solitary male sea goldie (Pseudanthias squamipinnis) keeps its distance from the swarm of females behind.

180-181 An overhang on the reef is the ideal position for a large soft coral; these corals are very variable in color and can increase their size by taking water into their tissue.

increased as a result of the formation of algae on the calcareous skeletons of the coral. In turn the population of predators has risen, although they still might not find much prey.

The smaller blocks of coral on the upper shelf are covered not only by soft corals but also by spongy masses of all shapes and colors. Feather starfish can be seen as far as the eye can reach. When the current is slower, in the middle of the day, the feather starfish hold out their tentacles to catch as much plankton as possible as they pass in the current. Around and below these blocks of coral you may find large numbers of scorpionfish or black jacks up to 16 inches (40 centimeters) long.

When the current is too strong to remain on the shelf, let yourself be taken at around 16 feet (5 meters) depth. The inflatable buoy should be attached by a cable that will float on the surface at this depth, so the boat crew can tell where you are while you are still underwater.

Letting yourself drift with the current can often bring unexpected and spectacular surprises. You may find yourself surrounded by huge schools of jacks or bump into mantas or eagle rays. You may also see small gray reef sharks or whitetip reef sharks; and when plankton is plentiful, a sighting of a whale shark is not a rarity.

Text and photographs by Vincenzo Paolillo

MALDIVES—ARI ATOLL
MAAYA THILA

In the Dhivehi language, *thila* means an isolated reef in the open sea. Maaya Thila, just such a reef, lies inside Ari Atoll. It is a coral formation that lies on a plateau at a depth of 100–150 feet (30–45 meters), rising to just 20 feet (6 meters) below the surface of the water. At this site, you have to take the current into consideration; if it is strong, it is best not to even enter the water as you will end up having to hold on to the coral and so damage it. If the current is only

182 top *From the plane, you can more fully appreciate the fascinating sight of the Maldive pass.*

182 bottom *This suggestive photo shows one of the numerous tourist villages found on the atoll of Ari.*

6 m
20 ft

25 m
83 ft

30 m
99 ft

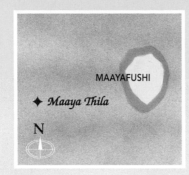

MAAYAFUSHI

◆ *Maaya Thila*

N

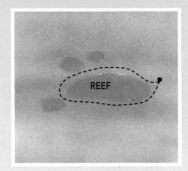

REEF

Illustrations by Domitilla Müller

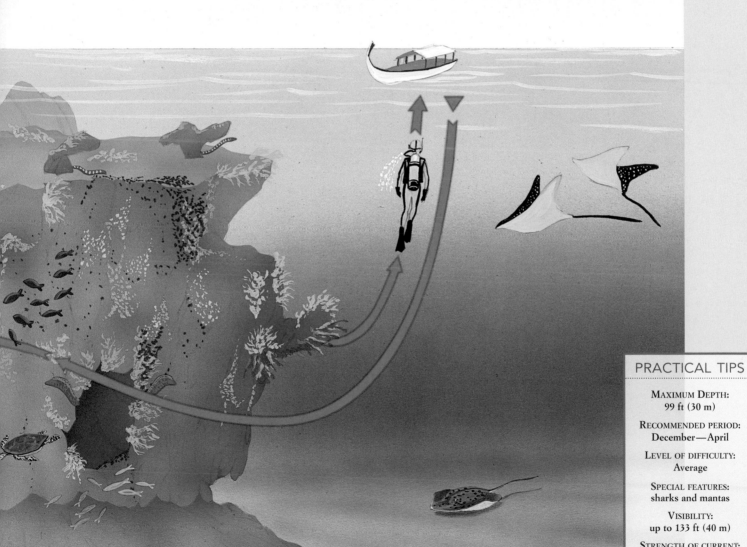

PRACTICAL TIPS

MAXIMUM DEPTH:
99 ft (30 m)

RECOMMENDED PERIOD:
December—April

LEVEL OF DIFFICULTY:
Average

SPECIAL FEATURES:
sharks and mantas

VISIBILITY:
up to 133 ft (40 m)

STRENGTH OF CURRENT:
Sometimes Very Strong

184-185 Characteristic of this dive are the colorful schools of tropical fish; these are bluestripe snappers (Lutjanus kasmira).

185 top left In the blue water above the diver's head, you can spot large deep-sea fish such as sharks and spotted eagle rays (Aetobatus narinari).

185 bottom left A dense group of oriental sweetlips (Plectorhynchus orientalis) finds shelter in a madrepore cave.

185 top right A beautiful sea fan (Gorgonia ventalina) extends itself toward the open sea.

185 bottom right This richly multicolored radial firefish (Pterois radiata) can boast of an extraordinary livery.

moderate, start by swimming against it so as not to end up too far from your departure point.

It is customary to start from the eastern end and go counterclockwise. The reef is not very wide, so it is not hard to do a complete circuit of the perimeter unless you decide to go deep or stop off for long periods—as always happens with photographers. The most interesting section, as is often the case, is the north side.

Descend quickly to the plateau, where blotched fantail rays *(Taeniura melanospilos)* lie. Raise your eyes and watch as gray reef sharks, enormous Napoleon wrasses, turtles, and spotted eagle rays pass overhead. Dense schools of bluestripe snappers *(Lutjanus kasmira),* moontail bullseye *(Priacanthus hamrur),* and Tiera batfish *(Platax teira)* encircle small rocks on the plateau. As you continue west, an enormous mushroom-shaped rock rising to nearly 80 feet (25 meters) harbors another shoal of snappers; several fine examples of anemones grow on its brow, populated by anemonefish. The south side is more uneven, with large rocks and cracks in which you may well find shoals of whitetip soldierfish *(Myripristis vittata)* and lovely gorgonians.

Returning to the east side, you come across more splendid sea fans and sea whips, an enormous titan triggerfish *(Balestoides viridescens)* or yellowfin triggerfish *(Pseudobalistes flavimarginatus)* nursing its eggs, and below an arch of coral, another shoal of oriental sweetlips *(Plectorhynchus orientalis).* Looking out toward the ocean, it is not unlikely you will see large rays and even whale sharks at the right season.

The beauty of this dive lies in its variety: migratory and nonmigratory fish, large predators, and small inhabitants of the barrier present a superb and certain spectacle.

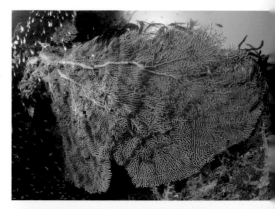

186 top left It's not easy for the photographer to get close to these humpnose bigeye bream (Monotaxis grandoculis).

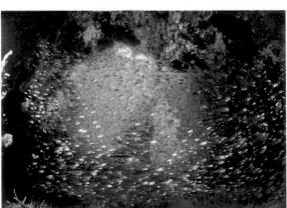

186 top right Small sea fans grow on the mushroom-shaped hard coral that surrounds the largest shoal.

186 center A blotched fantail ray (Taeniura melanospilos) lazily swims away, abandoning its hiding place in the sand, as the photographer approaches.

186 bottom Some beautiful caves found at the base of the shoal are filled with pygmy sweepers (Parapriacanthus guentheri).

186-187 In the photo, you can admire an incredible concentration of Maldive anemonefish (Amphiprion negripes) on a single sea anemone.

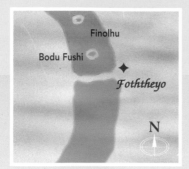

Finolhu

Bodu Fushi

◆ *Foththeyo*

N

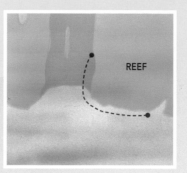

REEF

Text and photographs by Kurt Amsler

PRACTICAL TIPS

MAXIMUM DEPTH:
116 ft (35 m)

RECOMMENDED PERIOD:
December—April

LEVEL OF DIFFICULTY:
Expert

SPECIAL FEATURES:
arches with soft corals

VISIBILITY:
up to 133 ft (40 m)

STRENGTH OF CURRENT:
Often Strong

Illustrations by Domitilla Müller

FELIDU ATOLL

Foththeyo

Indian Ocean

MALDIVES—FELIDU ATOLL
FOTHTHEYO

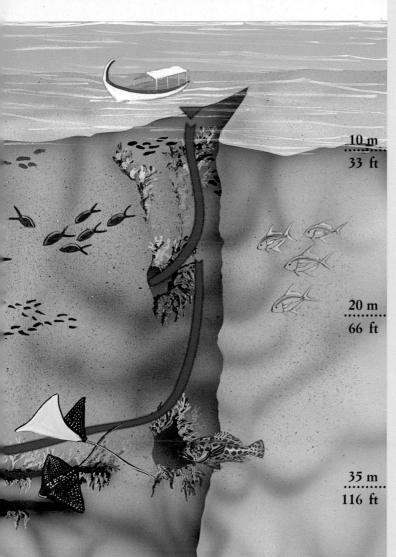

10 m
33 ft

20 m
66 ft

35 m
116 ft

S teep walls, grottoes, and overhangs are the major attractions for divers, not simply for the large variety of forms of life that inhabit them but also because they are homes to types of vegetation that are only rarely seen in exposed areas. One of these paradises of white coral is Foththeyo in the Maldives.

Foththeyo is on the east side of the outer coral bank of Felidu Atoll, where the main pleasure boats arrive that cruise the southern area of the Maldives. The diving centers on the tip of the southern atoll, Male, also organize daily excursions to Foththeyo. The immense outer coral bank is cut by a channel that ends in a lagoon. These sheltered waters are used as overnight anchorages by pleasure boats. From here, in just a few minutes a boat can reach a dive area that must be one of the most beautiful in the Maldives. The topography is magnificent. A gigantic plinth of coral—known in the Maldives

189 Foththeyo Reef has many hollows where soft corals of all hues grow; pastel shades predominate in the photograph, while the brighter colors on the wall are sponges and hand corals.

189

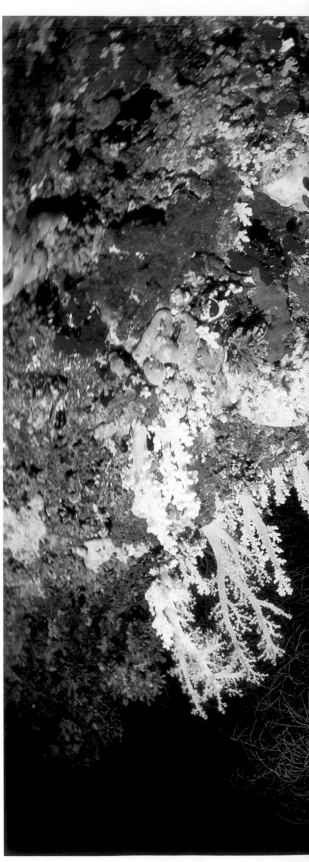

open sea. This requires proper buoyancy control to maintain specific depths. As a rule, safety during dives in this area requires solid diving experience.

A good dive is only achieved when the current arrives, bringing clear blue water; you can easily reach the *thila* before exiting, and maybe even the interior of the lagoon. The current, however, loses its force very quickly, and it is possible to cross the shallow sandy areas to descend again on the left or right side of the channel. The walls of the channel are home to many fish and are ideal for anyone wishing to use a still camera or video camera. As in the Maldives in general, every dive group at Foththeyo has to take an inflatable signal buoy. The buoy stands far out of the water and aids the crew on the boat in finding the diver even when the sun is very low.

As already mentioned, the steep wall and the side of the channel are completely covered with soft corals. Few places in the Maldives compare to this atoll.

In this zone, one type of soft coral predominates, white coral, which contrasts superbly against the blue of the water. As far as fish are concerned, large numbers of all kinds can be found. Off the steep walls cruise many examples of well-fed gray reef sharks and whitetip reef

as a *thila*—lies in the middle of the channel. Facing the open sea right in front of the outer coral bank, it reaches to 35 feet (10 meters) below the surface of the sea and then drops vertically to the deep. At about 120–130 feet (35–40 meters) down, the coral wall joins the interruption to the channel, creating grottoes and passages.

A dive at Foththeyo is an experience to remember and reveals a hugely varied underwater world to the visitor. Divers descending from a boat have to approach the side of the channel with the current flowing in from the

190 top The sturdy trunk of this gorgonian (Melithaea sp.) contrasts with its slim and intricate ramifications; this species is very widespread on the vertical walls and in the more exposed areas.

190 center Soft corals do not have the coherent skeleton that supports gorgonians, though both are members of the same group, the octocorals; a shared trait is that they both have polyps with eight finned tentacles.

190 bottom With its fins extended, a red lionfish (Pterois volitans) seems like a kite suspended in the water; it feeds mostly on small fish that it captures with rapid movements.

190-191 The reef is covered with cracks, gullies, and ledges in which the strong currents help soft corals grow to remarkable sizes.

190

193 top left A school of bigeye trevally (Caranx sexfasciatus) opens at the approach of a diver; the adults of this species often move in large numbers, while the young hide below floating objects.

193 bottom left As the giant manta (Manta birostris) swims, its two front appendices force water into its mouth; mantas feed on plankton and are often followed by other fish or, as in the photograph, carry sharksuckers attached to their bodies.

193 top right A red grouper waits for the small shrimp under its jaw to complete its cleaning. The the cleaners perform an important function for reef fish; experiments have shown that their absence causes an increase in ailments and parasites.

193 bottom right A turtle swims above the reef; unlike tortoises, turtles are unable to retract their neck and limbs into the protection formed by their carapace above, and plastron below.

sharks. A colony of spotted eagle rays spends time in the open sea around this area, and for years a giant sea bass has been seen that without any exaggeration is taller and fatter than an adult man. Escorted by a group of live sharksuckers, this giant passes by amazed divers. Such an encounter is certainly unforgettable, but that is as far as it goes; this creature cannot be caught on film from up close, as it stays at least 30 feet (10 meters) away.

A school of mackerel that can always be found on the coral plateau will call your attention to a small marvel of nature: you can swim through a natural arch about 70 feet (20 meters) high, completely covered with vegetation. Be especially careful here! The walls and roofs of the grottoes are covered with hard but brittle red and violet coral, which can break off at the lightest touch. To avoid this, maintain neutral buoyancy.

During morning dives, the sun lights up the whole of the wall, but in the afternoon the sun moves above or behind the coral bank. The degree and direction of the light and shade completely alter the appearance of the underwater scenes.

192-193 Gorgonians capture the current on the top of the reef, where organisms of all species vie for space with one another. The photo shows a diver behind an enormous gorgonian on the upper edge of which a dozen or so crinoids are attached; these echinoderms also collect food from the passing current, and the elevated position offered by the gorgonian is beneficial to them.

Indian Ocean

N

Mergui
Archipelago

● Mergui

Black Rock ◆

Andaman Sea

Phuket ●

REEF

Text and photographs by Roberto Rinaldi

PRACTICAL TIPS

MAXIMUM DEPTH:
133 ft (40 m)

RECOMMENDED PERIOD:
December—April

LEVEL OF DIFFICULTY:
Average

SPECIAL FEATURES:
mantas

VISIBILITY:
up to 66 ft (20 m)

STRENGTH OF CURRENT:
Strong

Illustrations by Domitilla Müller

Myanmar—Mergui Archipelago
Black Rock

195 top The color of the water at Black Rock and the density of fish change with the strength of the current. In this case the current carries with it a large quantity of nutrients, of which a swarm of chromis take full advantage.

195 bottom All the islands on Mergui Archipelago are rocky, either falling steeply into the sea or sloping gently, in which case they are covered with jungle and bordered by pale sandy beaches.

40 m
133 ft

The Andaman Sea is a stretch of the Indian Ocean well known by diving enthusiasts. Leaving from the Phuket Peninsula, you can find some glorious dive spots toward the various rocks that lie offshore; the water is rather murky but filled with an extraordinary quantity and variety of life. Out to sea lie the Similan Islands, huge, rounded, jungle-covered granite rocks surrounded by spectacular seabeds and often crystal-clear water. To the north lies mysterious Myanmar; closed to tourists for decades, it has only recently been reopened.

195

The map of the Myanmar coast shows a string of islands that rise from a shallow seabed and lead for miles out to sea, known generically as the Mergui Archipelago. Obviously, such a number of islands was a magnet to divers from the moment Myanmar decided to open its doors. It is also apparent that the only way to explore these many islands is by cruise ship, and *explore* is the right word; very little is known of their shallows. Today many dive sites have been identified, but cruise ships also like to take divers to areas that are still completely unvisited. One spot that has been known for some time and

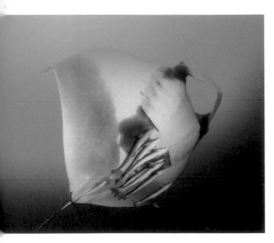

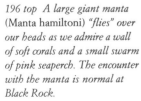

196 top A large giant manta (Manta hamiltoni) "flies" over our heads as we admire a wall of soft corals and a small swarm of pink seaperch. The encounter with the manta is normal at Black Rock.

196 bottom After a couple of minutes at a prudent distance, a giant manta plucks up courage and approaches us; a row of live sharksuckers (Echeneis nacrates), whose heads resemble cups, is attached to the manta's stomach.

196-197 Light soft corals (Dendronephthya sp.) cover the large rocks on the sandy bottom at the foot of Black Rock; yellow corollas of Tubastrea stand out in the riot of color.

196

197 bottom This close-up shows the delicate coloring of a starfish and soft corals that have found an ideal terrain on this stretch of seabed at Black Rock.

boasts superb underwater scenery is Black Rock, on the western tip of the archipelago that sticks out into the ocean.

As the name suggests, this is nothing more than a rock, not an island—a dark pinnacle that lies on a sandy, flattish bed about 130 feet (40 meters) down. One dive is probably not enough to complete a circle around the rock, as the currents are rather strong in these waters. Two dives will allow you to make the round trip, but they will not be enough to satisfy your desire to explore the depths in full.

Our arrival was celebrated by the spectacle of leaping giant mantas; rising completely out of the water, they created plumes of spray as they landed, but by the time we were ready to enter the water, they seemed to have disappeared out to sea. Underwater the walls of the rock are surprisingly rich in life and color. As elsewhere in the archipelago, entire rocks are lined with soft corals of thousands of hues; though small, they cover every square inch of the walls. Colorful large gorgonians also rise from the rocks, and dozens of crinoids cling on everywhere. While I was observing a wall of sea plants, I suddenly had the impression of a large UFO passing over me.

I looked up to see a truly huge giant manta sliding past just a yard above my head—just the beginning of a breathtaking spectacle during three or four dives a day over a period of several days. The mantas appeared in the water whatever its condition: clear and blue, or green and turbid. They flew in circles in pairs or three at a time

197 top The wall of the main rock is covered with gorgonians that stretch out toward the open sea in search of nutrients; notice the colonies of Tubastrea, *which open under cover of darkness.*

197 center At a certain distance from the walls of Black Rock, the rocks on the sand become smaller but are covered with an incredible number of sea lilies.

among an amazing company of live sharksuckers, also gigantic, but it was never possible to swim close to the giant mantas. They decided to come close to us spontaneously, sometimes as close as a few inches; on occasion we would find them the moment we put our heads below the surface, and on other occasions they would appear later during the dive. Never in our combined experience had any place been better for encounters of this kind.

Each dive along the rock bed that sticks out a little from the steep wall was affected by the direction and strength of the current. The memory of the dives at Black Rock will always remain in my mind, their fascination increased by the fact that this is such an unexplored place that it may well harbor other sensational surprises.

199 A large gorgonian rises from the rocks covered with soft coral; this is Melita squamata, *one of the loveliest gorgonians to be found in the tropics.*

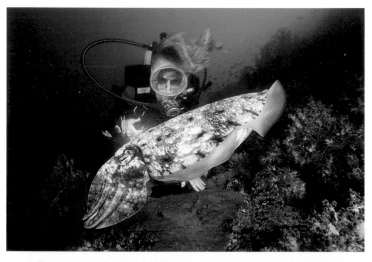

198 top left The diver's flashlight only partially does justice to the brilliant colors of the soft corals that populate the seabed at Black Rock.

198 center left A large cuttlefish (Sepia sp.) *camouflages itself among the soft corals; the diver's flashlight gives its presence away, but it remains still, confident of its camouflage.*

198 bottom left A leopard shark (Stegostoma fasciatum) *swims close to the colored reef.*

198 top right The current changes rapidly during dives and it may happen that the compact and heavy mass of green water is pushed away like a thundercloud in the sky, making way for clear water.

198 bottom right This scorpionfish (Scorpaenopsis sp.) *relies on its mimetic capability to survive; remaining still, it captures incautious prey that draws too near.*

N

Koh Bangu
KOH SIMILAN
Hin Pousar
Indian
Ocean
Koh Payu
Koh Miang
Koh Payan
Koh Payan

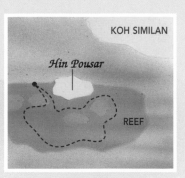

KOH SIMILAN
Hin Pousar
REEF

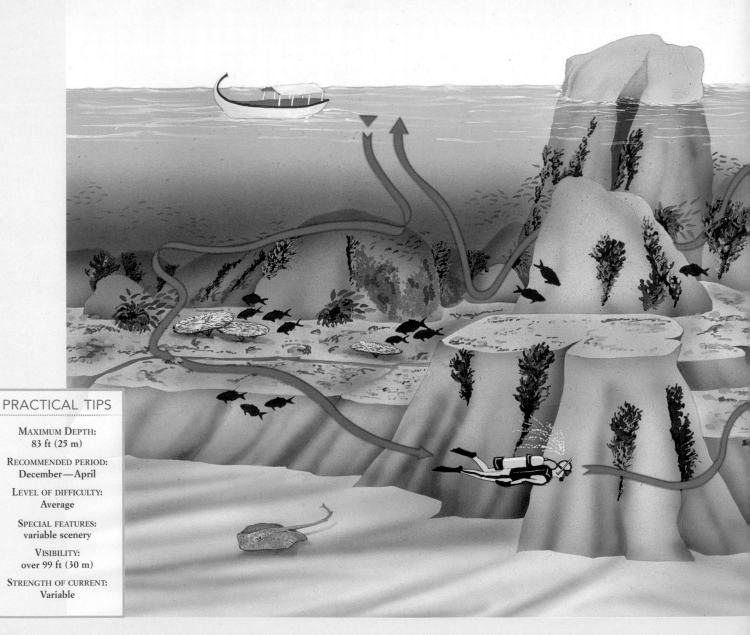

PRACTICAL TIPS

MAXIMUM DEPTH:
83 ft (25 m)

RECOMMENDED PERIOD:
December—April

LEVEL OF DIFFICULTY:
Average

SPECIAL FEATURES:
variable scenery

VISIBILITY:
over 99 ft (30 m)

STRENGTH OF CURRENT:
Variable

Text and photographs by Egidio Trainito – Illustrations by Domitilla Müller

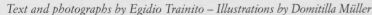

THAILAND—SIMILAN ISLANDS
HIN POUSAR

The Similan Archipelago lies along the northwest coast of Thailand about 70 miles (115 kilometers) north of the island of Phuket. It is an area of great interest because it is a marine park with the best water visibility in the country and because of the number of high-quality dives you can make around the nine islands of the archipelago. One of the best sites is now a classic destination for charter boats— Hin Pousar, also known as the Elephant's Head because of the shape of the rock where the dive takes place. The large blocks of smooth, dark granite fall sheer into the water, where they form varied scenery with plateaus, sudden projec-

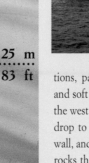

12 m
40 ft

25 m
83 ft

tions, passages, and arches covered with coral and soft corals. The best place for the descent is the west side of the smallest rock, where you can drop to 40 feet (12 meters), following the rock wall, and then move off west between the granite rocks that slope down to a depth of 80 feet (25 meters), where rays can be found in the sandy

201 top A small golden damselfish (Amblyglyphidodon aureus) swims above an enormous sea fan; many tropical gorgonians have ramifications that grow in all directions to create a tight mesh.

201 bottom The rock at Hin Pousar is also known as Elephant's Head, perhaps for its shape; as in all the other dive spots in the Similan Islands, anchorage is prohibited, and the park has provided mooring buoys.

201

202 *Two sea fans give shelter to a pair of redtail butterflyfish* (Chaetodon collare) *and a pair of brown-and-white butterflyfish* (Hemitaurichthys zoster).

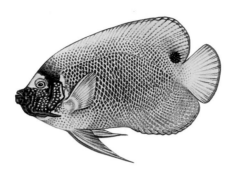

patches. Visibility often exceeds 80 feet (25 meters), and you can see in every direction: groups of oriental sweetlips hide under large umbrella-shaped acropora that grow on the rock, and banks of moontail bullseye *(Priacanthus hamrur),* some bright red, some silver with pinkish stripes, swim above the coral. The route turns back on itself toward the shallower rocks, where you begin a passage between them. The walls are covered with coral and soft corals that benefit from the channeling of the current. Crinoids of all colors stop in the most exposed areas even during the day, their arms extended in search of food. Here you can stop to watch the small shellfish that live between the arms of the crinoids and notice how they echo every tiny change of color of their hosts, although they are all the same species.

Where the water is shallower, stop to observe the tiny life forms that occupy each crack in the coral. There are small lobsters, nudibranchs, and spiral tubeworms, and you may even see a sea snake *(Laticauda colubrina)*—easily recognized by its black and blue transversal stripes and the white band along its belly—as it pokes its head into the cracks, searching for shellfish and other prey. It is a highly poisonous species, but the small size of its mouth makes it very unlikely that it could give a lethal bite to a diver. You can approach it without disturbing it, but remember that, as a creature with lungs, it has to return to the surface every now and then to breathe, which it does with great determination, disregarding anything in its way.

The final section of the dive continues counterclockwise around the largest mass, with an occasional foray into passages between the rocks. You will probably see large anemones fre-

quented by the skunk clownfish *(Amphiprion akallopisos),* yellowish orange with a central white band on its head and back. It inhabits areas limited to the East African coast and the Andaman Sea down to Sumatra and Java. You rise where you came in, perhaps meeting troops of rudderfish just below the surface, intent on nibbling the algae that cover the granite.

203 top *An* Amphiprion clarkii *swims above a* Cryptodendrum adhaesivum *and is under a* Paramuricea clavata: *on the rock, we see alcionari and red algae.*

203 bottom *An* Amphiprion ocellaris *among the tentacles of a sea anemone* (Heteractis magnifica): *the same species along the Australian coast is very dark and has white stripes.*

Hin Muang

Hin Daeng

N

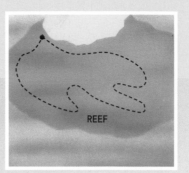

REEF

Text and photographs by Egidio Trainito

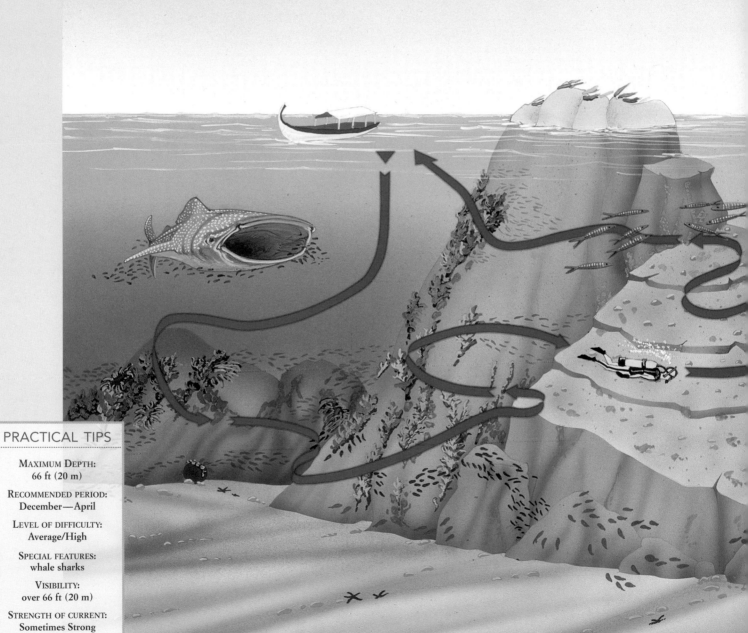

PRACTICAL TIPS

MAXIMUM DEPTH:
66 ft (20 m)

RECOMMENDED PERIOD:
December—April

LEVEL OF DIFFICULTY:
Average/High

SPECIAL FEATURES:
whale sharks

VISIBILITY:
over 66 ft (20 m)

STRENGTH OF CURRENT:
Sometimes Strong

Illustrations by Domitilla Müller

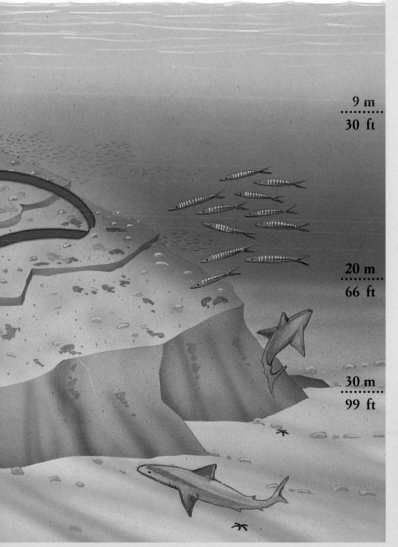

9 m
30 ft

20 m
66 ft

30 m
99 ft

205 top A pair of pennant coralfish (Heniochus acuminatus) *swims between the soft corals that cover a slope at Hin Daeng; the adults of this species often swim in pairs and feed mostly on zooplankton.*

THAILAND—KOH ROK ISLANDS
HIN DAENG

Seventy miles (115 kilometers) southeast of Phuket and roughly 40 miles (65 kilometers) from the coast that faces the area of Trang lie two small islands, Koh Rok Nok and Koh Rok Nai, almost united by a narrow stretch of sandy-bottomed sea, which with the surrounding shoals make up a protected area. Here you find the only shelters where you can stop before continuing to Hin Daeng, the Red Rock, which is 12 nautical miles to the west. Hin Daeng is a tiny piece of limestone jutting just a few feet above the

205 bottom A school of sea goldies (Pseudanthias squamipinnis) *easily recognizable by the bright orange coloring, swims close to the branches of an Acropora, a hard coral that offers a secure den to these shy fish.*

205

water, where the sea often does not permit you to stop. The higher rocks are covered with colored drapes that the local fishermen put there as propitiatory offerings for a good catch. Some hundreds of yards to the north of Hin Daeng, another piece of rock forms a huge spire that reaches to almost within 30 feet (9 meters) of the surface. It is called Hin Muang and rivals Hin Daeng for the superb quality of the dive.

Hin Daeng offers various diving opportunities, but without doubt the most important aspect of the site is the near certainty of meeting the largest fish in the world, the whale shark *(Rhincodon typus)*. Often the whale sharks at Hin Daeng are not of great size, but every now and then you come across more than one, which suggests that this area is a nursery for the species. It sometimes happens that while you are still preparing to begin your dive, the curiosity of the large fish stimulates it to start nosing around and under the boat, which gives you plenty of time to examine its size. The best way to meet the whale shark is to enter the water near the rock and

descend to one of the many terraces that form the bed on the north side. Wait there immobile, and with luck it will come close, intrigued by your bubbles. At this point, you can swim closer and observe its gray hide covered with white spots, its squat head, and its tiny eyes. You can follow as it swims below the water, often accompanied by large live sharksuckers or small jacks, but you will have to put a lot of effort into it, as one flick of its long tail gives it a lot of speed, however slowly it appears to go. The whale shark swims with its large mouth open, as it feeds on plankton and small fish, and is consequently harmless as far as the diver is concerned.

While you wait on the terrace, there is no chance of boredom: near the surface, needlefish dart back and forth continuously; farther below, large barracuda pass on the lookout for prey; while on the bottom, 70 feet (20 meters) or so farther down, large gray reef sharks swim in circles.

The southwest side of the almost vertical rock wall is the most spectacular you could hope to see: soft corals create a blaze of color, surrounded by pygmy sweepers and other small fish. The light penetrates obliquely during the middle of the day, and visibility can exceed 100 feet (30 meters). At times the fish are so dense that the light from above is obscured, creating continual plays of light and shade. You can rise counterclockwise toward the east face of the shallows, where several pinnacles are covered by large violet, orange, and blue anemones *(Heteractis magnifica)*. Some are completely open, with clown anemonefish *(Amphiprion ocellaris)* playing among the tentacles; others are closed and swollen, like large colored balls. The ascent continues as far as the shallows that surround the rock, where there is another multitude of organisms to discover: orange madrepore, nudibranchs, and large starfish trailing among the coral, while just above your head, on the surface, needlefish 3 feet (1 meter) long flit around looking for prey.

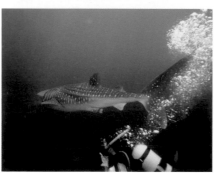

206 top left A small crab (Neopetrolisthes ohshimai) hides among the tentacles of a large anemone (Heteractis magnifica); it is an anomura and belongs to the same group as the edible crab, the pagurus.

206 bottom left At 100 feet (30 meters) down, a series of horizontally growing corals (Porites sp.) hosts some pale lilac soft corals; the raggy scorpionfish (Scorpaenopsis venosa) in the center is colored to blend in with the surroundings.

206 top right Two large soft corals (Dendronephthya sp.) have grown in one of the recesses where the current is funneled in; the small hollow teems with pigmy sweepers (Parapriacanthus ransonneti).

206 bottom right You can be fairly sure of an encounter with a whale shark (Rhincodon typus) at Hin Daeng, as they are curious and interested by the noise made by divers; a harmless creature that lives on plankton, the whale shark is the largest fish in the seas and can sometimes reach 60 feet (18 meters) in length.

206-207 The tip of the rock at Hin Daeng is washed by waves and currents and provides a home to adaptable creatures such us "the teeth of the dog;" on this calm day, some sea urchins nibble on algae, and a large crown of thorns (Acanthaster planci) is in search of some coral to prey on.

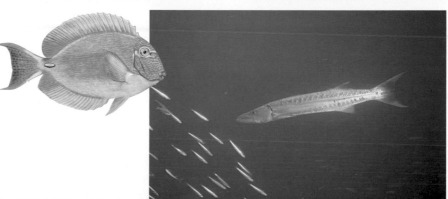

207 bottom You will find many predators around Hin Daeng and its surrounding rocks; needlefish as well as large solitary barracuda (Sphyracna sp.).

Asia

Hawaii Islands

Jessie
Beazley
Reef

Philippines

Pescador Island

Malaysia

South Point

Blue Corner

Gorgonian Forest

Likuan

South Ema

P o l y n e s i a

Indonesia

Papua
New Guinea

Mari Mabuk

Cod Hole

Tupitipiti Point

Tiputa Pass

Tulamben

Cod Wall

Australia

Fiji Islands

The Pinnacle

New
Zealand

Tasmania

Golden Bommie

P a c i f i c

PACIFIC OCEAN: INTRODUCTION

BY EGIDIO TRAINITO

The Pacific, the largest ocean in the world, stretches between Asia, Australia, and America. Its edges are lined with volcanoes, which form the so-called "belt of fire." It covers an area of 112 million square miles (180 million square kilometers) from north to south, between Arctic and Antarctica, meeting the Arctic Ocean at the Bering Strait, the Indian Ocean in the west in the seas of Indonesia, and the Atlantic to the southeast. It comprises many internal seas, especially along the western coasts: the Bering Sea, Sea of Ohotsk, Sea of Japan, Yellow Sea, East China Sea, South China Sea, the various seas in Indonesia (Java, Flores, Sulawesi, Moluccas, Ceram Banda, Timor, Arafura), the seas in the Philippines, the Sulu Sea, and the Coral Sea. All these are separated from the open ocean by a string of islands (the Aleutians, the Kurils, the Japanese archipelago, the Philippines, Indonesia, and so on). The lowest point on the surface of the earth is found in the Pacific, in the Mariana Trench's Vitjaz Deep, at a depth of 36,150 feet (11,020 meters) below sea level. Its waters Pacific have an average salinity of 36, decreasing with the increase in latitude and along the coasts where large rivers enter the ocean—the Yukon, the Columbia Fraser, and the Colorado in America, the Amur, the Yellow River, and the Chang Jiang in Asia. The superficial water temperature ranges between 77 and 82°F (25 and 28°C) in the equatorial area and falls off toward the poles. The band that includes temperatures that never fall below 68°F (20°C), and is home to formations of coral, tends to narrow when it comes into contact with the west coast of the American continent, where the presence of coral is limited to the Galapagos Islands and a few areas along the coast.

The waters between Australia and Asia, around the Philippines, Indonesia, Borneo, Papua New Guinea, and Malaysia, are home to a diversity of species at its greatest anywhere on the planet, with over 500 species of coral and 3,000 species of fish, and an endemic proportion over 30 percent.

Toward the east along the northeast coast of Australia, the Great Barrier Reef acts as a boundary to the Coral Sea. More than 2,500 reefs are strung along a front measuring 1,200 miles (2,000 kilometers) in length with a maximum width of 160 miles (250 kilometers) – one of the wonders of the world. Farther north and to the east, the tiny islands that form Melanesia, Micronesia, Polynesia and the Hawaiian archipelago are almost uncountable. In front of the South American coast to the east, the Galapagos Islands lie right on the equator.

If you could make a long dive right across the Pacific, you would see a progressive change in the biological and geological structure of the reefs. The presence of coral would decrease until you reached the American coast, where the life forms are quite different; for instance, in the Galapagos you would see sea lions and iguanas, and in California you would swim among tangled forests of kelp.

Every one of the thousands of islands in the Pacific offers myriad diving sites, but not all are similarly convenient. Some are difficult to reach, and some have no organized diving facilities. The highly efficient organization of floating hotels and magnificent boats that tempt thousands of divers to visit the Great Barrier Reef contrasts strongly with the precarious connections that allow you to visit some of the lovely areas of Indonesia. But many localities have now become obligatory destinations for divers in Malaysia, Sipadan, the Philippines, Fiji, and even French Polynesia. Some of these places require more than a day's travel to reach, but the beauty of the land and the magnificent underwater scenery are worth the effort and the expense.

PHILIPPINES

Cebu Island

N

◆ Pescador
Island

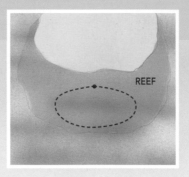

REEF

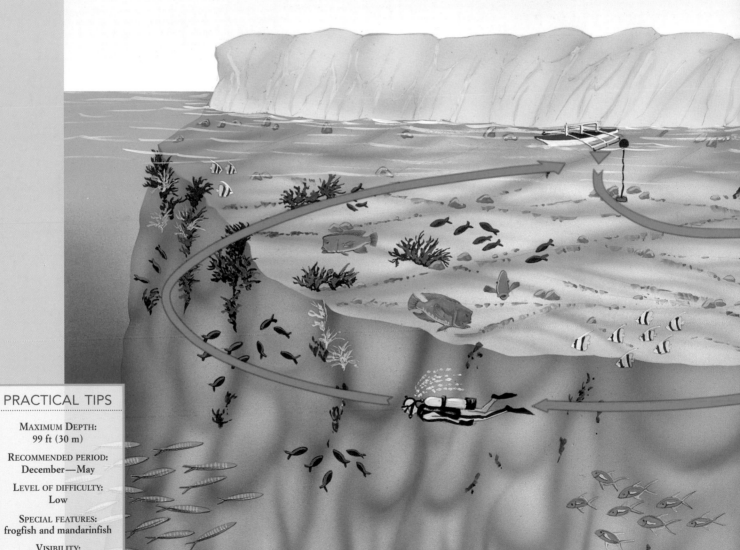

Text and photographs by Vincenzo Paolillo – Illustrations by Domitilla Müller

211 top A small yellowtail clownfish (Amphiprion clarkii) peeks out from the evanescent tentacles of the anemone with which it lives in symbiosis.

5 m
·········
17 ft

30 m
·········
99 ft

PHILIPPINES—CEBU
PESCADOR ISLAND

The coast of the island of Cebu faces the southern section of the strait of Tanon and is unquestionably an underwater paradise for divers, in particular the area of Moalboal. Anyone who has had the fortune to dive at White Beach, Copton Point, Ludo Point, and Sunken Island will long remember them, but the most famous dive site of all is Pescador Island.

This is a small island, no more than a pinnacle

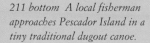

211 bottom A local fisherman approaches Pescador Island in a tiny traditional dugout canoe.

211

212 *A diver enters the water from a dugout canoe anchored close to the island.*

213 *top left The spotted turkeyfish is a beautiful but rare fish.*

213 *bottom left Finding a harlequin ghost pipefish (Solenostomus paradoxus) is a difficult task, but once discovered, it is easy to photograph.*

213 *top right A good-looking red crab freezes at the approach of a diver.*

that rises at most 35 feet (10 meters) from the sea, and lies 2 miles (3 kilometers) east-southeast of the coast of Tongo Point. It is possible to make a complete tour of Pescador Island if you don't dawdle, and you are sure not to be disappointed.

The most interesting part of the dive is the area between the south and east of the island, for its spectacular variety. You enter the water from a buoy positioned over a sandy coral plateau no more than 15 or 20 feet (5 or 6 meters) deep, on which you will see splendid elkhorn coral; in the middle of this, each evening, it is likely you will catch a glimpse of an elusive dragonet *(Synchiropus picturatus)*, the superb blenny that is the despair of underwater photographers, and leatherback coral on which you may see a shellfish out for a stroll. Huge numbers of anemones of all types and colors live on the sand, attached to small coral formations and, of course, escorted by anemonefish and

brightly colored nudibranchs.

Descend on the south side, where the slope is gentle and populated by coral, all kinds of sponges, and soft corals. You will see an extravaganza of scorpionfish decked out in pink, yellow, and red costumes, some with light blue shading, darting hither and thither or absolutely still on large sponges.

No farther down than 35 feet (10 meters), you can be fairly sure of meeting frogfish. I came across two enormous specimens of Commerson's frogfish *(Antennarius commersonii)*, one brown and the other black, so still I could photograph them from all angles. Farther out, schools of jacks and barracuda circle.

213 *bottom right The diver's flashlight illuminates the extraordinary vegetation that proliferates on the walls of Pescador Island.*

Heading east, the rock wall becomes steeper; enormous trees of black coral, barrel and tube sponges, gorgonians, brightly colored soft corals, and crinoids appear, all densely populated by small fish and crabs that would be difficult to find elsewhere. All around are Napoleon wrasses, morays, pufferfish, starfish, and butterflyfish. You don't need to be particularly observant to notice the nudibranchs, yet more frogfish (I found one no more than 3 inches [8 centimeters] long, colored a wonderful red and with white-edged fins that I simply fell in love with), harlequin ghost pipefish (*Solenostomus paradoxus*), leaf scorpionfish, and more.

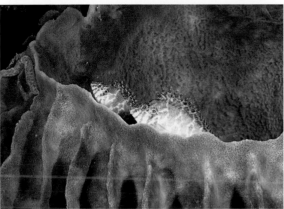

Because of the phenomenal variety of life forms, if you look around with care, you risk using up your air before you can go deeper (the seabed is only 100 feet [30 meters] or so deep here), or even reaching the point where you head up onto the plateau to return to the boat.

And that is only daytime! When I went out at night, all the inhabitants of the reef were out on the hunt or simply for the exercise, and I went through a roll of film in record time. Among others, you are certain to see several examples of Spanish dancers (*Hexabranchus sanguineus*).

214-215 This giant Commerson's frogfish (Antennarius commersonii) *tries to hide itself on a candelabra sponge in vain.*

215 top left Two small morays poke their heads out of a fissure in the reef.

215 center left Two spotted hawkfish (Cirrhitichthys aprinus) *take refuge in a large barrel sponge.*

215 top right A leaf scorpionfish (Taenianotus triacanthus)*, a master of camouflage, rests immobile among the coral formations.*

215 bottom This is another of the many Commerson's frogfish that populate the waters of Pescador Island; it is waiting in ambush between two sponges.

North Reef

Jessie
Beazley
Reef

TUBBATAHA REEF

South Reef

N

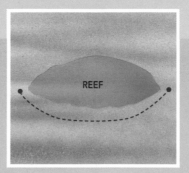

REEF

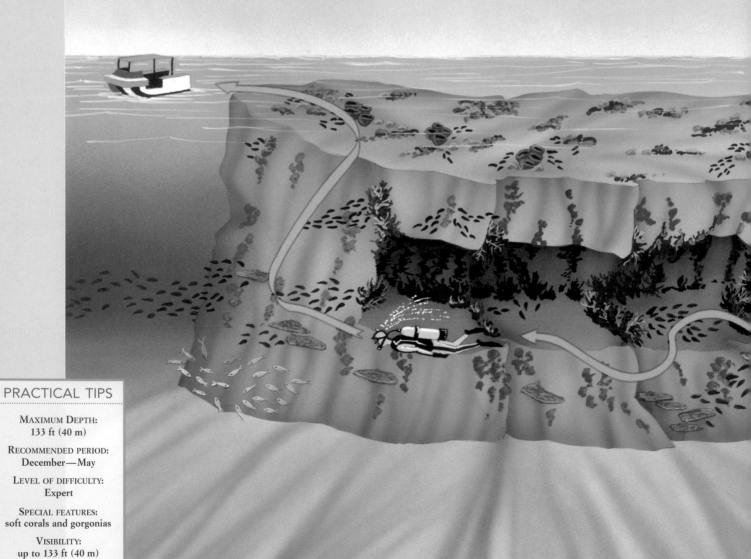

Text and photographs by Roberto Rinaldi – Illustrations by Domitilla Müller

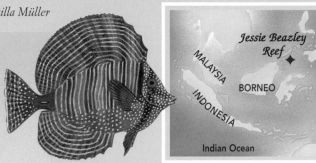

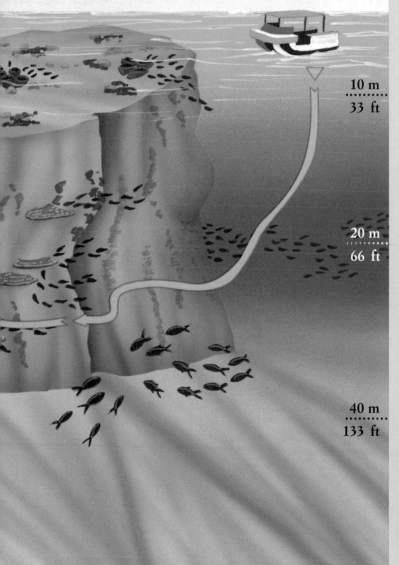

PHILIPPINES—TUBBATAHA REEF
JESSIE BEAZLEY REEF

The vast Philippine archipelago offers an infinite number of fascinating sites for divers. There is an impressive variety of seabeds, some still to be explored, available to divers in one of the richest seas in the world. The archipelago, volcanic in origin, was created in the Pacific right on the edge of one of the deepest chasms on the planet: the Mariana Trench. This gives an indication of just how difficult it is to summarize the abundance and

10 m
33 ft

20 m
66 ft

40 m
133 ft

217 left In their small canoes, the Filipinos face dangerous trips over the open ocean. We meet more than a few, miles from the coast.

217 right Vertical walls, teeming with colorful gorgonians and corals: a summary of the sea bottoms of Jessie Beazley. In the photo you can see a branch of Siphonogorgia sp.

217

218 top A giant Arothron stellatus over a garden of madrepore and soft coral.

218 bottom A giant barrel sponge (Xestospongia sp.) showing its open mouth (oscula).

218-219 At sunset, clouds of pink Anthias surround this colony of madrepore.

the variety of marine beds covered in the area. It is difficult to choose, but one place stands out for its uniqueness and for its unquestioned isolation, which keeps it protected and little visited by either tourists or fishermen.

This is Tubbataha Reef, a coral system that emerges right in the center of the Sulu Sea, and which has for some time been part of a vast national park.

The departure point is Puerto Princesa, a town on the island of Palawan from which you have to steam 113 miles (182 kilometers) southeast to reach the atolls. A remote place, it is made even more difficult to reach in that only the months of March to June give favorable sailing and diving conditions.

Tubbataha Reef can be divided into two main sections: South Reef, an elliptical atoll that surrounds a lagoon, with only a small rock, called Black Rock, emerging to the north; and North Reef, which lies on the other side of a channel about 4 miles (6 kilometers) northeast. North Reef offers a lengthy wall that runs southwest to northeast. It contains a long and narrow lagoon in which a sandy island emerges from the coral at the northern tip, where the rangers in charge of the park live. It is clear that on such a long and continous coral reef as the one that bounds the two atolls, there is an infinite number of dives that are difficult to identify separately.

The reef is at all points rich and varied, adorned by hard corals for the first few yards, then by gorgonians and soft corals in abundance. But to find a site that is truly special, you have to visit a small isolated reef, Jessie Beazley Reef, which lies to the west of the northern atoll. This column of coral rises from the bottom to just touch the surface of the sea, showing from above as a greenish, circular fringe no more than some tens of yards across. Two dives are all it requires to circle the reef. Arriving by boat, you soon realize that the water is crystal clear, though washed by strong currents. From the top of the reef, the corals slowly drop away to about 35 feet (10 meters), where a dense ecosystem exists. You will find beautiful acropora, tabular corals, green "lettuce corals," and a huge number of soft corals. The sea is literally teeming with reef fish, including squirrelfish, garibaldis, unicorn fish, emperor fish, and tropical umbrines.

Looking out to sea, you will no doubt catch sight of banks of tropical dentex and jacks, but that is for later. First, swim along a wall that in a single swoop reaches a rocky bottom around 130 feet (40 meters) down.

The wall is absolutely vertical and sheer for long sections. It is here that you will see why this reef has been chosen as the loveliest of the Tubbataha coral system, as you find yourself over a spectacular bed of soft corals and gorgonians that make gloriously colorful photographs.

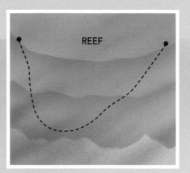

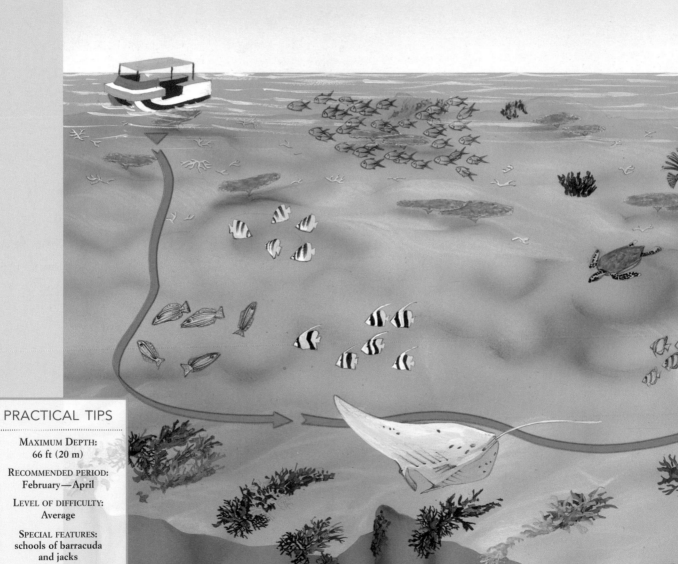

PRACTICAL TIPS

Maximum Depth:
66 ft (20 m)

Recommended period:
February—April

Level of difficulty:
Average

Special features:
schools of barracuda
and jacks

Visibility:
up to 133 ft (40 m)

Strength of current:
Often Strong

Text and photographs by Vincenzo Paolillo – Illustrations by Domitilla Müller

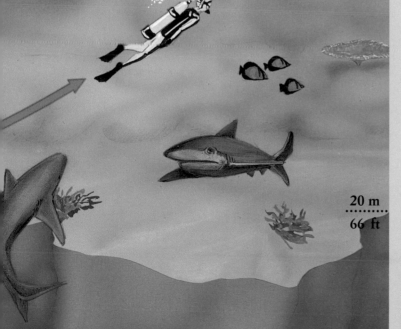

5 m
17 ft

20 m
66 ft

MALAYSIA—SIPADAN
SOUTH POINT

The reef that surrounds the small island of Sipadan is rather curiously shaped like a large angelfish. South Point represents the face of the fish, and it is here that we find the loveliest dive in the area.

The current reigns supreme at all hours of the night and day, sometimes running one way, sometimes the other, and in its midst swim two

221 top Enormous numbers of turtles live, nest, and reproduce at Sipadan; in particular the green turtle (Chelonia mydas) and the hawksbill turtle (Eretmochelys imbricata).

221 bottom Pulau Sipadan Rock lies off the east coast of Malaysian Borneo in the Celebes Sea.

221

222 top *Various groups of Tiera batfish* (Platax teira) *change color to match their background on the ledge.*

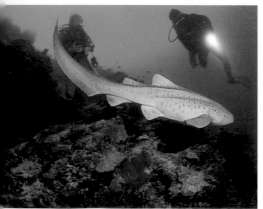

amazingly large shoals of fish—one of barracuda, the other of bigeye trevally. They have no fixed itinerary, so it is necessary to watch the surface of the sea from a boat until you see a large dark cloud, then jump in quickly. It may be either of the two shoals, but there is no need to worry; the two travel close together, sometimes blending into one another before separating again. If you find one, you will certainly see the other.

Great barracuda *(Sphyraena barracuda)* and bigeye trevally *(Caranx sexfasciatus)* are enormous fish, certainly far over the average, and in this case travel in huge numbers, in their thousands. The schools are very dense. Sometimes they turn in on themselves to form huge spinning balls; sometimes they lengthen, wrap around the diver, and

spin above him like a vault. It is a wonderful experience to enter their shoal and cut through it.

The water is rarely deep, and the fish swim at a depth of between 15 and 70 feet (5 and 20 meters). If they move out to sea, they soon return; the problem is simply the current, which is often very strong, and both shoals always have to swim against it.

222 bottom *Disturbed, a leopard shark* (Stegostoma fasciatus) *heads off into the deep.*

222-223 *An immense bank of bigeye trevally* (Caranx sexfasciatus) *halts off the edge of South Point.*

The current is also a challenge to the diver, which raises another issue: at one time the bed was covered with marvelous elkshorn coral, but today it is almost a cemetery. The local guides say that this is because of sea storms, but I have my doubts. Having seen how divers hang on to coral to resist the power of the current and take a moment to get their breath back, I urge any of you fortunate enough to find yourselves in this place to take special care.

If you are unable to follow the barracuda or the jacks, do not hold onto the bottom, just

223 top There are huge numbers of pufferfish in the waters off South Point; this is a starry toadfish (Arothron stellatus).

223 bottom A large school of great barracuda (Sphyraena barracuda) *forms extraordinary shapes.*

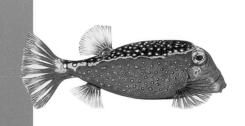

224-225 At around 70 feet (20 meters) depth you come across gorgonians, sometimes of huge size.

225 top left One of the most curiously shaped fish, the warty frogfish (Antennarius maculatus).

hang in midwater and leave what remains of the coral undisturbed, and the two shoals will return before long.

But South Point is not just barracuda and trevally: on the deeper terraces, you may find a zebra shark basking among the gorgonians and branches of red coral with her white-finned young, or out to sea you may catch a glimpse of mantas or spotted eagle rays.

Rising up the terraces toward the island, you will undoubtedly see green or hawksbill turtles searching for food or places to rest. And at a depth of 10 to 13 feet (3 to 4 meters) you will find yourself among a shoal of Tiera batfish *(Platax teira)*. They rummage around on the seabed, changing color to match their surroundings: grayish blue when on the sand, brown among the rocks.

Closer to the surface, have the patience to search out a leaf scorpionfish *(Taenianotus triacanthus)* among the enormous sponges, or a ribbon eel *(Rhinomuraena quaesita)* peeping out of its hole. Then there are also lovely nudibranchs, scorpionfish, unusual crabs, pufferfish, angelfish, and many, many others.

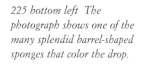

225 bottom left The photograph shows one of the many splendid barrel-shaped sponges that color the drop.

225 top right Large sea fans characterize the dive down to about 130 feet (40 meters).

225 bottom right This is a fine example of a leaf scorpionfish (Taenianotus triacanthus), camouflaging itself against its background.

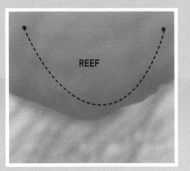

Text and photographs by Vincenzo Paolillo

PRACTICAL TIPS

MAXIMUM DEPTH:
133 ft (40 m)

RECOMMENDED PERIOD:
March—June

LEVEL OF DIFFICULTY:
Expert

SPECIAL FEATURES:
gorgonias and sea serpents

VISIBILITY:
over 133 ft (40 m)

STRENGTH OF CURRENT:
Strong

Illustrations by Domitilla Müller

5 m
17 ft

20 m
66 ft

40 m
133 ft

MALAYSIA—LAYANG LAYANG
GORGONIAN FOREST

Seen from outside, Layang Layang doesn't look inviting. It is no more than a hotel and a large airstrip on a field almost devoid of vegetation, where seabirds, mostly gannets, make their nests. But below the surface, the magnificent environment and uncontaminated coral formations are like few other places on earth, and the concentration of deep-sea and sedentary life rapidly makes you forget how little of interest lies outside the hotel windows.

Gorgonian Forest is probably the best dive at Layang Layang, particularly during the spring months—more than in most places, here the differences between seasons are truly striking. At that time of the year, an encounter with dense

ranks of barracuda or gray reef or hammerhead sharks is almost certain, even if not at a range suitable for photography. In the summer, however, the increase in water temperature drives away not only large predators but also all the shoals of other fish, nevertheless leaving one of the most densely inhabited underwater environments in the world.

We are on the east side of Layang Layang

*227 left As a rule, a school of bigeye trevally (*Caranx sexfasciatus*) can be found close to the wall.*

227 right Rows of gorgonians are typical of the deepest part of this dive.

228 bottom left You may come across a handsome leopard shark (Stegostoma fasciatum) on a step at about 100 feet (30 meters) deep.

228 top left This photograph clearly explains the origin of the name given to this reef at Layang Layang; the gorgonians that live in these waters are innumerable.

228 center left Gorgonian Forest is also the site of a number of grottoes; the one in the picture is home to more gorgonians.

reef. The current is constant, the visibility exceptional. At first the slope descends in small steps on which towers of madrepore grow, but then it drops away sharply toward canyons, balconies, and small fractures.

Here is a forest of incredibly colored and varied gorgonians: fields of enormous Anthotelidae, Acanthogorgidae, and Melithaeidae follow one another without interruption, often mixed with clumps of soft corals and festoons of crinoids, sometimes inhabited, if you have the patience to wait, by groups of feasting shrimps.

Yet this is a site where you pay less attention to the fish than to the extraordinary forms and colors of the underwater forest.

There are fish, of course: schools of bigeye trevally (Caranx sexfasciatus) and larger members of their family move among the sea fans, while a shoal of green humphead parrotfish (Bolbometopon muricatum) could well pop up from the bottom for a moment before disappearing at the same speed, to the photographer's despair. On the balconies at depths lower than 130 feet (40 meters), it is not impossible to catch sight of a sleeping nurse shark or a zebra shark, enormous yellowbanded or painted sweetlips (Plectorhincus lineatus or P. pictum) slowly shifting away.

As we ascend to a depth of 70 feet (20 meters), the gorgonians make space for enormous sponges (Xestospongia testudinaria) and tube-shaped sponges in which it is not uncommon to find sizable groupers.

Closer to the surface, there are beautiful anemones with their customary partners, anemonefish, crabs (Neopetrolisthes ohshimei), and an incredible number of mollusks of all sizes, pufferfish, scorpionfish, and all the varieties of coral fish.

It is not unusual to sight sea serpents (Lauticauda colubrina) wriggling quietly but unceasingly between the rocks, on the sand, and from one hole to another, probably on the lookout for small prey.

228 top right The photograph shows the structure of one of the many large barrel shaped sponges in Gorgonian Forest.

228 bottom right Small, long-bodied bigeye barracuda (Sphyraena forsteri) rise almost to the surface to play among the breakers.

229 Sea fans are used as a stepladder by sea lilies so that they can better reach the plankton-filled waters that the current washes past.

Text and photographs by Vincenzo Paolillo

N

Tulamben

Bali

REEF

PRACTICAL TIPS

MAXIMUM DEPTH:
66 ft (20 m)

RECOMMENDED PERIOD:
May—September

LEVEL OF DIFFICULTY:
Average

SPECIAL FEATURES:
gorgonias, black coral
and barrel shaped sponges

VISIBILITY:
up to 133 ft (40 m)

STRENGTH OF CURRENT:
Variable

INDONESIA—BALI
TULAMBEN

Tulamben, on the northeast coast of the island of Bali, is a beautiful bay surrounded by luxuriant vegetation with the highest mountain on the island, Gunung Agung, behind it. A hotel right on the beach also operates as a diving center.

You can start right from the hotel with the tanks on your shoulder or have them carried down to the water's edge by one of the porters. Then you must choose whether to go left toward a lovely wreck or toward the open sea, following

20 m
66 ft

the shoals, and then turn to the right toward the head of the bay. The latter is the best dive, as it covers a range of experiences: a huge number of small life forms make it a real paradise for macro-photography, and the scenery is of great interest.

After crossing the few yards of beach in front

231 top Note the pebble beach and dugout canoes pulled up out of the water in front of the headland where the Tulamben dropoff is located.

231 bottom A massive red gorgonian lives on the inner part of the wall.

231

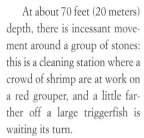

232 Here you will find enormous barrel shaped sponges (Xestospongia testudinaria) and gorgonians growing alongside one another.

233 top left Large numbers of leaf scorpionfish (Taenianotus triacanthus) hide among the coral.

233 center left A splendid example of a harlequin ghost pipefish (Solenostomus paradoxus) appears to pose for the photographer.

233 bottom left Yellowbanded sweetlips (Plectorhynchus lineatus) mill in groups and singly near the surface just off the promontory.

233 top right Another of the splendid sea fans that grow on the wall at the end of the east gulf.

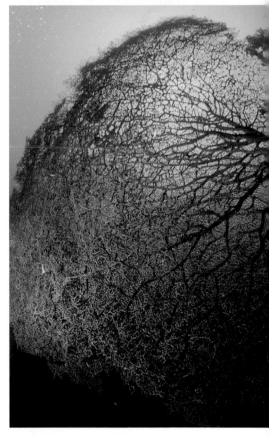

of the hotel (the pebbles hurt your feet if you are carrying the tanks, weights, and photographic equipment), you enter the water among large rocks that lie on a black lava sand bottom. It's worth stopping for a moment, as it would be a pity to miss the highly colored nudibranchs at large on the sand.

The plateau descends more quickly in a series of undulations perpendicular to the slope. In the hollows you are likely to find nudibranchs, sole, gobies living symbiotically with shrimps cleaning out the lair, lizardfish, and perhaps even black seahorses or tiny young yellow boxfish with black spots.

On the ridges you will see small gorgonians, leatherback corals, and crinoids on and around which exists an incredible variety of creatures; each crinoid is occupied by periclimenes shrimp, but there may be also shellfish or a splendid harlequin ghost pipefish *(Solenostomus paradoxus)*. A lovely leaf scorpionfish *(Taenianotus triacanthus)* rests on a piece of coral, while a superb porcelain crab *(Neopetrolistes maculatus)* can be seen on an anemone. You will also notice a crowd of fire gobies *(Nemateleotris magnifica),* and all the usual inhabitants of the sand.

At about 70 feet (20 meters) depth, there is incessant movement around a group of stones: this is a cleaning station where a crowd of shrimp are at work on a red grouper, and a little farther off a large triggerfish is waiting its turn.

You have to wrench yourself away from these marvelous sights and head right (south) at the same depth. In just a few moments you arrive at a wall covered with gorgonians; an enormous reddish violet specimen will undoubtedly attract your attention. But there are many other things: other gorgonians, large branches of black coral, and huge barrel sponges. It is as well to look among the outer cracks in the rock, as you may find a pink hairy crab *(Laurica* sp.).

Toward the point, the wall drops less steeply in large steps where many different fish are milling around: mullet, tropical umbrines, more groupers and triggerfish, morays in their lairs, and everywhere mollusks, crayfish, crabs, nudibranchs, and the occasional frogfish.

If you look out to sea, you may catch a glimpse of some sharks or opahs.

233 bottom right Holyfish of various colors find refuge between the branches of this splendid, flowered gorgonian.

Text and photographs by Vincenzo Paolillo – Illustrations by Domitilla Müller

INDONESIA—MANADO
LIKUAN 2

Manado is one of the underwater paradises of Indonesia. Fundamentally, it offers two dive areas: the Lembeh Channel, where shallows offer the lover of macrophotography everything he could dream of, and the island of Bunaken, where enthusiasts of the environment and large fish will not be disappointed. There are numerous dives around the island, but the most beautiful are those along the

234 top One of the village beaches on the island of Bunaken.

234 bottom Splendid sea fans can be seen on this dive.

6 m
20 ft

9 m
30 ft

40 m
133 ft

234

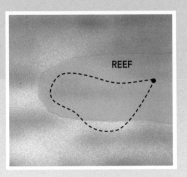

N

Likuan

Manado

SULAWESI

REEF

PRACTICAL TIPS

MAXIMUM DEPTH:
133 ft (40 m)

RECOMMENDED PERIOD:
April—October

LEVEL OF DIFFICULTY:
Expert

SPECIAL FEATURES:
anemones and six species
of clownfish

VISIBILITY:
up to 133 ft (40 m)

STRENGTH OF CURRENT:
Average

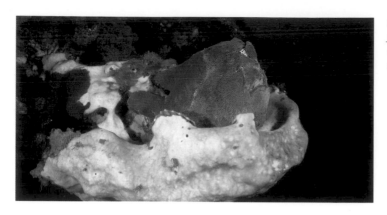

236 top *A giant Commerson's frogfish* (Antennarius commersonii) *rests in the hollow of a sponge.*

236 bottom *A green turtle* (Chelonia mydas) *is surprised at it rests on a rock among black coral.*

236-237 *This extraordinary photograph shows one of the many huge sponges, surrounded by hundreds of fish.*

vertical Likuan wall that stretches 1 mile (1.5 kilometers) along the south slope with frequent changes of direction. Three dives—Likuan 1, Likuan 2, Likuan 3—have similar characteristics, except that Likuan 1 is nearly always washed by a current, being the outermost of the three. For that reason, we will choose Likuan 2, where the gorgonians are perhaps less beautiful and there are fewer migratory fish, but there is more likelihood of meeting curious inhabitants of the reef.

Descend to the coral platform among the rock masses and the corals. Here it is common to find nudibranchs, mollusks (including the splen-

did cowrie with its black covering), and lots of blue-and-yellow ribbon morays *(Rhinomuraena quaesita)* that, when young, are completely black, a true test of the photographer's skill.

Soon you will come across the characteristic species of this area, a variety of differently colored anemones—yellow and white—six species of anemonefish, and many stonefish of unusual colors and forms. Then there are many species of chetodonts, scarids, labrids, and pomacentrids.

We begin our descent of the wall, passing over shelves, clearings, vertical faces, and strips of sand. You will see gorgonians and, above all, giant sponges in all shapes: organ pipes, barrels, and cups.

Angelfish, Moorish idols *(Zanclus cornutus)*, enormous porcupinefish, curiously colored trumpetfish, and frogfish of different colors hide among the cracks or can be glimpsed in the hollow of a sponge. Nor is it rare to see turtles—perhaps at rest on the black coral—groupers, and barracuda.

The large shoals, however, stay farther out, like sharks, save the occasional loner asleep in a long, shallow, horizontal crack. The drop descends to 130 feet (40 meters) before the seabed gently slopes away toward the open sea.

It is time to rise, carried by the current, but the panorama is the same elsewhere; if you have sharp eyes, though, you may notice some truly unusual sights: gobies on the branches of the sea whips, bizarrely shaped crabs, and, on the gorgonians, the unusually shaped pygmy seahorse, the same shade as his support.

Wangi Wangi

Kaledupa

Mari Mabuk ✦ Tomia

N

Binongko

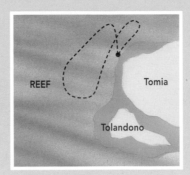

REEF

Tomia

Tolandono

Text and photographs by Egidio Trainito

PRACTICAL TIPS

Maximum Depth:
86 ft (26 m)

Recommended period:
All year

Level of difficulty:
Average

Special features:
large variety of organisms

Visibility:
over 165 ft (50 m)

Strength of current:
Weak

Illustrations by Domitilla Müller

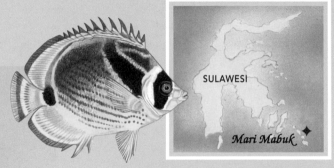

SULAWESI

Mari Mabuk

INDONESIA—WAKATOBI
MARI MABUK

Southeast of Sulawesi—one of the innumerable islands of Indonesia—a string of small islands only accessible by boat reaches toward the south. The region is called Tukang Besi, but the local name is Wakatobi, from the combination of the first syllables of the four main islands: Wangi Wangi, Kaledupa, Tomia, and Binongko. To the west of the last two, a vast barrier reef over 93 miles (150 kilometers) stretches almost intact, only visited by a few fishermen who fortunately don't use explosives in their fishing, as

10 m
33 ft

18 m
60 ft

26 m
86 ft

239 left The beach of Tolandono takes on special colors when the last monsoons brush the islands of the Wakatobi Archipelago.

239 right Corals, sponges, sea lilies, and swarms of small fishes populate one of the many complicated architectures of the Indonesian depths. The sea lilies search for elevated positions to better capture floating material with their plumed arms.

many fishermen do in the western Pacific. All the zones of the reef offer excellent diving and have two things in common: the clarity of the water, sometimes allowing visibility in excess of 160 feet (50 meters), and the extraordinary diversity of species, which makes each stretch of

240 top left *On the sloping bottom of the Indonesian seabed, creatures of all kinds crowd together: among the coral and sponges are tunicates (shown in the middle of this photograph).*

240 top right The complex design of this bluegirdled angelfish (Pomacanthus navarchus) is different from the juvenile pattern, as in all species of the larger angelfish.

240 bottom left A giant barrel sponge (Xestospongia testudinaria) dominates the passage of the reef. The sponge's rough body greatly increases its surface area, allowing it to filter more of the water from which it harvests the organic materials it feeds on.

the reef a seething mass of life forms, all deserving of attention.

A dive site in front of Tomia Island encapsulates all the characteristics of the area: called Mari Mabuk, it is a long coral spine with a slope on either side that offers as many different dives as you could wish for. It is usual to moor at a fixed buoy and drop about 70 feet (20 meters) along the west side of the shoal, which has the shallower areas (about 35 feet [10 meters]). Descending from the buoy, you reach a barrel sponge (*Xestospongia testudinaria*) so large that you can enter it completely. Heading south, you come across a jumbled sequence of soft corals and gorgonians, creating microenvironments teeming with sponges, sea squirts, and an infinity of other invertebrates. Swarms of brightly colored fish swim in every direction, but you will rarely see anything large; small is beautiful here, though a slowly passing turtle is an exception to prove the rule. Approach it carefully, and it will not take fright.

If you continue in this direction, you will reach one of the loveliest points on the coral spine, a large area covered by hard coral in the shapes of fans or cups, which look like enormous roses with their petals open. Intact, with no sign of fractures, they are surrounded by the usual swirls of small fish and the occasional moontail

bullseye. Return toward the buoy along the other side of the spine over expanses of coral, vivid sponges, and sea squirts of various species and colors, until you reach a zone colonized by large sea fans. Various species pile on top of one another, covered in turn by vivid crinoids and branched or stick sponges, while scorpionfish meander between the branches and starfish with puffy arms (*Choriaster granulatus*) seem to look for shelter. You could also search for a rarity, like a pair of glassfish with their amazing camouflaging ability. This is a dive you wish would never finish, and fortunately you will have some time left for the final shallows, where you might like

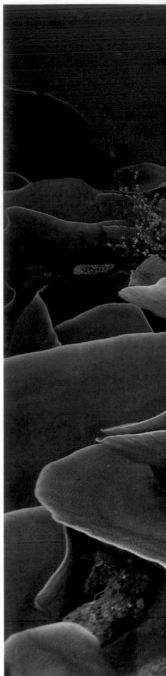

240 bottom right A rank of yellow and blueback fusiliers (Caesio teres) slides above the intricate ensemble of barrier organisms, formed of carnation corals, gorgonians, and hard coral. This species of fusilier, distributed throughout the Indo-Pacific as far as Australia, was described for the first time in 1906.

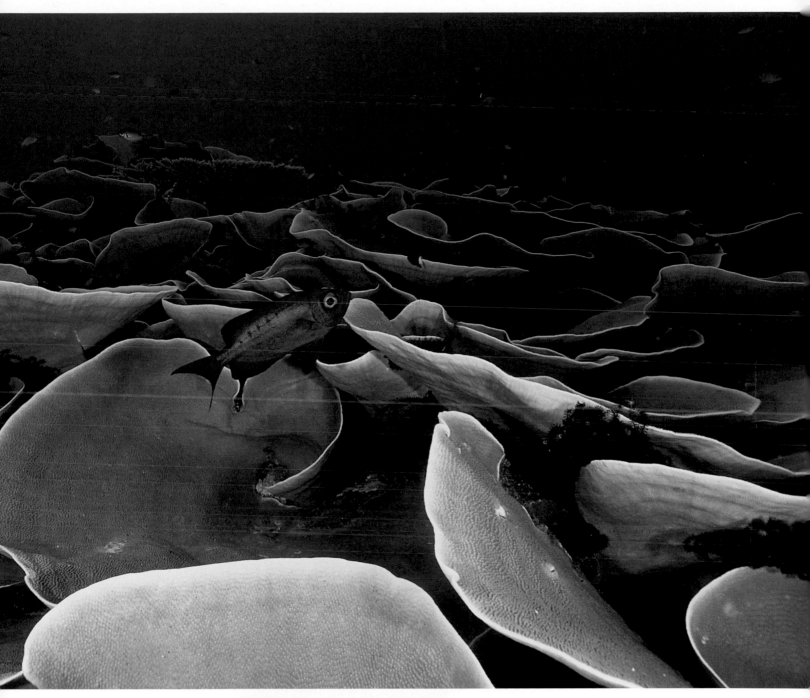

240-241 *A moontail bullseye* (Priacanthus hamrur) *swims above the Rose of Mari Mabuk: a colony of hard corals (perhaps genus* Turbinaria) *shaped like the petals of a rose.*

241 bottom *In the clear water, a diver swimming above the Rose of Mari Mabuk allows you to appreciate the size of this enormous coral construction. In fact, the sheets of coral cover a large section of the seabed.*

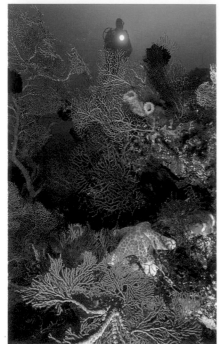

to follow a particular theme: for instance, you can look for nudibranchs, and if you find many species, you can go for endemic species of fish. Then there are other wonders that live on the dead coral, like the ribbon moray eels *(Rhinomuraena quaesita)* that often poke their heads out of their holes in pairs, likewise pairs of fire gobies *(Nemateleotris magnifica)* and blueband gobies *(Valenciennea strigata)*. The dead coral is also often the place where you might find a sea serpent *(Laticauda colubrina)* in search of prey. An hour underwater at Mari Mabuk passes quickly, and always leaves you with a desire to return.

242 top left In the close-up picture the leaf scorpionfish (Taenianotus triacanthus) *is perfectly visible, but in* *ambient light its camouflage at times makes it almost impossible to identify in the complexity of the reef.*

242 center left This starfish (Choriaster granulatus) *is posed on the coral reef among a great variety of gorgonians and other small organisms.*

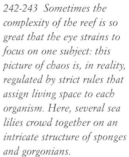

242-243 *Sometimes the complexity of the reef is so great that the eye strains to focus on one subject: this picture of chaos is, in reality, regulated by strict rules that assign living space to each organism. Here, several sea lilies crowd together on an intricate structure of sponges and gorgonians.*

243 top *The large dimensions of this anemone* (Heteractis magnifica) *make the clown anemonefish* (Amphiprion ocellaris) *seem even smaller, lost in its intricate tentacles.*

243 bottom *A red sponge seems to have generated a beautiful gorgonian just as red, on which little white polyps provide contrast: around them are vivid branching sponges, sweetlips, and hard corals.*

242 bottom left *Two large coral umbrellas dominate a slope of the reef. Their size is largely due to the great* *luminosity and limpidness of the water: often the visibility is greater than 200 feet (60 meters).*

Garove Island

Capo Hollman

N

South Ema

Kimbe

NEW BRITAIN

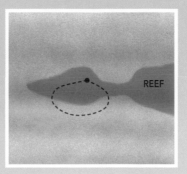

REEF

Text and photographs by Vincenzo Paolillo

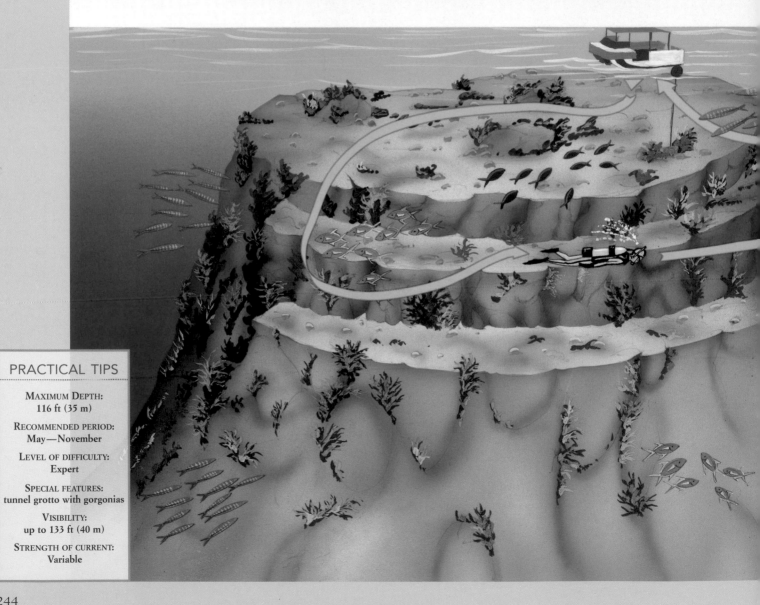

PRACTICAL TIPS

MAXIMUM DEPTH:
116 ft (35 m)

RECOMMENDED PERIOD:
May—November

LEVEL OF DIFFICULTY:
Expert

SPECIAL FEATURES:
tunnel grotto with gorgonias

VISIBILITY:
up to 133 ft (40 m)

STRENGTH OF CURRENT:
Variable

Illustrations by Domitilla Müller

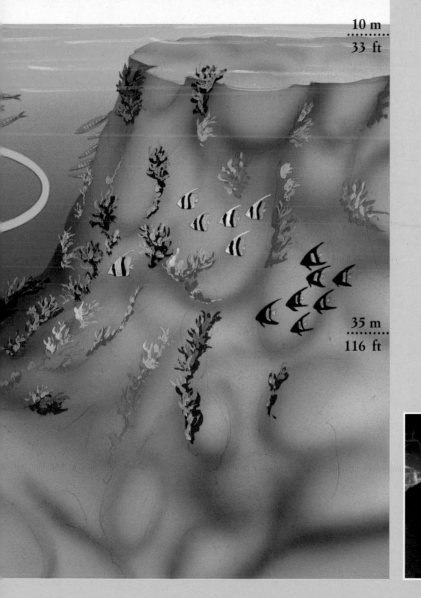

10 m
....
33 ft

35 m
....
116 ft

SOUTH EMA

There are many interesting dives in the Gulf of Kimbe, where Walindi is located, but the most beautiful, if only because the most complete, is South Ema. There is a large reef that rises from a depth of over 330 feet (100 meters) to within 10 feet (3 meters) of the surface. An unusual outcropping in the shape of a rounded, upside-down vase extends from

245 top Fields of large, highly colored gorgonians characterize this dive.

245 bottom A small cardinalfish spends the night hidden among the polyps of the soft coral.

245

246 *A magnificent forest of coral captures plankton, the organism's favorite food, transported by the current.*

247 *top left* *The elephant-eared sponge, typical of the waters off Papua New Guinea, is a favorite with photographers. Here, we see an enormous one which seems to be sculpted by the current.*

247 *top right* *Gorgonians and sea lilies often live in perfect symbiosis.*

the reef; its narrow neck is attached to the seabed about 100–115 feet (30–35 meters) down, while its rounded belly reaches up to about 35–40 feet (10–12 meters) from the surface. A buoy is attached to the south side of the body of the vase, and you make your way down its chain before deciding which way you wish to go. The choice is to head off toward the point following the steps that descend into the depths, or to remain on the plateau. If you choose the first, you will find magnificent gorgonians and elephant-ear sponges, and you can hope to find gray reef sharks *(Carcharhinus amblyrhynchoides)*, silvertips *(Carcharhinus albimarginatus)*, or schools of barracuda; if you choose the second, among enormous barrel sponges and red sponges you will find fields of anemones, usually accompanied by spinecheek anemonefish *(Premnas biaculeatus)* colored impossibly red and with three equally spaced bands. You may see lovely mantis shrimps *(Odontodactylus scyllarus)*, or gobies that live on the sand in symbiosis with cleaner shrimps, or enormous starfish paired with shrimps that echo their color *(Periclemenes* sp.).

There are other choices, though. If you descend toward the neck of the vase, at about 125 feet (38 meters) depth you will encounter a lovely grotto adorned with festoons of sea fans and, at the exit, an explosion of red sea whips. The neck of the vase is covered with sea fans, adorned with crinoids and sponges of all shapes and hues. If now you follow the neck of the vase, you arrive once more at the main shoal.

Here are yet more anemones in large numbers, populated by various anemonefish: the yellow clownfish *(Amphiprion sandaracinos)* has a white stripe from its face to the tail along the upper part of its body, and the lovely clown anemonefish *(Amphiprion ocellaris)*, a more vivid orange, displays three wide white bands, edged in black like its fins.

Everywhere you will find species living in symbiosis. It is not rare to find longnose hawkfish or large Chinese trumpetfish among the gorgonians, shrimps among the crinoids, and small fish hidden among the soft corals.

The variety of this dive makes it worth repeating, especially for the photographer who uses a range of lenses.

247 *bottom right* *The soft corals at South Ema are especially luxuriant.*

247

PALAU ARCHIPELAGO

Blue Corner

N

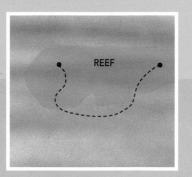

REEF

Text and photographs by Roberto Rinaldi

PRACTICAL TIPS

MAXIMUM DEPTH:
99 ft (30 m)

RECOMMENDED PERIOD:
October—April

LEVEL OF DIFFICULTY:
Expert

UNUSUAL FEATURES:
large tunnel grotto

VISIBILITY:
up to 133 ft (40 m)

STRENGTH OF CURRENT:
Very Strong

Illustrations by Domitilla Müller

PHILIPPINES

Palau Archipelago

Blue Corner

INDONESIA

PAPUA
NEW
GUINEA

MICRONESIA—PALAU
BLUE CORNER

10 m
33 ft

17 m
56 ft

30 m
99 ft

The islands of Micronesia extend for hundreds of miles across the Pacific Ocean along a strip between 10 degrees latitude north and the equator. The first islands on a route from the Philippines heading east are those of the Palau Archipelago. This corner of the world is particularly spectacular, with a multitude of tiny islands lying inside an elliptical belt of coral that lies north-south. Some of these are simple coral islands, fringed by white sandy beaches and covered in thick jungle. Others, limestone islands covered with thick, impenetrable jungle, have been violently eroded; the plentiful rainwater, made acid by the decomposition of this rich organic matter, has carved an infinity of open channels through the

limestone cliffs, forming grottoes, narrow but remote bays, and round saltwater lakes more or less in contact with the open sea.

For divers, the most interesting areas lie outside the reef in the extreme southwest. Leaving the lagoon through an artificial canal through the coral called the German Channel,

249 left The archipelago of the Seventy Islands is formed from the unmistakable limestone islands that emerge from the great Palau Lagoon. Beyond the external barrier, the submerged Blue Corner promontory extends toward the open sea.

249 right At first we saw only two or three holes in the barrier, but when we penetrated into the grotto, we found ourselves in this cavity in the face of the reef wall at a depth of about 100 feet (30 meters).

250 top The outer buoy of the southern slope is the place where we most often met thick schools of tropical seabream, much larger than the jacks they live with.

250 center In the plain on the summit, one can have close encounters with sea turtles.

250-251 Several divers descend into Blue Holes, lost in the interior of what seems to be an enormous cathedral. The sunlight filters through from above and is reflected from the white sandy bottom, illuminating the scene with a pale and fantastic light.

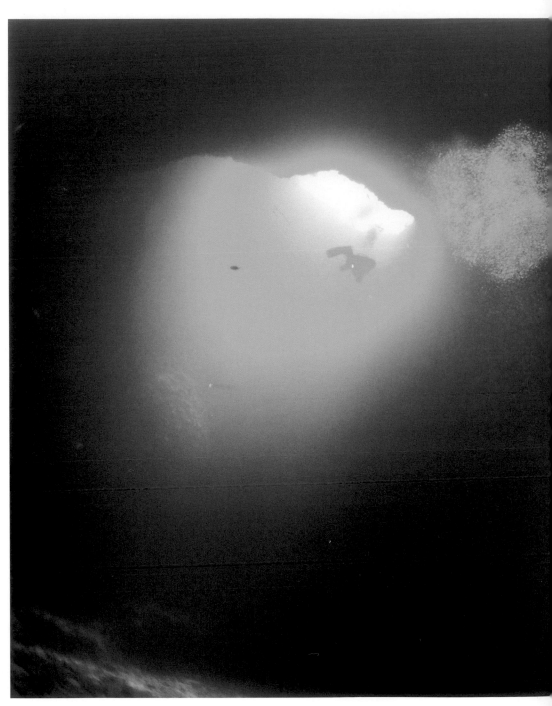

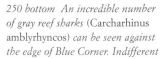

250 bottom An incredible number of gray reef sharks (Carcharhinus amblyrhyncos) can be seen against the edge of Blue Corner. Indifferent to the violent current that we struggle against, they swim with an elegance that, more than aggression, seems to define them.

with the reef on your right, you head for a section where the seabed is especially beautiful. This may be due to the particular morphology of the reef, which at this point juts out toward the open sea, away from the general mass of the reef. This wedge of coral interrupts and intercepts the flow of the currents, along with the plankton they carry.

The origin of the name Blue Corner is made clear when you look at the site. Four buoys are fixed along the edge of the two sides of the "corner." You are advised always to enter the water at either of the two outer buoys, depending on the current, which can have immense power. Let's imagine we start on the south side. Moor on the buoy fixed to a flattish bed about 35 feet (10 meters) from the edge of the dropoff. Enter the water and descend along the wall. You will immediately be surrounded by a cloud of fish, often this area is inhabited by a dense shoal of small bigeye trevally and an equally dense school of dentex. Near the mooring buoy you will see a lovely small grotto, which forms the summit of a wide vertical gully in the wall. This is worth spending a few moments in, especially if you like photography, as here there is an abundance of large gorgonians of every hue.

Make sure you do not go deeper than 80 to 100 feet (25 to 30 meters); there is nothing here that you cannot see higher up, and you will lose valuable time. You also have to

251 bottom Here colors no longer exist, with the exception of a thousand gradations of blue that dissolve to black in the rocky walls or to white on the sandy bottom.

251 top The thick schools of bigeye trevally (Caranx sexfasciatus) are perhaps the loveliest spectacle of the waters of Blue Corner. Usually they are rather small individually, but very dense and fast, and they are particularly spectacular when they swim, throwing silver flashes, among the gorgonians.

251

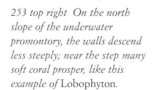

252 Among the shadows in the depths of Blue Corner, a small chromis seeks refuge for the night in a thatch of whip coral.

253 top left Characteristic of almost all the dives along the external reefs of Palau are the red whip corals of the Ellisellidae *family.*

*253 bottom left A doughboy star (*Choriaster granulosis*), easily recognised by its rounded, stumpy arms, settles on the multicoloured reef at Blue Corner.*

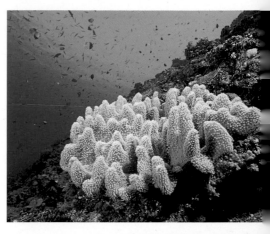

253 top right On the north slope of the underwater promontory, the walls descend less steeply; near the step many soft coral prosper, like this example of Lobophyton.

bear in mind that on most days the current will not allow you to return to the mooring buoy, and that the dropoff is always between 35 and 60 feet (10 and 17 meters). It is therefore impossible to make stops for decompression if you do not wish to be carried away by the current.

Once past the gully, continue along the wall quickly until you come to a patch of isolated gorgonians and vivid soft corals, which are certainly lovely but nothing to what is to be seen farther ahead. Throughout this dive you will be literally surrounded by an incredible abundance of fish. Really extraordinary!

As you swim on, keep an eye on the ledge above your head, and at a certain point you will notice that its straight line is broken by a sharp indent where a second gully opens in the wall. You have arrived at the most beautiful spot of the dive. Note the gigantic gorgonians and beautiful colonies of soft corals and sponges. Above your head, dozens of sharks crisscross, and off toward the deep there is nearly always a shoal of large barracuda. Stop here for a few moments, and then rise toward the other side of the gully. Now you are right on the outermost tip of the Blue Corner. The dropoff lies at a depth of 56 feet (17 meters) exactly. The current is usually very strong, so it is best at this point to take out the reef hook from your jacket. Fix the hook to a projection of the reef (but not on a living coral, of course!) and let the current carry you. Suspended in midwater, you will be able to enjoy the fantastic experience of sharks coming up close, barracuda immobile in the water, and carangids suffering from the attacks of dogfish. It is a wonderful feeling!

After a few minutes, swim toward the shelf. In the past I was always convinced that this was a waste of time, but now I realize that you will almost surely come across a large eagle ray, various turtles, and a gigantic but distrustful Napoleon wrasse.

The opposite side of Blue Corner is less steep but still filled with life. Continue along the wall until the wedge joins the main body of the reef, and you will find another great dive spot: Blue Holes. These are four large holes in the flat section of the reef that lead inside a wide grotto with a sandy bottom at a depth of 100–130 feet (30–40 meters). Enter the grotto through the holes and then exit through the opening, which takes you to the outer coral wall. From here, if the current is favorable, you can reach Blue Corner again, and you will have combined two dives in one.

253 bottom right The diver gives scale to the notable dimensions of this great fan of Melitea squamata, *which extends toward the open sea in the crystalline waters of Blue Corner.*

Text and photographs by Kurt Amsler – Illustrations by Domitilla Müller

AUSTRALIA—LIZARD ISLAND
COD HOLE

Almost parallel to Australia's Pacific Coast, from Bundaberg in the south to Cape York in the north, runs the Great Barrier Reef of Australia. Fourteen hundred miles (2,300 kilometers) long, with a greater surface area than England, this reef chain is the longest in our planet.

This eighth wonder of the world consists

254 top The Australian Great Barrier Reef extends for a length of over 1,400 miles (2,300 kilometers) and varies in width from 37 to 168 miles (60 to 270 kilometers): to the north, in the Cairns area, Lizard Island stands alone, surrounded by coral reefs.

254 bottom The granite rocks of Lizard Island are an exception in the over 2,500 reefs that form the Great Barrier Reef: covered in thick tropical vegetation, the island is surrounded by white coral beaches.

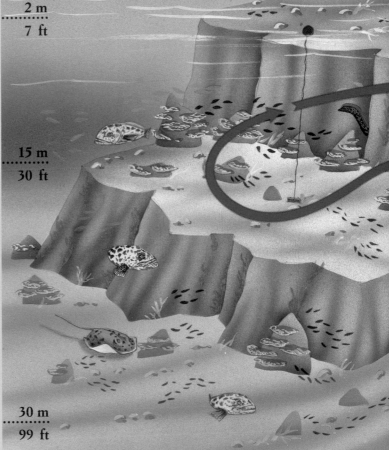

2 m
7 ft

15 m
30 ft

30 m
99 ft

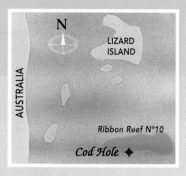

AUSTRALIA

N

LIZARD
ISLAND

Ribbon Reef N°10

Cod Hole ✦

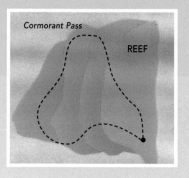

Cormorant Pass

REEF

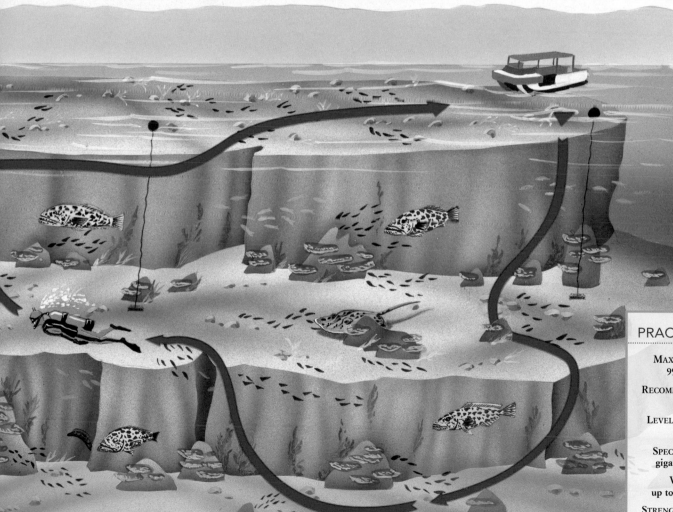

PRACTICAL TIPS

MAXIMUM DEPTH:
99 ft (30 m)

RECOMMENDED PERIOD:
All year

LEVEL OF DIFFICULTY:
Average

SPECIAL FEATURES:
gigantic groupers

VISIBILITY:
up to 133 ft (40 m)

STRENGTH OF CURRENT:
Often Strong

256 top left At times the groupers chase each other in territorial squabbles: the agility with which they move is impressive.

256 bottom left A great stingray (Taeniura melanospilos) slides just above a patch of bright white sand: the rays spend a lot of time hidden in the sand, as revealed by the thin layer that still covers this one.

256 bottom right The grouper carousel begins to swim to the middle water to meet the divers: in the clear water the keel of the boat seems to loom over the great fish.

256 top right Smaller potato cod weigh about 180 pounds (80 kilograms), while the larger ones are over 440 pounds (200 kilograms) and 7 feet (2 meters) in length.

256-257 The groupers of Cod Hole (Epinephelus tukula), often called potato cod or potato groupers, come to greet the divers as soon as they reach the bottom: they are accustomed to receive food from charter-trip dive masters.

of 2,000 individual reefs and 69 islands. Seen from the air, it is like a ribbon, shimmering emerald green to turquoise blue, on which islands look like green-and-white fried eggs and sandbanks like bleached boomerangs.

The Great Barrier Reef is home to a vast range of life forms, and thanks to the tropical temperatures hundreds of different coral species thrive. Unmatched in any other place are the innumerable, varied snails and mussels, together with worms, sponges, crabs, and echinoderms. Thanks to strict protective measures, the Barrier Reef is a refuge for many types of animals threatened with extinction. Humpback whales swim enormous distances from the Arctic to the Barrier Reef to bring their young into the world undisturbed in the warm water. Six out of seven of the sea turtles still living on our planet lay their eggs in the sand of the reef's numerous uninhabited islands and sandbanks. In the north, sea cows are still to be seen, the so-called dugongs, together with saltwater crocodiles, which live in the shallow lagoons and the mangrove coasts.

For naturalists the Great Barrier Reef is a never-ending fascination and challenge. Many research stations devote themselves to studying geology, currents, and plant and animal life under the water. A large research station is found on Lizard Island, which lies in the immediate vicinity of our diving spot and can be recognized by its

landmark, the 1,280-foot (390-meter)-high Cook's Look. From this mountain in 1790 Captain James Cook, shut in behind the reef after his discovery of the Australian continent, found a passage through to the open sea.

The famous Cod Hole lies on Ribbon Reef No. 10. Here live enormous groupers that, because of the black spots on their backs, are called potato cod or potato groupers (Epinephelus tukula). For generations these fish have lived around a plateau sloping to the east, which for a long time has been declared a protected area. Since the fish have never been hunted, they have reached amazing proportions. As an example, fish weighing 330 pounds (150 kilograms) and as long as a fully grown person are not a rarity. Potato groupers have absolutely no fear; in fact, they are very curious and will follow divers wherever they go. In the interest of the fish, however, the diver should avoid actually touching them; parasites can immediately take advantage of any damage to their skin's protective mucus layer, causing pain to the animal.

If you can spend several days diving at Cod Hole, do not fail to be in the water at the first rays of the morning sun. At the full moon is the best time to see groupers mating. Normally black and white, the fish become snow white, and at the first light they commence their lovemaking.

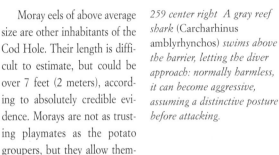

259 top right Laminar coral serves as a base for the branches of a fire coral, surrounded by a cloud of little silverfish. Fire coral is not a madrepore but belongs to the group of hydrozoans, despite having a calcareous skeleton.

258 Though the groupers claim attention with their comings and goings, there is no lack of glimpses of subtle beauty as well; a whip coral (Ellisella sp.) extends from a cleft in the reef.

259 left The diver's flashlight gives evidence to the delicate structure of the branches of one of the numerous gorgonians that proliferate in the waters of Cod Hole.

Moray eels of above average size are other inhabitants of the Cod Hole. Their length is difficult to estimate, but could be over 7 feet (2 meters), according to absolutely credible evidence. Morays are not as trusting playmates as the potato groupers, but they allow themselves to be observed at a near distance and photographed.

In the channels that flow inward from the external reef, the conditions of the currents are ideal to meet the large predators of the coral sea. Above all the gray reef sharks hunt here, but you may also often see blacktip reef sharks. On rare occasions you might happen upon tiger sharks, but they are not aggressive and ignore divers in their territory. On the stretches of sand inside the reef, carpet shark rest in the sand.

Cod Hole can be reached not only from the adjacent Lizard Island Resort but also from diving boats that cruise the North Coral Sea. Trips are also offered from the mainland. It is a day's journey to reach the area.

In connection with Cod Hole, other dives are offered in this area, among them drift diving in Dynamite Pass. The current, initially strong, becomes gradually weaker as you pass through a channel filled with swarms of small and large fish into the lagoon. In this spot the diver can also meet the classic inhabitants of the territory; most notably, where the current is strongest, confrontations with large sharks and other big fish are always possible.

259 center right A gray reef shark (Carcharhinus amblyrhynchos) *swims above the barrier, letting the diver approach: normally harmless, it can become aggressive, assuming a distinctive posture before attacking.*

259 bottom right A thick group of yellowbanded sweetlips (Plectorhynchus lineatus) *surrounds a coral pinnacle like a "ring-around-the-rosy": lazy during the day, the sweetlips feed at night, mostly on crustaceans.*

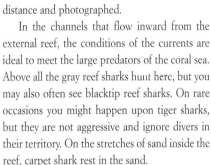

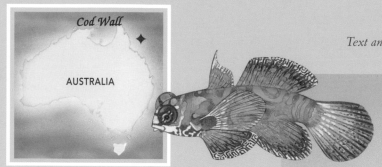

Text and photographs by Roberto Rinaldi

AUSTRALIA—FLINDERS REEF
COD WALL

5 m
17 ft

20 m
66 ft

45 m
149 ft

T he Australian Great Barrier Reef has always been a diver's dream. Yet sailing in these waters, we discovered that we had to leave this extraordinary living wall to make the best dives. The Barrier Reef, which delineates a wide lagoon between itself and the continent, drops into the depths of the Pacific Ocean. Soon after leaving the last flourishing coral and sailing a few miles east, you encounter seabeds over 1,330 feet (1,000 meters) deep. It is here, in the heart of the Coral Sea, that the madrepores, for a moment,

260 top After the first drop, the wall brings us to an inclined sandy plane where sponges and large gorgonians prosper, together with some isolated coral.

260 bottom Schools of jacks swim in the open water, moving with their noses turned against the currents that rage through these waters. The water is crystalline, making it very entertaining to photograph these fish.

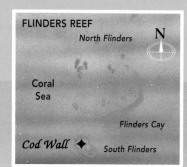

FLINDERS REEF

North Flinders

N

Coral
Sea

Flinders Cay

Cod Wall ◆ South Flinders

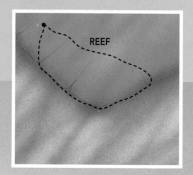

REEF

Illustrations by Domitilla Müller

PRACTICAL TIPS

MAXIMUM DEPTH:
149 ft (45 m)

RECOMMENDED PERIOD:
All year

LEVEL OF DIFFICULTY:
Expert

SPECIAL FEATURES:
enormous gorgonias

VISIBILITY:
over 133 ft (40 m)

STRENGTH OF CURRENT:
Very Strong

take over from the muddy, flat bottoms that characterize the oceanic abysses. A few dozen miles from the end of the Barrier Reef, imposing towers of coral rise vertically, almost breaking the surface. These mighty, audacious towers have nearly vertical walls that are more than 1,330 feet (1,000 meters) high. Columns more than 10 miles (16 kilometers) in diameter delimit a rather shallow, calm lagoon with seabeds that alternate between the whitest sand and spectacular castles of coral. The diving here is splendid, but even more spectacular is jumping into the abyss from the outside edge of the atoll. We are at Flinders Reef, and here

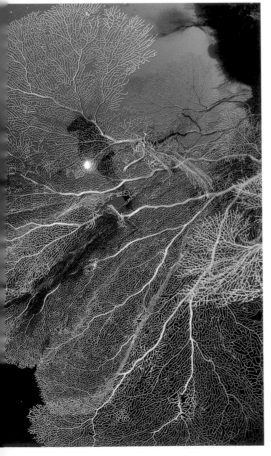

262 top Before the plain, the walls that descend over the step of the reef are clothed in thick forests of fan gorgonians, with their classic shape, and tufts of fiery red whip gorgonians, like those in the photograph.

262 bottom Gorgonians (Subergorgia sp.) of exceptional dimensions are one of the common characteristics of the walls of Flinders Reef. This one certainly measured more than 10 feet (3 meters).

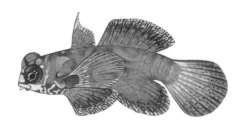

263 bottom left *Diving in the forest of gorgonians at Cod Wall really gives you the impression of being an elf lost in a forest of giant trees.*

263 top right *On the plain, even the sponges can reach truly remarkable sizes. They are delicate creatures, unable to withstand great pressure and therefore adapted to life in areas far from the energy of the waves.*

we decide upon a special dive, one among the many possibilities along the external wall of the coral tower. In reality, we will dive into the water of a southern layer of Flinders Reef, a small tower that has recently shifted south of the main reef, called South Flinders or South Boomerang. Our dive will enable us to explore an immense wall, rich in scarcely credible fauna and flora as well as fish. It would seem that here you can find a perfect sampling of all the creatures that populate these waters, even though the wall is not as impressively and absolutely sheer as in other sections of the external reef. The current is a constant concern during this dive, but the position of the mooring buoy makes it possible to avoid problems. As soon as we are in the water, we realize that the mooring cable is fixed to coral where the external barrier forms an angle, at a depth of about 35 feet (10 meters). The clarity of the water is simply baffling; from the surface, we can see the seabed some 130 feet (40 meters) below us. We dive quickly to avoid being pulled by the current before the wall offers us protection and calm waters. We immediately find ourselves in a forest of sea fans: enormous clumps of

262-263 The rich sandy plain, where a large orange soft coral (Dendronephya sp.) sticks up among the gorgonians and whip coral.

red whips alternate with gigantic golden-yellow fans. Everywhere around us, we see schools of barracuda and jacks, swimming in circles in the limpid water. With the desire to discover something extraordinary, we head for the angle at the base of the wall. On the sand at about 130 feet (40 meters) grows the largest sea fan anyone has ever seen. The crew of the *Spoilsport* measured its width as 16 feet (5 meters)! This gigantic sea fan is, however, not

263 bottom right *In the land of the "giants," it can often be surprising to take a careful look at the microscopic world, as in this case, where we discovered a small chromis hidden within the soft branches of a carnation coral.*

264-265 This giant gorgonian is the largest that I have ever seen in my life. According to the men in the boat that placed us at Cod Wall, it measures more than 16 feet (5 meters). This is without doubt a required destination for this dive.

265 top left The sea lilies are extremely abundant on the seabed of Flinders Reef. Here a yellow Oxycomanthus bennetti *is well attached to a coral.*

*265 bottom left Rising toward the top of the reef, we run into a school of trevally (*Caranx *sp.). At Cod Wall it is easier to meet these fish near the surface than at noteworthy depths.*

265 top right The observation of tiny life on the bottom at Cod Wall also provides great satisfaction. This coral was shot with a special lens that provided a field of one by one-half inch (2 centimeters by 1).

the only extraordinary creature to populate this steep terrace; we find other sea fans, gigantic sponges that look like elephant ears, more clumps of coral with bright red whips and white polyps. Beyond the terrace, the wall drops vertically into the abyss. We are in the ideal place to spot the large outlines of gray reef and hammerhead sharks, alone in the immense blue of the water.

After several minutes, we slowly begin to rise, swimming along a wall covered by a dense forest of sea fans. We are probably surrounded by barracuda and carangids as we head toward the ridge that we see above our heads. Now we have to direct ourselves toward one of the distinct channels that open in the wall. There, at about 70 feet (20 meters), we encounter an abundance of sponges and sea fans in an area made even more interesting by its many natural arches, caves, and passageways. Careful not to be swept away by the current, we then head for the mooring point, where we will rise to the surface, holding onto the cable.

*265 center right The blackfin barracudas (*Sphyraena qenie*) are the true rulers of the surface waters of Cod Wall. This is a stationary school, and an encounter is therefore guaranteed at depths between the surface and 100 feet (30 meters).*

*265 bottom right These hammerhead sharks (*Sphyrna *sp.) cross extremely deep, far off in the blue under our fins, hardly visible in the crystalline waters made dark by the depth.*

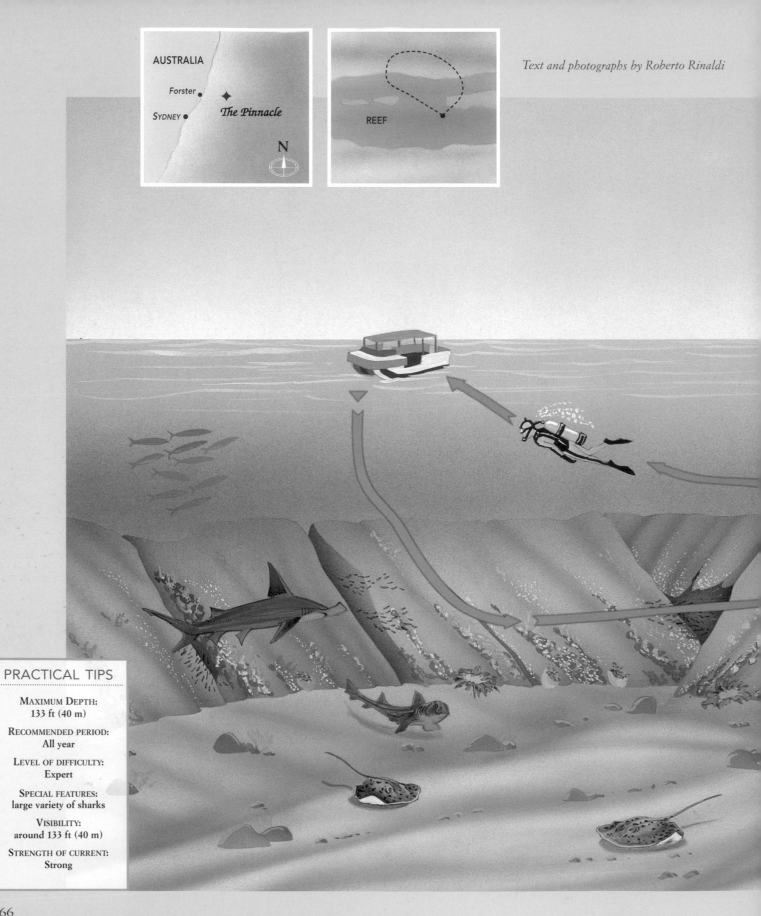

AUSTRALIA

Forster

SYDNEY

The Pinnacle

N

REEF

Text and photographs by Roberto Rinaldi

Illustrations by Domitilla Müller

AUSTRALIA

The Pinnacle

AUSTRALIA—MID NORTH COAST
THE PINNACLE

267 top *At the bottom of the shallows, a low fin lifts several yards above the surrounding seabed. Two sharks are beginning to circulate around a school of kingfish on the bottom, and will end with a series of precise and deadly attacks.*

267 bottom *A wobbegong shark is immobile on the bottom of a fissure, perfectly camouflaged. As often happens, it shares its home with a thick school of silverfish.*

24 m
80 ft

35 m
116 ft

40 m
133 ft

While the swift aluminum catamaran makes some headway climbing a seemingly unending wave, insidious breakers beat noisily against its hull, leaving white puffs of foam under a lead-colored sky. I hadn't imagined that I was about to make one of the best dives of my career as a globetrotting diver. I am on the open sea off Forster, a fish-

ing village three hours north of Sydney by car. My companions and I may seem somewhat perplexed, with the waves tossing the boat about and the engines screaming while we slide rapidly toward the chasm beyond the crest of the wave. Ron steers his boat with assurance. Perhaps he is even somewhat amused by our dumbfounded expressions and our silence. We soon arrive at an imprecise point. Far from the coast, we find ourselves alternately within a deep valley, with slopes of heavy, gray water surmounted by crests streaked by the white of the foam, and atop the crest, admiring the panorama of the two valleys that open on our sides. From the blanket of lead in front of us, an impenetrable gust of rain advances violently, flattening even the crests of foam. A small group of boats is already in the same area. They rise and fall, disappear in the valleys, and appear climbing on the crests. "Shark hunters," Ronnie announces while he holds us in balance, extracts the anchor from the forepeak, and moors the boat. We quickly get ready to jump into the water. The gust of rain, so intense, seems to have lifted the leaden blanket of clouds and opened a window of light that illuminates the water below us. We dive quickly, moving along the anchor cable, and approach an immense black rock. Below us is a school of kingfish, silvery, powerful fish, each more than 3 feet (1 meter) long. But we don't interrupt our dive. We want to reach the bottom quickly before the current pulls away the anchor cable and makes us surface far away at an unknown point.

We are in a place known as "the Pinnacle," a rocky shoal that rises from the deeper seabed surrounding it. In reality, instead of the pinnacle that we expected, we find ourselves in front of a long, separated rocky ridge, jagged and fragmented into a series of channels and rather high peaks. The

seabed around the ridge varies in depth from 115 to 130 feet (35 to 40 meters), while the highest peaks rise up to 80 feet (24 meters) from the surface. The rocks on the bottom are flat, hollowed out, polished and cleaned by the fury of the impetuous currents that pound these waters and that probably cause the extraordinary abundance of fish here. Within a few seconds we have a disturbing demonstration of this abundance, con-

268 top A group of Port Jackson sharks rest immobile in the deepest, most tranquil seabed of the Pinnacle. These completely harmless sharks are not very good swimmers.

268 bottom A meeting with the large black stingrays in perennial motion on the bottom is practically assured, and is certainly one of the more spectacular encounters, in view of the dimensions that these creatures often reach.

268-269 This wobbegong is enormous, over 10 feet (3 meters) long for sure. I approached cautiously: it crouched on a smooth, round rock, not much higher than the surrounding bottom, where I myself rested on a level with its nose.

firmed by a mighty burst from the simultaneous flipping of thousands of powerful tails, which at the same moment force the school to make a sudden change of direction. What attracted us to the Pinnacle was not the wealth of fish in general but specifically the abundance of every kind of shark. At the Pinnacle we found the very timid Port Jackson sharks, with round heads and inoffensive mouths, aggressive mako sharks, which are wonderful swimmers, mimetic wobbegongs, with heads embellished by protuberances and tails with a powerful whip, and impressive Toro sharks, which boast a frightening set of teeth. At the Pinnacle, hammerheads are at home, as are great white sharks, regularly seen in these waters. Among the rocky gorges, we discover large orange, branched sponges, decorated by clusters of white squid eggs, while the rocks around are covered by flowering coelenterates such as the bright yellow *Parazoanthus* and vivid pink jewel anemones with small diaphanous circles around their tips. After reaching the anchor, we dive to the level bottom. The imposing ridge protects us from the current, and we can swim freely here without effort. A rhythmic movement of a large dark mass attracts our attention. We go closer and discover that it is a dense school of silverfish, each as large as the palm of my hand, that live in the entrance to a small cave. The sides of the fish glint, hit by the light of our flashlights, while hundreds of individuals move together in an orderly manner, with no hesitation, like dancers who have learned their steps perfectly. Only the light of our torches

allows us to discover a large wobbegong reclining on the bottom of the cave, perfectly immobile and camouflaged. I go within a few inches of its face and assault it with a strong flash. It remains immobile and doesn't move until my presence becomes too obstinate. Then it shakes itself, arches its back, rocks its head right and left, with difficulty raises the rest of its body, and passes in front of me, pushing me against the wall of the cave. It parades its entire length, certainly more than 10 feet (3 meters), in front of my eyes, smacking me with the movement of the water from its last tail flip. We then leave the cave and discover a group of two or three Port Jackson sharks, lying lazily on the bottom. None of them recalls its fearsome, predatory relatives. They stay there, calmly, with their large, round, disproportionate heads leaning on the rocks, their breathing labored when we get too close, exposing their fear. On the same seabed live enormous black trigoni, measuring up to 7 feet (2 meters) in diameter. We raise our eyes and discover the unmistakable outline of a group of Toro sharks, just above the rocky ridge. Instinctively we swim clos-

269 top Colors are not abundant on the sea bottoms of the Pinnacle. From this point of view, the most representative forms of life are these orange sponges. Here a squid has chosen to lay its eggs on the sponge.

269 bottom Tiger anemone is the name of these fascinating coelenterata that colonize the skeletons of whip gorgonians or others like them.
Found in abundance, they are as big as a small coin.

er, leaving our shelter, and find that we have to fight the current to reduce the distance. The sharks mind neither us nor the current. They continue swimming lazily, with exasperating slowness, each one, however, remaining at a certain distance from the others. There are six or seven, ranging from 7 to 10 feet (2 to 3 meters) long, large, powerful, and majestic when their skin reflects the light of the flashlights with bronze gleams. With their mouths partially open, their big, long, curved teeth sharp as blades, they intimidate us quite a bit. We know very well that these creatures only appear lazy and innocuous; in reality they are capable of unpredictable and deadly precise lightning strikes. I am thinking about all of this while I try to get closer from below to photograph the ferocity expressed in those frightening mouths. All of a sudden, I realize that six or seven sharks, still keeping a certain distance between themselves, have begun to rise from the bottom. I rise with them, swimming like a man obsessed in the strong current, very much hindered by the cumbersome photographic equipment I am carrying. I try to stay near them, to maintain contact, while the current does its best to carry me away. I try to get closer, to reduce the distance, but I can't. A few yards above, a large black cloud hovers, a school of kingfish. The sharks begin to swim around the school slowly,

with exasperating, almost stubborn slowness. The silver fish move closer and closer, crowding together. Above and at the sides, they squeeze together, side to side and back to stomach. In an instant the school is transformed into a gigantic ball of living beings that evidently senses aggressive intention in the movement of the sharks. Meanwhile a large shark has stopped a few yards away and remains immobile in the water, moving its tail only enough to resist the current and stay in the same place. The movement of the other sharks is faster and closer to the ball of fish, which is letting itself drift with the current. Closer and closer they come, while the fish in the school withdraw more and more decisively, until the isolated shark is seen in the middle of the ball. A loud crack, an instant after, the uproar of the simultaneous flipping of a thousand tails. And a sharp, protracted noise, the sound of someone violently biting into an apple. The isolated shark, helped by the others, has captured a kingfish and now, with a series of terrible bites, is devouring it. The final act of this spectacle lasts for only a few seconds. The ball re-forms immediately while a second shark remains immobile in the water and the others begin swimming in circles. I swim harder against the current to record this impressive moment in the life of the sea. The hunting scene repeats itself several times before my eyes as the sharks help each other to capture their prey. Only a few times do I get close enough to take a photo. The taste of the air becomes metallic in my throat because I am breathless after swimming so long against the current. It is time to leave; one final effort, and I reach the cable and begin to rise. Now I'm convinced. This really was the best dive of my career. I have returned to the Pinnacle, but I have never, for any reason, thought of changing my mind.

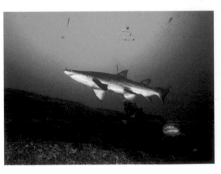

270 left These sweepers are very common: they can be seen in almost every crack, under every rock that can offer them protection.

270 top right This photo shows the climax of the hunt: the sharks lock the school of kingfish into a sphere, then take turns pushing the sphere toward the mouth of the shark that will attack.

270 bottom right The sharks mostly congregate along the ridge of the Pinnacle.

270-271 A close encounter with a large shark shows a mouth armed with sharp teeth and a nose scarred by a violent clash.

Bicheno
TASMANIA
Golden Bommie

N

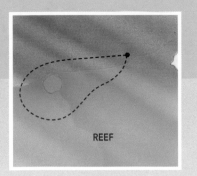

REEF

Text and photographs by Roberto Rinaldi

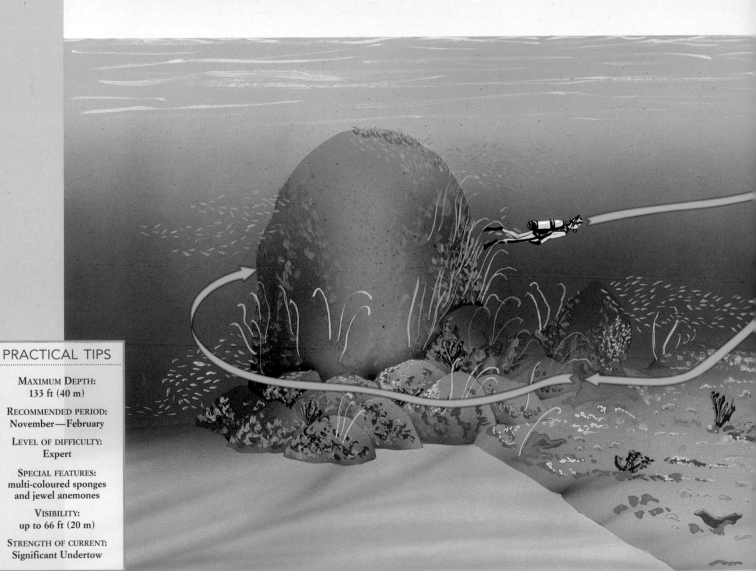

PRACTICAL TIPS

MAXIMUM DEPTH:
133 ft (40 m)

RECOMMENDED PERIOD:
November—February

LEVEL OF DIFFICULTY:
Expert

SPECIAL FEATURES:
multi-coloured sponges
and jewel anemones

VISIBILITY:
up to 66 ft (20 m)

STRENGTH OF CURRENT:
Significant Undertow

Illustrations by Domitilla Müller

AUSTRALIA

TASMANIA

Golden Bommie

AUSTRALIA—TASMANIA

GOLDEN BOMMIE

10 m
33 ft

25 m
83 ft

40 m
133 ft

Dives in Tasmania are full of surprises. Generally, to a diver Australia means the Great Barrier Reef, but the island to the south of the mainland that faces the Antarctic and is situated in the sea of the famous "Roaring Forties" offers some of the most intriguing dives anywhere on the planet.

Tasmania is a small granite island. Its luscious green covering is separated from the mainland by the Bass Strait, known for the number of ships that have gone down in its dangerous waters. The island has a number of spectacular and rocky mountains, and enormous areas are covered with thick green forests, in which ground and bark are lined with soft moss. On the lower slopes, mountain streams of clear icy water cross green meadows. If ten travelers were to spend a week on Tasmania, at the end they would all give a different description of

273 top Sponges and whip coral prosper on the flat sea floor around the main rocky structure. This seabed is rich with life and color at every point.

273 bottom Governor's Island and the diving area: the rock zone begins beyond the "flowering rocks," toward the open sea, and Golden Bommie is the last important peak before the sand covers the bottom.

273

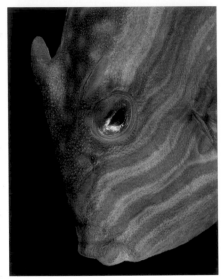

Governor's Island the bed quickly reaches depths of 80–130 feet (25–40 meters). The island is large and flat and greatly endowed with marine life. The backwash can at times be very strong, preventing approach to the rocks closest to the surface. If conditions permit, it is worth organizing a descent to view a rather special environment formed by various types of seaweed. One species in particular, characterized by extremely thick leaves that easily resist the violence of the waves, is not commonly found elsewhere. The sight of the leaves moving to the rhythm of the waves is very beautiful.

An interesting spot in the flat granite scene is an isolated pinnacle that rises from a depth of about 130 feet (40 meters) and is surrounded by large boulders and channels 6 or 7 feet (2 meters) deep, where the vast rocky seabed meets the sand. If you enter the water here, you will not believe your eyes, especially if you are lucky enough to have clear water; from that day on you will just laugh when anyone tells you that tropical seas are the most colorful. This is not a tropical garden of coral but a garden of sponges. The bed below you is covered with them—yellow, red, black, and violet. If you look carefully, you will see small sponges that line the rocks, others branched or in the shapes of plates or organ pipes. This scenery is set alight by the bright colors of porifers and the vivid yellow of coelenterates of the genus *Parazoanthus*, like small yellow daisies that cover entire underwater rocks.

Yet lovelier, and typical, are the yellow anemones, also coelenterates, in the shape of small flowers that line the rocks in soft pink, yellow, and white. In certain areas, especially where the sides of the main rock meet the large rounded rocks resting on the bottom, you will see a thick forest of pale sea whips, which are extremely spectacular when washed by the current. The fish population is also varied and dense, with a large number of strangely attired fish that you would have only expected in tropical waters but which have evidently become adapted to the relatively low temperatures of this sea. And you will be accompanied throughout the dive by a dense and dramatic shoal of large silverstreak goldies.

the island. As the saying goes, on Tasmania each day has four seasons; one might equally expect heavy rain and splendid sunshine on any day of the year. The same thing might be said of the sea here, where the water offers visibility of up to 130 feet (40 meters), but at times can be reduced to a few yards (1 or 2 meters). I once made a dive to a wreck on the southern tip and found I could not even see 3 feet (1 meter). Discouraged, I made the same dive the next day, and found to my surprise that I could make out the outline of the ship 130 feet (40 meters) below as soon as I entered the water.

What has remained with me is the constant and incredible variety of scenery and fauna that the waters offer. One of the loveliest places to dive is off the town of Bicheno on the east coast. The coastline is a series of white sandy bays and stretches of low, round granite rocks. As the seabed stretches out to sea, it offers the diver no steep wall or other outstanding feature, but around a large rock known as

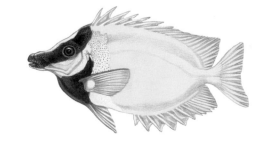

274 top and bottom The cowfish, the symbol of the Tasmanian Sea, is unique in that the male is brown, and the female, blue.

274-275 One of the masses at the base of the pinnacle. Here the life at the bottom is more exuberant with scores of species competing for space: Parazoanthus *are climbing on the sponges, while a colony of jewel anemone (*Corinactis *sp.) seems to cover a whip gorgonian.*

275 bottom Among the masses at the base of the main rocks, an Axinella *sponge leans out from the rock to capture nutriments. The wall is covered with* Parazoanthus.

Text and photographs by Kurt Amsler

POLYNESIA—RANGIROA
TIPUTA PASS

276 top Two gray reef sharks (Carcharhinus amblyrhynchos) approach the outcropping of the reef where the photographer is hiding: the shark's eye is always impressive, with its cold gleam.

276 bottom In aerial pictures one immediately identifies the pass, characterized by the intense blue color of the water, which contrasts with the lighter tones of the bottom and the reef: the strong current is very visible, even rippling the surface.

F rench Polynesia is divided into the Society Islands, the Tuamotu Archipelago, and the Gambier and Marquesas Islands. Tuamotu is unquestionably the best area for diving, as it is formed exclusively by coral atolls, unlike the Society Islands, where marine volcanoes still exist, surrounded by lagoons and coral rings.

Stretched over an area of sea measuring 750 by 370 miles (1,200 by 600 kilometers), the Tuamotu form the largest group of coral atolls in the world. The dive described in this chapter is to be found on one of these atolls, Rangiroa, which lies 125 miles (200 kilometers) from Papeete International Airport and can be reached via Air Tahiti in about half an hour. The atoll, with its aquamarine lagoon, measures 48 by 15 miles (78 by 24 kilometers), with a perimeter of

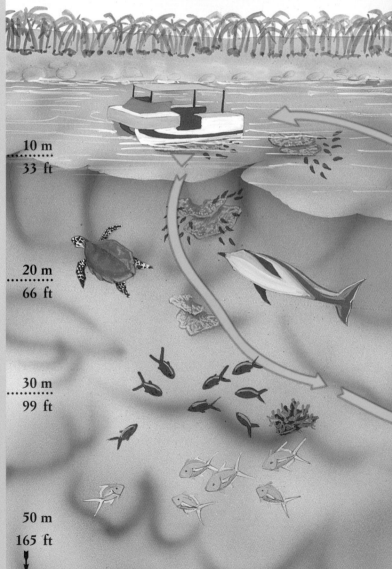

10 m
33 ft

20 m
66 ft

30 m
99 ft

50 m
165 ft

RANGIROA ATOLL

Tiputa Pass

N

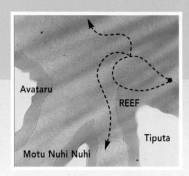

Avataru

Motu Nuhi Nuhi

REEF

Tiputa

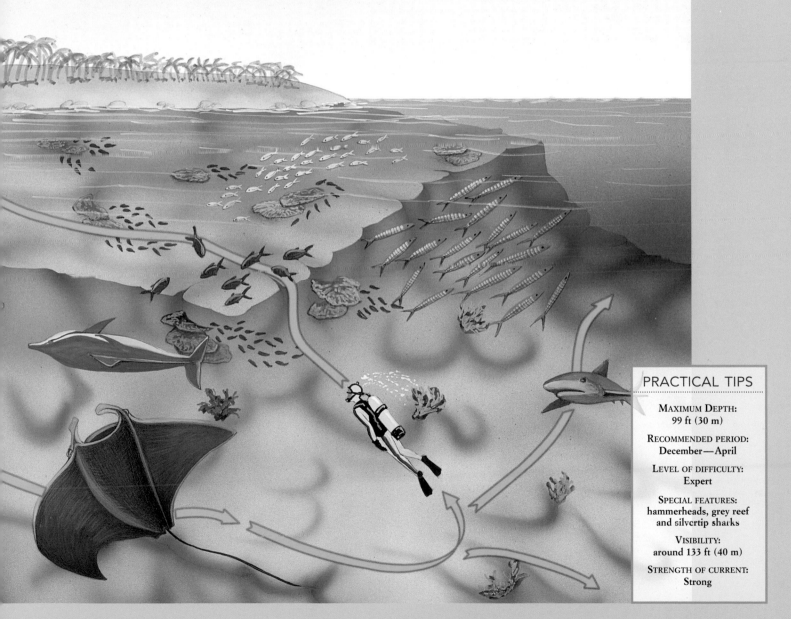

PRACTICAL TIPS

MAXIMUM DEPTH:
99 ft (30 m)

RECOMMENDED PERIOD:
December—April

LEVEL OF DIFFICULTY:
Expert

SPECIAL FEATURES:
hammerheads, grey reef
and silvertip sharks

VISIBILITY:
around 133 ft (40 m)

STRENGTH OF CURRENT:
Strong

277

173 miles (278 kilometers) of unexplored coral.

Rangiroa Island—which takes its name from the atoll—is 4 miles (7 kilometers) long and only 1,000 feet (300 meters) wide. It lies between two deep channels, Avataru Pass and Tiputa Pass, through which millions of gallons of water pass with the rhythm of the tides. Both channels are superb dive sites and offer everything a diver could wish for: steep walls, luxuriant coral vegetation, shoals of fish, mantas, barracuda, leopard rays, and hammerheads, and, naturally, the entire range of Pacific reef fish.

One very special place is the west side of

Tiputa Pass, which faces the ocean and where an interesting underwater phenomenon is to be seen. Without doubt, Tiputa Pass is the capital of the gray reef shark. "In my opinion, there is no other place in the world with a population of gray reef sharks comparable to the one here," declares Erich Ritter, a famous shark expert at the University of Miami. Between 150 and 300 examples of this elegant predator lurk in this corner of the channel, and in the entire channel there must be thousands. This spectacle offers a thrill to even the most blasé shark fans.

Normally, you enter the water when the current arrives; this provides the best conditions and carries you along the channel. Sharkpoint, a prominent corner on the coral wall, is characterized by a projection similar to a grotto. Here divers, protected from the current, can watch the numerous sharks as they swim back and forth.

The gray reef shark has the classic features of a predator fish: a pointed nose, dorsal fin, yellow eyes, and a crescent mouth. Its scientific name is *Carcharhinus amblyrhynchos;* though not as well known as the great white, the gray reef shark is a close relation.

The gray reef sharks of the southern seas are known for being specially aggressive in certain circumstances, but at Rangiroa these animals are extremely peaceful and completely uninterested in divers. This behavior is confirmed by Yves Lefevre, owner of the Ray Manta Club on Rangiroa, who has been diving here for fourteen years.

There is no certain scientific explanation for the large shark population in these waters. Is it because there is so much food available to them or because the current makes their life comfortable? Not having branchial muscles, sharks are forced to swim all their lives just to breathe.

Gray reef sharks are not the only attraction at Tiputa Pass. Here you can see at least five other types of shark; for example, *Sphyrna mokar-*

278 top left This little grouper (Epinephelus sp.) displays teeth, prominent eyes, and nostrils formed by a U-shaped pipe of olfactory cells.

278 center left A large group of shadowfin soldierfish (Myripristis adusta) and whitetip soldierfish (Myripristis vittata) swims over the reef: these species normally live alone or in small groups.

278 bottom left Several hundred barracuda (Sphyraena qenie) file tranquilly in front of the divers: this species normally gathers in schools during the day.

278 top right A Quoy's parrotfish (Scarus quoyi), rests during the night in a cavity of the reef: its teeth are visible, fused in two semicircles that form a strong "beak," with which it crunches the coral to feed on the algae that live there in symbiosis.

278 bottom right A young giant manta (Manta birostris) swims alongside a diver: the mantas are cartilaginous fish, unmistakable with their large triangular "wings," which serve for swimming and to direct water and plankton to their mouths.

278-279 *A thick group of butterflyfish* (Heniochus diphreutes) *allow themselves to be approached without fear: while the young of this species swim near the reef, the adults swim in the middle zones, feeding on zooplankton.*

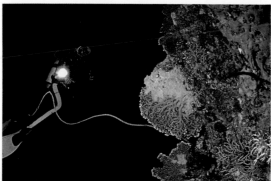

279 bottom *The vertical wall of the reef extends down into the dark, covered with carnation coral, sponges, and above all lace coral; these hydrozoans, unlike fire coral, do not have symbiotic algae and display brilliant coloration.*

280-281 *Numerous examples
of blacktip reef shark (Carcharhinus melanopterus)* swim in
the middle zones: this species
is commonly seen here,
recognizable by the black top of
its dorsal fin, with a white
band.

280 bottom *A silvertip shark*
(Carcharhinus albimarginatus)
swims in the blue; it lives in
coastal environments, both in
the open and at notable depths,
and is considered potentially
dangerous.

281 bottom A pair of small gray reef sharks approaches the photographer with apparent aggression: they are probably motivated only by curiosity, as demonstrated by the tranquillity of the other fish species swimming around them.

Sharkpoint, let yourself be carried by the current along the canal as far as the rock fall. Crossing the channel is a great attraction of this dive site. Keep your eyes open all around as well as below and above you, as you don't want to miss the chance to see large manta and eagle rays swimming against the current in the open sea. With a little luck, you will also come across a large hammerhead shark.

ran can reach the respectable length of 13–20 feet (4–6 meters). These gigantic but docile creatures live at a depth of 130–160 feet (40–50 meters) and are extremely shy.

When the tide turns, the splendid silvertips (Carcharhinus albimarginatus) arrive in the channel with the ocean current. The Polynesians calls this shark "Tapetee," and it is the incarnation of what people think a shark should be, its steely muscle-bound body covered with a shining golden skin made for maximum speed. The Tapetee behave much more like an animal of prey than the gray reef sharks; particularly impressive is the way that they register everything that is going on around them and react immediately to every change.

Large nurse sharks can be seen below the overhangs and in the fissures while, higher up, whitetip sharks and young blacktip sharks live around the coral bank. After a stop at

Generally, this dive ends on a small island inside the lagoon that is also a superb point of entry, teeming with the loveliest examples of Pacific coral fish. It is called Aquarium, and is deservedly a popular diving site.

281 top A numerous group of gray reef sharks swims on the barrier: the gray reef shark can attack divers, but after biting it normally swims away, causing nonlethal wounds.

281 center A gray reef shark, swimming against the coral, makes his way among hundreds of tiny fish of the barrier: even if he has no aggressive intentions, his appearance is threatening.

Text and photographs by Kurt Amsler – Illustrations by Domitilla Müller

POLINESIA

Tupitipiti Point

FIJI ISLANDS

FRENCH POLYNESIA

NEW ZEALAND

POLYNESIA—BORA BORA
TUPITIPITI POINT

Bora Bora is the most photographed zone in French Polynesia. The larger island, 16 miles (10 kilometers) long, is surrounded by a lovely lagoon that contains many *motus*, or tiny islands. Bora Bora is enclosed by a coral bank; ships can only pass through a single passage to the open sea. The symbol of the island is unquestionably the volcano Otemanu, 3,285 feet (727 meters) high, which keeps watch over the thickly covered mountain slopes and the lagoon of changing colors.

The local airport was built by the Americans during World War II on a nearby island. It was on

Bora Bora that the tourism began that led to the excessive commercial development of French Polynesia today.

Dives can be made in the lagoon as well as off the outer coral bank, so you can set out regardless of weather or sea conditions. The lagoon contains a huge quantity of fish and is home to innumerable mantas, which congregate for the "manta dance" not far from the Calypso Club diving cen-

282 top The atoll of Bora Bora, seen from the plane, is surrounded by a cobalt blue sea that contrasts with the emerald green of the interior lagoon; before we set down in the water, the island sinks again into the blue.
Photograph by
Philippe Bacchet.

282 bottom The reef is riddled with caves and outcroppings: here the flow of water is greatest, making them ideal sites for the large gorgonians.

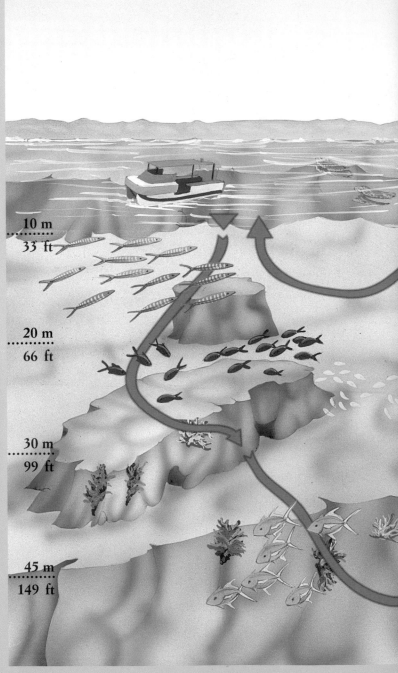

10 m
33 ft

20 m
66 ft

30 m
99 ft

45 m
149 ft

BORA
BORA

*Tupitipiti
Point*

N

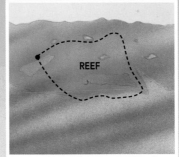

REEF

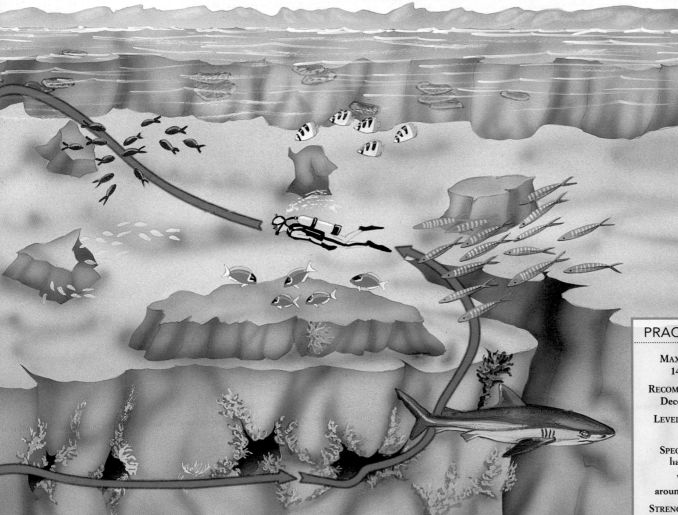

PRACTICAL TIPS

MAXIMUM DEPTH:
146 ft (45 m)

RECOMMENDED PERIOD:
December—April

LEVEL OF DIFFICULTY:
Expert

SPECIAL FEATURES:
hammerheads

VISIBILITY:
around 133 ft (40 m)

STRENGTH OF CURRENT:
Strong

ter. Even beginners are allowed to dive in the lagoon, whereas proven experience is necessary for trips to the outer coral banks.

The dive spot we describe here, however, with the musical name Tupitipiti Point, is at the southeast corner of the island on the outer coral bank. The single canal that passes from the enormous lagoon to the sea cuts diagonally across the atoll, making the trip to Tupitipiti Point by boat rather long. The direction of the wind is also important: if it blows from the east, the breakers crash against the coral, and the dive cannot be made. When the wind blows from the south, the journey is less pleasant, but the dive is possible. The best conditions are without question when the wind is from the north or the west.

The topography of the dive point is dramatic. The coral bank, which sometimes rises above the surface of the water, first drops straight down 35 feet (10 meters), then a flattish shelf composed of blocks of rock leads to the proper dropoff point, which is truly worthy of the name: the walls descend vertically to depths far out of sight. Generally the water here is perfectly clear and the sunlit underwater seascape offers a strong contrast to the deep blue of the sea.

When the sea is calm, the dive boat can be moored close to one of the large blocks of rock, or it is possible to do a drift dive, which is more convenient, as you can descend with the current

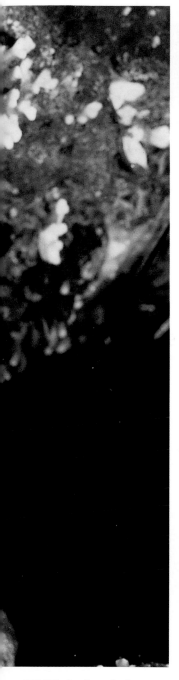

magnificent experience.

There is a wide variety of corals. First of all there is *Distichoporas* in a range of colors. All the overhangs are covered with small branches of coral, particularly in shades of violet. Larger branches of all colors grow in the grottoes of the steep wall at a depth of 115 feet (35 meters) and more.

Large fish are always present, as the southeast corner is particularly exposed to the current. On the plateau or below the overhangs close to the surface, you may well come across whitetip or blacktip reef sharks. Looking out to sea from the coral bank, you will often notice large shoals of bigeye jacks, which produce a silvery glint in the water with their swollen bodies. Then there are often scalloped hammerheads, which are generally rare in this area of French Polynesia.

There are also barracuda of respectable size, mainly found around the rocks of the shelf. And certainly in November and December, though not necessarily in other months, you will find enormous schools of triggerfish.

You can also count on seeing mantas and eagle rays, although it is not possible to know with certainty where, as they swim along the entire length of the atoll and do not stop in particular points, as they do in the lagoon. With a little luck, the diver at Tupitipiti Point will see a school of eagle rays or even a giant manta.

without having to worry about the way back to the boat.

The best feature of this spot is that it is suitable for divers of all levels of experience. The less experienced can explore the surface areas, while the more expert can go deeper. What makes this site exceptional are the grottoes with multihued corals about 150 feet (45 meters) down. Even relatively inexperienced divers will find diving at Tupitipiti Point satisfying, and dives made along the coral bank at 70–100 feet (20–30 meters) and among the huge rocks on the plateau have much to offer. To best witness the extraordinary colors and the huge number of species in the cracks and below the overhangs, you are advised to take a flashlight with you. The rules of diving, which dictate that the upper areas be explored first, can be perfectly respected thanks to the site's ideal topography. The dive along the overhangs at a depth of 35 feet (10 meters) contributes to the

284-285 A yellow-edged moray (Gymnothorax flavimarginatus) *hidden in a cavity displays his fine teeth.*

285 top left A huge mass near the surface, covered with gorgonians and other invertebrates, seems a disordered tableau: in reality, all these organisms obey very rigid rules for their survival.

285 center left Hundreds of bluestripe snappers (Lutjanus kasmira) *form a compact school.*

285 bottom left A number of butterflyfish (Heniochus diphreutes) *swim in the middle depths.*

285 top right Several blacktip reef sharks (Carcharhinus melanopterus) *are surrounded by a cloud of snappers and many other fish: evidently the sharks are not displaying any aggressiveness and, therefore, do not represent a danger for the smaller fish*

285 bottom right Four large live sharksuckers (Echeneis naucrates) *are allowing themselves to be carried by a manta. The sharksucker adheres to its host by means of a sucker disk on its back, a transformation of its dorsal fin.*

Pacific Ocean

◆ *Ocean Pinnacles*

Carmel Bay

N

CALIFORNIA

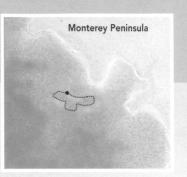

Monterey Peninsula

Text and photographs by Brandon Cole

PRACTICAL TIPS

MAXIMUM DEPTH:
97 ft (30 m)

RECOMMENDED PERIOD:
Summer to Autumn

LEVEL OF DIFFICULTY:
Average—High

SPECIAL FEATURES:
hydrocorals and kelp forests

VISIBILITY:
32—80 ft (10—25 m)

STRENGHT OF CURRENT:
Average/Strong

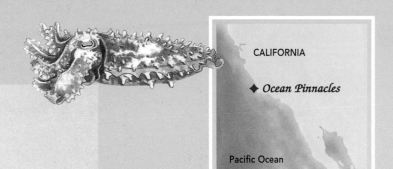

CALIFORNIA

♦ *Ocean Pinnacles*

Pacific Ocean

CALIFORNIA—CARMEL BAY
OCEAN PINNACLES

12 m
39 ft

15 m
49 ft

18 m
59 ft

The Ocean Pinnacles is widely considered to be one of the premier dive sites in California. It comprises a series of undersea mountains three-quarters of a mile off the Monterey Peninsula. They are marked by a lush kelp forest which sprouts from jagged peaks thrusting up from more than 100 feet (30 meters) below.

It is a perfect September day with no wind and only a gentle swell. I have anchored my small inflatable in 40 feet (12 meters), over a ridge lying to the west of the shallowest pinnacles whose crowns rise to within 15 feet (4 meters) of the surface. Executing a back-roll entry, I plummet down to find myself in the middle of a jellyfish storm. The cool 55° F water is thick with them, pulsing, spinning by me in the current. The largest are purple and white, one foot in diameter with stringy tentacles trailing 10 feet behind. The smallest, thimble-sized, number in the thousands and dance about chaotically.

The riot of color and motion atop the reef calls me downward. I descend to 50 feet (15 meters) and swim along the edge of a canyon whose steep walls are overgrown with bright clusters of hydrocoral. Splendid in purple, pink, red, and orange hues, hydrocoral favors offshore reefs such as these in Carmel Bay, which are bathed by clean, nutrient-rich water. Searching among the delicate branches I find hermit crabs, ringed top snails, brittle stars, and tiny fish such as sculpins and kelpfish.

Dipping down into a sand channel at 80 feet

287 top and bottom Two notable encounters in Ocean Pinnacles: a rare luminous jellyfish (Pelagia noctiluca), *top, and a giant* Pycnopodia helianthoides *starfish, bottom.*

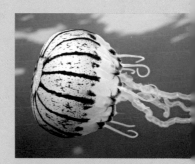

(25 meters) I spy flounder and a huge sunflower sea star with 13 arms. Continuing eastward and upward, poking along the wall's face, I come across a ling cod perched on a ledge at 60 feet (18 meters). Baring its impressive teeth, this three-foot long predator hungrily surveys the shadows below. Right next door a male cabezon rests his big fat head on a pile of green eggs. A staunch protector of his brood, Mr. Mom never even flinches when I zoom in on his ugly mug.

It is a challenge to find a section of rock not already claimed. Bryozoans, tunicates, and sponges in bold colors share substrate with the ubiquitous strawberry anemone. I try to photograph a decorator crab as it clambers from a patch of pink anemones over a barricade of barnacles. The crab is stylishly sporting camouflaging tufts of feathery hydroids. Rockfish, perch, and greenlings dart between the kelp holdfasts and scoot over the turf. Nudibranchs are everywhere. My list includes lemon peels, spanish shawls, dendronotids, and a dorid laying egg coils. There are also cup corals, feather duster worms, spotted rose anemones, and coralline algae in abundance.

At the 45-minute mark, I ascend for my safety stop. Sunbeams needle down through the kelp forest canopy. I feel as if I am floating in a cathedral. A squadron of 200 blue rockfish hover beside me amidst the towering kelp stalks. I spend my last few moments gazing out into open water. On past dives I've seen boisterous sea lions, ocean sunfish, and even a blue shark once. The Pinnacles hold many surprises.

The Ocean Pinnacles are accessible only by boat. Many local charters dive the site regularly when conditions permit. (www.cypress-charters.com, www.montereyexpress.com,

www.montereyscubadiving.com, www.divecentral.com, www.beachhopper2.com) If you have your own boat, you can launch from either the Breakwater in Monterey (a long, sometimes rough, 10-mile (16-kilometers) run) or from Whaler's Cove in Point Lobos State Reserve (a much shorter ride, although reservations are required: http://ptlobos.parks.state.ca.us, tel: 831-624-8413). Expansive kelp beds mark the Pinnacles in the summer, as well as a square tower-like building directly onshore called Castle House. Summer and fall usually promise the best diving weather. Visibility improves into the fall (30–80 feet/9–25 meters) as the summer's plankton blooms subside. Because of depth, currents, swell, and surge, the Ocean Pinnacles are recommended as an intermediate to advanced dive only. Note that there is another great dive site, the Outer Pinnacles, a quarter of a mile south of here.

Text and photographs by Vincenzo Paolillo

CALIFORNIA — CATALINA

AVALON'S CASINO POINT DIVE PARK

C atalina is an island of 122 square miles (197 square kilometers) in the Pacific Ocean off the Californian coastline, halfway between Los Angeles and San Diego. An unusual feature of this island is that it is 95 percent privately owned, at one time by the owner of the Wrigley chewing gum company and today by the foundation he created, the Santa Catalina Island Conservancy, whose task it is to protect the island and its natural environment.

A small part of Catalina is occupied by the town of Avalon, a modern base for tourists who come to fish, dive, and sail. On the west side of

290 *left It is quite common to run into seals in these waters.*

290 *right The most common inhabitant of the kelp forest, a symbol of this sea, is the garibaldi* (Hypsypops rubicundus). *Photograph by Gianfranco D'Amato.*

Avalon is a casino, and in front of this building a small section of the sea measuring 650–1,000 by 164 feet (200–300 by 50 meters) is a protected area known as the Casino Point Dive Park, off limits to fishermen and boats. You prepare on the square in front of the casino, climb over the parapet, and descend the rocks to the sea. The descent is not easy, as the rocks are sometimes slippery; a few small waves and a little backwash are enough to make entry difficult, because you must first

8 m
26 ft

15 m
50 ft

CATALINA ISLAND

Point
Dive Park

Avalon's Casino

N

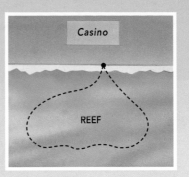

Casino

REEF

Illustrations by Domitilla Müller

JACQUES
COUSTEAU

PRACTICAL TIPS

MAXIMUM DEPTH:
50 ft (15 m)

RECOMMENDED PERIOD:
April—October

LEVEL OF DIFFICULTY:
Easy

SPECIAL FEATURES:
kelp forests

VISIBILITY:
around 66 ft (20 m)

STRENGTH OF CURRENT:
Variable

292 *top left* *The three characteristic colors of this dive are the green of the kelp, the red of the garibaldi, and the orange of the gorgonians.*

pass through a thick mass of brown kelp (*Macrocystis pyrifera*), a giant seaweed; commonly 50 to 70 feet (15–20 meters) long, it can grow up to 330 feet (100 meters) in length! Its enormous green leaves stay afloat by the ingenious device of small air bubbles within them.

As the rock drops steeply for 23–26 feet (7–8 meters), the kelp extends from the seabed to the surface, not leaving even a square inch of space between the rocky shore and the open water. Push your way through the weeds that wrap themselves around you and almost prevent you from submerging until, after 35 feet (10 meters) or so, the forest thins a little, and it is possible to descend to the bottom and enjoy the spectacle. Rays of light filter down through the leaves, creating wonderful patterns through which huge numbers of fish pass, including the marvelous garibaldi (*Hypsypops rubicundus*), a damselfish of unusual size, up to a foot (30 centimeters) in length, and a magnificent color somewhere between red and orange that forms a glorious contrast with the green leaves of the seaweed. It is even prettier when young, as it is then edged and spotted with light blue.

Moving right, you descend to 50 feet (15 meters) and, at the feet of the kelp, find lovely gorgonians; a little farther out is a plaque dedicated to Jacques Cousteau, and then the wreck of a boat.

The stems of the kelp rise all around, providing a habitat to the garibaldi, shoals of two types of grunts, the kelp bass (*Paralabrax clathratus*) with its pale belly, gray-speckled back,

and green eyes, and the colorful California sheephead (*Semiconyphus pulcher*), with a square head like the cutwater of a boat and sharp teeth. The kelp bass remains idle among the kelp leaves and only moves when approached by the photographer; the sheephead, by contrast, is in continual movement.

If you are lucky, you will come across a dense shoal of Pacific sardines (*Sardinops sagax*), swimming close to the surface over your head, or perhaps a curious sea lion that has abandoned the port of Avalon, where despite the ban, they are fed by tourists. Maybe he is interested in you, or just looking for a snack.

On the rocks of the seabed, you may well find a colorful member of the goby family: a bluebanded goby (*Lythrypnus dalli*) with its orange body and blue head, or a zebra goby (*Lythrypnus zebra*), distinguished from its bluebanded brother because the two colors alternate in stripes. Then there are lobsters, scorpionfish, and crabs.

If you play close attention among the seaweed that covers the bottom, you might see a small shark known as the horn shark (*Heterodontus francisci*), no more than 16 inches (40 centimeters) long and a sort of grayish brown with small dark spots. Be careful not to let his immobility tempt you to touch him; on his back, just in front of the two fins, he has two small triangles that bear extremely sharp spines.

The dive has no particular itinerary, as it is best to remain in a small area and return to the shore where you entered. It is dangerous to surface too far away from the shore; if your head pops up outside the restricted area, you stand a fair chance of being decapitated by one of the hundreds of motorboats in the area. The only negative factor associated with a dive in this tiny paradise is the noise of their motors.

292 *bottom left* *Shoals of blue-bronze sea chubs* (Kyphosus analogus) *often haunt the forests of kelp.*

292 *top right* *California morays* (Gymnothorax mordax) *can be made out between the rocks.*

292 *bottom right* *The smallest known shark is the horn shark* (Heterodontus francisci), *which hardly reaches 3 feet (1 meter) in length; it gets its name from the two stings just in front of its dorsal fins.*

293 left The kelp's leaves are
held up by tiny bubbles of air.

293 right Lovely gorgonians
grow at the feet of the
enormous brown kelp
(Macrocystis pyrifera).

Text and photographs by Vincenzo Paolillo — Illustrations by Domitilla Müller

GALAPAGOS ISLANDS

◆ *Roca Redonda*

Isabela

GALAPAGOS—ISABELA
ROCA REDONDA

17 m
56 ft

30 m
99 ft

50 m
165 ft

About 15 miles (24 kilometers) from the northern tip of Isabela, the largest island in the Galapagos, the large rectangular rock named Roca Redonda rises in the middle of the sea. Its walls are so steep that it is impossible to understand how the sea lions manage to climb up there to spend the night after passing all day in the water.

The location of the rock makes it a meeting place for many pelagic species. The north side is usually frequented by hammerhead sharks, unless the warm waters of the Niño force them away (as last happened in 1997–98). The south side offers a wider variety of encounters and the chance to enjoy a curious phenomenon.

294 top Harlequin wrasse (Bodianus eclancheri) are variously colored; the predominant hue may be red, yellow, or white.

294 bottom Roca Redonda is a rectangular rock that rises steeply from the middle of the sea.

294

Roca Redonda

PACIFIC OCEAN

N

Isabela

REEF

PRACTICAL TIPS

MAXIMUM DEPTH:
99 ft (30 m)

RECOMMENDED PERIOD:
January—May

LEVEL OF DIFFICULTY:
Average

SPECIAL FEATURES:
sea lions and sharks

VISIBILITY:
up to 99 ft (30 m)

STRENGTH OF CURRENT:
Variable

296 top right A large number of hammerhead sharks (Sphyrna lewini) can be seen near the walls of Roca Redonda.

296 bottom right This lovely scorpionfish (Scorpaena plumieri mystes) is surrounded by myriad barbier.

296-297 A meeting with sea lions is one of the most exciting experiences at this site.

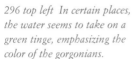

296 top left In certain places, the water seems to take on a green tinge, emphasizing the color of the gorgonians.

296 center left This green turtle (Chelonia mydas) is about to leave its safe hiding place on the reef; it has probably been disturbed by the diver.

296 bottom left The leather bass (Dermatolepis dermatolepis) is very common in the Galapagos Islands.

Enter the water on the east side of the island, where you will immediately see huge rocks covered with seaweed, the favorite habitat of the sea lion. If you don't stop to look at them or photograph them, they will try to attract your attention with frequent lunges or by encircling you as they playfully attempt to make friends.

The rocks are populated by an incredible number of migratory and nonmigratory fish. Commonly seen are Moorish idols (Zanclus cornutus), the characteristic leather bass (Dermatolepis dermatolepis), shoals of golden-eyed grunts (Haemulon scuderi), and razor surgeonfish (Prionurus laticlavius)—although these are not so numerous as to be seen in the tranquil waters of the archipelago—but above all harlequin wrasse (Bodianus eclancheri) in various colors, yellow and red in particular.

Continuing along the south side of the rock, you come across the phenomenon mentioned above: a stream of hot water slowly rises from below the bed toward the surface, demonstrating the continuing volcanic activity in this area.

Farther along, the rocks disappear, and the bed on which the Roca Redonda stands slowly descends from a depth of 56 feet (17 meters) out toward the open sea. Occasional visitors are passing giant mantas, green turtles resting on the bottom, or a blotched fantail ray (Taeniura meyeni) or whitetip stingray

(Dasyatis brevis), which will only swim away if seriously disturbed. Branches of black coral colored green grow on the edge of the dropoff, inhabited by swarms of fish.

You arrive at the western tip, where the rock wall drops suddenly to 70 feet (20 meters) before slowly sliding gently downward into the deeps. Here you will find an enormous shoal of pelican barracuda (Sphyraena idiastes), which like to hug the rock. They are not as large as you would find elsewhere, as at Sipadan, but their numbers are truly impressive.

If you still have enough air, before returning to the boat, take a last look at the seabed, where you may find morays, pufferfish, scorpionfish, and perhaps an unusually large damselfish.

INDEX OF PLACES

300 The seabeds of Ras Umm Sid, only a few hundred yards from the port of Sharm el-Meya, are particularly rich and fascinating.

DIVE the WORLD
the most fascinating diving sites

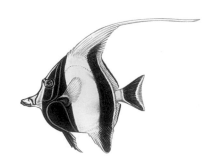

© 1997 White Star s.p.a.
Via Candido Sassone, 22/24 - 13100 Vercelli, Italy
www.whitestar.it

New extended and updated edition in 2007

TRANSLATION: C.T.M. Milan

ISBN 978-88-544-0216-4

REPRINTS:
1 2 3 4 5 6   11 10 09 08 07

Color separation by: Fotomec, Torino
Printed in Cina